FROM NIMBIN TO MARDI GRAS

MAR '98

354.9400854 H393f

ENTERED JAN 1 7 1995

Other titles in the series

Australian Television
Programs, pleasure and politics
Edited by John Tulloch and Graeme Turner

Dark Side of the Dream
Australian literature and the postcolonial mind
Bob Hodge and Vijay Mishra

Fashioning the Feminine
Girls, popular culture and schooling
Pam Gilbert and Sandra Taylor

Featuring Australia
The cinema of Charles Chauvel
Stuart Cunningham

Framing Culture
Criticism and policy in Australia
Stuart Cunningham

From Pop to Punk to Postmodernism
Popular music and Australian culture from the 1960s to the 1990s
Edited by Philip Hayward

Myths of Oz
Reading Australian popular culture
John Fiske, Bob Hodge, Graeme Turner

National Fictions
Literature, film and the construction of Australian narrative
Graeme Turner

Resorting to Tourism
Cultural policies for tourist development in Australia
Jennifer Craik

Stay Tuned
The Australian Broadcasting Reader
Edited by Albert Moran

Temptations
Sex, selling and the department store
Gail Reekie

Australian Cultural Studies
Editor: John Tulloch

Columbia College Library
600 South Michigan Avenue
Chicago, IL 60605

FROM NIMBIN TO MARDI GRAS
Constructing Community Arts

Gay Hawkins

ALLEN & UNWIN

354.9400854 H393f

Hawkins, Gay.

From Nimbin to Mardi Gras

© Gay Hawkins, 1993

This book is copyright under the Berne Convention.
No reproduction without permission. All rights reserved.

This publication has been assisted by the Commonwealth Government
through the Australia Council.

Australia **Council**
for the Arts

First published in 1993 by
Allen & Unwin Pty Ltd
9 Atchison Street, St Leonards, NSW 2065 Australia

National Library of Australia
Cataloguing-in-Publication entry:

Hawkins, Gay.
From Nimbin to Mardi Gras.

Bibliography.
Includes index.
ISBN 1 86373 466 X.

1. Australia Council. Community Arts Program—
History. 2. Federal aid to the arts—Australia.
3. Community art projects—Australia. 4. Australia—
Cultural policy. I. Title. (Series: Australian cultural studies).

354.9400854

Set in 10/11 pt Times by DOCUPRO, Sydney
Printed in Malaysia by SRM Production Services Sdn Bhd

10 9 8 7 6 5 4 3 2 1

General editor's foreword

Nowadays the social and anthropological definition of 'culture' is probably gaining as much public currency as the aesthetic one. Particularly in Australia, politicians are liable to speak of the vital need for a domestic film industry in 'promoting our cultural identity'—and they mean by 'cultural identity' some sense of Australianness, of our nationalism as a distinct form of social organisation. Notably, though, the emphasis tends to be on Australian *film* (not popular television); and not just *any* film, but those of 'quality'. So the aesthetic definition tends to be smuggled back in—on top of the kind of cultural nationalism which assumes that 'Australia' is a unified entity with certain essential features that distinguish it from 'Britain', the 'USA' or any other national entities which threaten us with 'cultural dependency'.

This series is titled 'Australian Cultural Studies', and I should say at the outset that my understanding of 'Australian' is not as an essentially unified category; and further , that my understanding of cultural is anthropological rather than aesthetic. By 'culture' I mean the social production of meaning and understanding, whether in the inter-personal and practical organisation of daily routines or in broader institutional and ideological structures. I am *not* thinking of 'culture' as some form of universal 'excellence', based on aesthetic 'discrimination' and embodied in a pantheon of 'great works'. Rather, I take this aesthetic definition of culture itself to be part of the *social mobilisation of discourse* to differentiate a cultural 'elite' from the 'mass' of society.

Unlike the cultural nationalism of our opinion leaders, 'Cultural Studies' focuses not on the essential unity of national cultures, but on the meanings attached to social difference (as in the distinction between 'elite' and 'mass' taste). It analyses the construction and mobilisation of these distinctions to maintain or challenge existing power differentials, such as those of gender, class, age, race and ethnicity. In this analysis, terms designed to socially differentiate people (like 'elite' and 'mass') become categories of discourse, communication and power. Hence our concern in this series is for an analytical understanding of

v

the meaning attached to social difference within the *history* and *politics* of discourse.

It follows that the analysis of 'texts' needs to be untied from a single-minded association with 'high' culture (marked by 'authorship'), but must include the 'popular' too—since these distinctions of 'high' and 'popular' culture themselves need to be analysed, not assumed. Gay Hawkins in *From Nimbin to Mardi Gras* challenges these distinctions centrally, examining their development in the context of 'the power of ideologies about culture and value'. She emphasises the importance of analysis that shows 'how the field of culture is mediated by classes and class factions . . . How cultural distinctions are invoked by dominant groups to legitimate some cultural practices and not others; to credit some cultural forms with the status of taste, quality, aesthetics and Art; to win government subsidy for some cultures and not others'. As Hawkins argues, 'The major effect of expanded government support was that the separation between art and mass culture became a cornerstone of this new public cultural field . . . Arts funding has generated a whole set of meanings for art based on the rejection of the techniques for mass distribution and on the capabilities of mass audiences'. In particular, Hawkins examines how 'excellence' and 'nation' as terms of discourse have been mobilised to attribute value to 'Art' and to the upper middle class audiences which 'appreciate' it. 'The primary function of discourses of value is social differentiation'; and this 'process of valorising art, specifically through the winning of subsidies for it, has consolidated class differences and power . . . Arts funding, then, has to be seen as a field in which art and its audience are continually constructed in relations of power and difference . . . In subsidising the pleasures of upper middle class city dwellers, arts funding effectively disenfranchises large sections of the citizenry whose cultural pleasures are either ignored or devalued by current mechanisms of support'.

The focus of this book on the Community Arts Program inevitably requires, then, 'a documentation of how "community" was placed in relation to the dominant discourses structuring support for the arts'. As Hawkins says, to trace the invocation of 'community' in community arts is 'a case study of the tensions involved in trying to reconcile policies which address the nation as an undifferentiated whole with those that seek to address specific groups that are represented as "other", as outside the nation, as communities of difference'.

In contrast to the art of 'excellence', community arts could be valued 'because they were a mechanism for maintaining collective identity of consciousness among different groups. They were a way of asserting and celebrating difference'. At the same time, though, the book asserts the importance of re-evaluating left discourse in relation to the 'progressive' nature of community arts. In her critique both of dominant ideas of artistic 'excellence' and of left notions of the authenticity of 'community', Gay Hawkins traces the 'deeply ambiguous' history of the Community Arts Program.

Culture, as Fiske, Hodge and Turner say in *Myths of Oz*, grows out of the divisions of society, not its unity. 'It has to work to construct any unity that it has, rather than simply celebrate an achieved or natural harmony.' Australian culture is then no more than the temporary, embattled construction of 'unity' at any particular historical moment. The 'readings' in this series of 'Australian Cultural Studies' inevitably (and polemically) form part of the struggle to make and break the boundaries of meaning which, in conflict and collusion, dynamically define our culture.

JOHN TULLOCH

Foreword

As anyone who has had much to do with them will know, the concepts of art and community are each of them capable of generating a multiplicity of conflicting meanings and interpretations. When the two are brought together, therefore, a good deal of semantic friction is bound to be generated. For those who view art as the product of individual creativity, the very notion of community art is a contradiction in terms. There are others, however, for whom community art is the only true art in view of the nourishment it supposedly draws from its close association with the wellsprings of popular creativity.

Unfortunately, however, a good deal of what has been said and written about the community arts has shown scant appreciation of the discursive minefields which await the unwary in this area. Unsurprisingly, perhaps, the most extensive discussions of community arts theory and practice have been offered by its enthusiasts. The resulting advocacy function and orientation of much of this writing has meant that it has tended to make light of the semantic density of their terms 'community' and 'art'—and of the conditions of their combination—in favour of simple, commonsense definitions which can be operationalised easily for policy purposes.

From Nimbin to Mardi Gras stands out from this literature in the trouble it takes to theorise its object rather than simply take it for granted. For Gay Hawkins' purpose in this study is neither to praise community arts nor, assuredly, to bury them; rather it is to understand them—and to understand them in the complexity of their historical formation, and in their differences and particularities, as the outcomes of a varied set of policy, political, aesthetic and ideological circumstances and calculations.

This involves, at one level, a history of the emergence of the community arts as an administrative and funding category within the Australia Council—a story Hawkins tells with great skill and with an impressive command of her documentary sources. At another level— and it is here where her study is most significantly innovative—it is a history of the discursive categories that have informed different conceptions of the community arts while also supplying the policy rationales which have been called on to justify the development of special forms of consideration and support for those arts. Against those who see the community arts as already there, a self-originating field of creative and artistic expression, this approach allows Hawkins to view the community arts as an administrative field—that is, as a set of policy objects and targets brought into being by and through the activities of government arts and cultural policy bodies, agencies and programs.

It is, moreover, an administrative field that has been characterised by a good deal of mobility and variability so far as its legitimating rhetorics have been concerned. Put another way, there is no single thing the various activities that are called community arts have in common— except for the fact of this being their administrative designation. The range of community arts, as Hawkins describes it, stretches from the annual celebration of Nimbin's hippie version of rural community to Sydney's gay Mardi Gras—a range in which the way art and community are envisaged and combined with one another varies significantly, and in which the rationales for government involvement have varied from aesthetic through social empowerment.

None of this, of course, in any way detracts from the reality of the community arts. They may achieve, embody, represent or establish communities in various ways, just as they may encompass a multitude of artistic forms, relations and practices. Hawkins does not neglect these issues. Having considered the administrative and discursive processes through which the community arts have been shaped into being, she then offers a detailed—and very clear-eyed—assessment of the main community arts programs that the Australia Council has supported. While refusing to romanticise the community arts, Hawkins is equally careful to distance herself from those who view the community arts as a bureaucratically administered culture which serves merely to detach the people from their true artistic interests. Instead, what is offered is a balanced but sympathetic account fully alert to the important gains that the community arts have produced in promoting more widespread participation in, and recognition of, a broadened range of cultural and artistic activities.

For all these reasons, then, *From Nimbin to Mardi Gras* is an important book. Firmly grounded in a full and rich understanding of the history of Australian cultural policy, the book also breaks new ground theoretically in its sophisticated application of contemporary cultural theory to the community arts. Its concerns, in this regard, go beyond the Australian context in bringing new light to bear on many issues that have been at centre stage in the international theory and practice of the community arts. Just as important, Hawkins sets new standards for the field of cultural policy studies more generally through the deft and telling manner in which she interrelates theoretical, political and policy questions.

Tony Bennett
Faculty of Humanities, Griffith University
December 1992

Contents

Abbreviations

AC	Australia Council
ACFTA	Australian Council for the Arts
ACTU	Australian Council of Trade Unions
AETT	Australian Elizabethan Theatre Trust
ALP	Australian Labor Party
AR	Annual Report
AWL	Art and Working Life
CAB	Community Arts Board
CAC	Community Arts Committee
CAO	Community Arts Officer
CCDC	Community Cultural Development Committee
CCDU	Community Cultural Development Unit
CEAD	Community Environment Art and Design
DASET	Department of the Arts, Sport, the Environment and Territories
HAW	House About Wollongong
LOP	Land of Promises
MM	Mothers' Memories Others' Memories
NCAC	National Community Arts Co-operative
NESB	Non-English speaking background
RDS	Retrenchment—Denying Skills
SPF	Special Projects Fund
WCAC	Workers Cultural Action Committee

Plates

Tables

Acknowledgements

This history of the Community Arts Program of the Australia Council began life as a PhD. (That should not deter the reader.) I am indebted to numerous people and organisations who have supported this study in both its thesis and its book form. I express my great appreciation to past and current staff involved with community arts in the Australia Council for their continual help and encouragement. Staff provided me with information on the Community Arts Program, a space to work in, and much assistance and advice. Their enthusiasm for the project was a great source of support, especially when I felt like I was drowning in archives. Thanks to Andrea Hull, Antigone Kefala, Deborah Mills, Jon Hawkes and Jenny Bissett for making themselves available for interview, often on a number of occasions. Many other people involved with the development of the Community Arts Program were also an enormous help. Thanks to all the artists, arts organisers and bureaucrats who gave up their time to be interviewed, lent me documents and shared their insights and anecdotes. Thanks also to the staff of the Australia Council library who run one of the best arts policy information centres in the country.

A grant from the Community Cultural Development Committee funded the conversion of the thesis into a book. I am extremely grateful for this assistance and for the CCDC's commitment to seeing the study reach a wider audience, even though they may not agree with many of its assessments.

Sheila Shaver and Elizabeth Jacka, who supervised my doctorate, were a constant source of intellectual stimulation and encouragement. Sheila's detailed reading of numerous drafts and her suggestions and criticisms are deeply appreciated. I am extremely grateful to Liz for remaining involved with the project long after she had left the academy, and for her generosity with time and ideas. Thanks also to Pauline Johnson who filled in while Sheila was on leave. I would also like to extend my thanks to various friends and colleagues who offered comments on my work, especially Tim Rowse, Rob Lynch, Felicity Collins,

Kerry Carrington and Ann Game. Special thanks go to Tony Veal for his tireless computing assistance. Elizabeth Weiss of Allen & Unwin made very useful editorial suggestions and was ever helpful and encouraging. Stuart Cunningham, Tony Bennett and Sophie Watson were the examiners for my doctorate. Their comments were generous, insightful and rigorous. They gave me new enthusiasm for the project and valuable critical feedback.

I am also indebted to my family for their endurance, good humour and childcare. Thanks especially to my brother Andrew, for providing me with a room to work in, and to my children Nina and Louis for sleeping all night, most of the time. My greatest appreciation goes to my partner Warwick Pearse, whose patience, ideas and affection sustained me through the long haul.

Note: Some parts of the book have appeared as articles in *Media Information Australia*, *Artlink* and *Culture and Policy*.

Introduction

The great grey giant was a grotesque, 5m long papier mâché construction
that required eight pallbearers. A procession of the giant and pallbearers
led by the Hermit of Blue Knob moved through Nimbin at sunset on New
Year's Eve. Every so often it stopped and the hermit would call for the
citizens to bring out their vile memories of the old year—tax returns, old
love letters, jaded theses etc—and stuff them in the belly of the giant.
(Dunstan, 1979: 19)

The first contingent roaring out of the dark and onto Oxford Street was the
motorcycle cops. Not the Cocteau or even the Genet version; these cops
were bearers of light, beaming their mega-headlamps before them, blinding
the crowd with a stage technique Grace Jones had perfected in her 1978
cabaret tour. As the irises of more than 100,000 spectators readjusted
(estimates vary wildly—it seemed the whole city was out), there was a
burst of glitz, a shatter of disco sound, then an improbable assortment of
people throwing condoms to begin Sydney's 10th Annual Gay Mardi Gras.
(Michaels, 1988b: 4)

Nimbin and Sydney's Gay and Lesbian Mardi Gras are both notorious,
lingering in popular memory even amongst those who have never
witnessed them, let alone participated. For hippies and homosexuals,
these cultural events have functioned as public expressions of
'community', as celebrations of difference through the pleasure and
spectacle of carnival. They have also shared a common patron: at
various stages of their histories each has received a grant from the
Community Arts Program of the Australia Council.[1]

The history of this arts funding program is the focus of this book,
and Nimbin and Mardi Gras can serve to establish its general boundaries. The first, located in the idyllic paddocks of the north coast, was
and remains quintessentially early 1970s in its celebration of nature,
the age of Aquarius and pre-industrial communality. The second, taking
place in the heart of the city, was, by the 1990s, a carnival for the
performance of homosexuality revelling in excess and hedonism.

Between these two events the story of the Community Arts Program
has unfolded. A story marked by controversy over funding decisions,
innumerable definitions of community arts, internal tensions within the

Australia Council, patronage of some extraordinary cultural activities and persistence in the face of many attacks. The Community Arts Program survived the demise of Whitlam and Fraser's razor and remains an irritant in Commonwealth arts funding; a persistent challenge to the status of *Culture* in cultural policy.

The invocation of 'community' in arts policy is both recent and symptomatic of wider developments. The historical context of the Community Arts Program is shaped not only by the emergence of various social movements, from the counterculture to sexual liberation, but also by new trends in social policy. In the late 1960s and early 1970s the category 'community' spread like a virus through many areas of public administration. Child welfare departments were renamed Youth and Community Services, the Commonwealth Schools Commission began funding programs to foster school/community involvement, health bureaucracies were besieged by demands for community health services and the Australian Council for the Arts (ACFTA) established the Community Arts and Development Committee. The very ambiguity of the term 'community' was perhaps the source of its appeal. From education to health to welfare to the arts, 'community' was invoked in different ways with different effects.

This account argues that 'community arts' were a creation of government policy, an official invention. Despite nostalgic claims that they are 'as old as civilization' (O'Neill, 1984) the category 'community arts' had no real currency in Australia until it appeared in federal arts policy as a separate funding program in 1973. The evolution of the Community Arts Program formed part of the Whitlam Government's conversion of the ACFTA into the Australia Council. The program was not a response to an organised social movement, nor was it designed to support a specific cultural form. It was, instead, framed within the social democratic demand for increased access to and participation in the arts. This demand was not foreign to arts funding. The need to spread the 'civilising benefits' of culture had been mobilised in previous arguments for government support. But Whitlam gave access and participation new emphasis. In the 1973 Annual Report of the ACFTA, fostering a wider spread of interest and participation in the arts was placed next to the encouragement of excellence and the promotion of national identity as a key objective of arts support (ACFTA, AR, 1973: 9). Unlike earlier government gestures, Whitlam produced money as well as rhetoric. The creation of a separate program responsible for access and participation was an innovation in the organisation of arts funding.

Attaching the title 'community arts' to this program was an indicator of both the popularity and the ambiguity of the term 'community'. It was strategic. In the absence of a fixed referent community arts signified a heterogeneous field of cultural activity. But this ambiguity was also the source of the program's ongoing identity crisis. In fact, if there is one question that has been asked repeatedly of the Community Arts Program since its inception it is: what exactly is it? The answers to this question come thick and fast, ranging across a vast array of cultural forms and constituencies. Community arts are murals, craft workshops in prisons, agitprop theatre, a migrant women's embroidery group, regional arts centres, local government cultural officers, a photo exhibition of a miners' strike, a mask-making project with children. The list goes on and on but little is clarified. Instead, a vague boundary is established that distinguishes community arts from both 'high' culture and mass culture. Community arts are located out on the cultural fringes where marginal groups produce marginal art. Often it is easier to characterise 'community arts' by what it is not; forms with the status and authority of Art and the upper middle class audience that enjoys them escape this classification. Clustered around this elusive term are notions like 'amateur', 'local', 'political', 'authentic', 'social concern', 'welfare', 'therapy' and 'worthy', notions which are at once the source of community arts' opposition and marginality. While the amateur and the local may challenge the hegemony of the professional and the national in arts policy they are also invoked as terms of derision and dismissal, as signs of aesthetic fiascos and cultural lack.

Recognition of the multiple and contradictory representations of community arts does not mean that dominant meanings cannot be identified. The fact of state funding demands rules of inclusion and exclusion with which to assess applications. As a source of funds for some cultural activities and not others, the Community Arts Program has had to establish a *field* of patronage. The construction of the Community Arts Program through the practice of patronage and the construction of a set of meanings about community arts are deeply involved with one another.

The power of the Community Arts Program of the Australia Council to prescribe certain meanings for community arts is one of the main concerns of this inquiry. Unlike theatre or literature or painting which have both 'histories' and various institutional and economic structures, community arts was initially constituted only by government policy and money. The Community Arts Program was the sole source of economic support. This does not mean that there was no cultural activity of this sort until the establishment of the program. On the contrary, an immense variety of pre-existing cultural organisations and workers were attracted to this fund and were accepted as community arts thanks to the ambiguity of the earliest funding guidelines. The funding body was constitutive in the sense that it established a field with wide references under which a multiplicity of disparate activities and discourses were gathered together and *re-presented* as community arts.

The funding institution, however, is not the sum of community arts

but only one of many registers. Patronage is enabling. Grants for
'community arts projects' have supported a vast diversity of cultural
activities and workers. Projects, then, provide an important key to the
complex outcomes of funding. And it is for this reason that they have
been accorded a place in this history. A focus only on administrative
arrangements and policy discourses would exclude a consideration of
the effects of the Community Arts Program outside the micro-politics
of the Australia Council. The relationship between policy, the types of
projects funded and the texts which emerge from these is a central
preoccupation of this account.

Projects are also an indicator of how much community arts is
constituted not as a distinctive cultural form or aesthetic but as a
particular cultural practice. In tracing how four projects funded by the
Community Arts Program have invoked 'art' and 'community' it is
possible to consider how knowledges of community arts have been
produced at the level of local cultural practice and how policy and
projects interact.

As the primary source of funds the Community Arts Program of the
Australia Council has played a significant role in the establishment of
other forms of economic and organisational support. For example, since
the late 1970s all state and some local governments have established
community arts funding programs and since 1983 state networks of
community art workers have received federal funding. The meanings
and practices privileged in the national program have had a major
influence on these initiatives. So, from the invocation of 'community'
in federal arts policy in the early 1970s, to the 1990s, a community
arts complex has developed, characterised by state and local policies
and funding programs, community-based arts organisations, associations of community art workers, journals and the discourses which
circulate within and between these various sites.

To different degrees these developments are part of the Community
Arts Program's constituency; they are tied to it either economically or
ideologically or both. However, detailed analysis of this wider community arts movement is outside the scope of this account. What is of
concern here is the network of relations between the Community Arts
Program and its constituency. These relations are not fixed; they shift
within a field marked by expectations, dependencies and power. The
funding institution is both active and acted upon. The central task is
to trace the *productive* effects of patronage, to explore its interrelation-
ship with community arts projects and community arts practitioners.

Documenting the Community Arts Program

In order to trace the shifting and often contradictory meanings for
community arts and the conditions which produced them this account
deploys a method that is dynamic. It refuses the constrictions of a

single theoretical model and, instead, uses concepts which highlight how the object has been constituted and which allow several lines of analysis. Michel Foucault's (1980a) idea of the 'toolkit', of an engaged theory that emerges not as a system but as an instrument for step by step reflection is extremely useful. It allows for an interpretation to be developed through the process of constructing a history of the Community Arts Program and some of its projects.

Foucault's various studies of the emergence of institutions to administer and reform populations acknowledge the specificity of discourses and power relations. In his approach state institutions are understood in and through their particular histories, orders and productivities. The notion of discourse is particularly relevant to this investigation of the Community Arts Program. It offers a way of understanding how the institutional practices of the Australia Council have both codifying effects regarding what is to be known about 'the arts' and prescriptive effects regarding what is to be done in terms of promoting and funding them (Foucault, 1981: 5). Discourse analysis concentrates on the conditions which produce knowledges and practices and their constitutive effects. It provides a method for tracing how certain ideas and practices have come to signify community arts and how these meanings both shift and are reiterated over time. According to Foucault this approach lays no claim to totality, nor does it seek to universalise. Instead, it is a method which privileges a multiplicity of historical processes (Foucault, 1981: 5).

While this inquiry is concerned to trace historical patterns it does not assume any hidden logic behind the evolution of the Community Arts Program. Such an assumption neutralises discourse and makes it a sign of something else, of hidden meanings and intentions. As Stuart Cunningham (1989) has argued, deterministic accounts reduce discourse to a symptom or expression of a purposive drive by some abstracted force such as the state. They 'treat policy discourse as simply another object for the surveilling eye of cultural critique' (Cunningham, 1989: 8).

Discourse must be represented in its consistency, it must emerge in its own complexity, if we are to understand why and how statements appeared when and where they did. Tracing the formation of the Community Arts Program, then, involves the description of power relations at work at particular historical moments and the patterns of discontinuity and continuity in ideas and practices. It also involves a description of the discursive fields in which the policies for community arts were produced, and the ways in which these policies emerged in relations of displacement and differentiation from other policies enunciated within the Australia Council. As the program responsible for encouraging greater access and participation in the arts the Community Arts Program interpreted its mission in different ways at different times. But this took place always in relationship to the discourses on art and culture enunciated in the rest of the Australia Council.

The production of a field of knowledge about community arts is inextricably caught up with the play of power. In much of Foucault's work the study of institutions is organised around the description of their specific power relations (see Foucault, 1977). Power relations are defined as 'the way certain actions may structure the field of other possible actions' (Foucault, 1982: 223). Power is not something above society, or possessed by individuals, or controlled from one point of view (Wickham, 1987: 148). It is a process, an activity, a shifting set of relations. Foucault refuses to accept the idea of an aggregation of power within a final source such as the state or the economy. He argues for analyses which recognise how power relations are elaborated, transformed and organised within specific sites. This does not mean a denial of the reality of the state. Foucault is attentive to how power relations have been governmentalised, rationalised and centralised under the auspices of various state institutions (1982: 224). But this does not lead him to a representation of the state as a monolithic, one-sided, controlling apparatus.

Annette Kuhn (1988) identifies two significant strengths in Foucault's conceptualisation of power. Firstly, it offers a way of under-standing the unevenness, resistance, conflict and ongoing transforma-tion in relations of power. Secondly, it recognises that power can be productive in certain ways. Both these strengths avoid negative and deterministic definitions of power. The relevance of Foucault's notion of power for this study is that it facilitates an analysis attentive to how the Community Arts Program was produced within the practices and power relations of federal arts funding. And how this program, in turn, produced a variety of new constituencies for arts funding that had for so long been ignored or persistently devalued.

As we will see shortly, Foucault's approach influences the shape of this book. In Part I the political field of arts funding is explored. The emphasis is on the structures which underpin state support for the arts and their effects. Understanding this historical and discursive context is crucial for assessing the nature of community arts' challenge. In Part II the story of the Community Arts Program is set down. This section provides both a document of the program and a critical evaluation of its success in contesting some of the more undemocratic aspects of arts policy. Part III shifts from policy to projects. Using case studies of key issues in the formation of community arts, the focus is on how projects recreate meanings for community arts within the specific context of local cultural production.

Cultural policy studies

Several recent critiques of cultural studies have argued for a more pragmatic political orientation to be established within this field (Bennett, 1989b; Cunningham, 1992). In opposition to the search for progressive texts, resistant subcultures and active audiences, studies of cultural *policy* are hailed as the source of a more applied and interventionist approach. In arguing for the insertion of 'policy' between 'culture' and 'studies' Tony Bennett (1989b) insists that the purpose is not to identify another object for the scrutiny of the cultural critic, but rather to produce urgently needed critical knowledges about governmentality and culture. For Cunningham (1992) 'cultural policy studies' offers a fundamental challenge to the left idealism and political irrelevance of much existing work in cultural studies.

Central to this task is the production of concrete, historically detailed accounts of the various institutions and agendas which shape the cultural sphere. The emergence of cultural policy studies signals the possibility of useful interaction between cultural analysis and cultural administration. It also highlights the importance of review and reform of cultural policy that emerges from a close understanding of how meanings for culture are produced and managed. Without investigations of the emergence and operations of government interventions in cultural activity present practice is difficult to assess. Critical knowledges of the past are an important resource for understanding how the present is formed. This does not mean a search for origins but rather an analysis attentive to how past discursive structures are 'thought' in the present.

This history of the Community Arts Program is motivated in part by these demands for positive knowledges about cultural policy formation. It is also motivated by the ongoing demand for democratic reform of cultural administration. A fundamental question shaping this account is: what does the history of the Community Arts Program yield in terms of more equitable approaches to public intervention in culture?

Beyond this is a series of related issues concerning why this program was established in the early 1970s, what shape it took during the years under review and how its various bureaucratic and discursive practices produced meanings for 'community arts'. There is also a concern to explore how the Community Arts Program was accommodated within the Australia Council, how its staff and constituencies negotiated the internal tensions within this institution over its uncertain status and legitimacy. Apart from this there are the projects, the outcomes of patronage. How were policy objectives expressed through local cultural activity?

An historical record of the Community Arts Program is important. Without this the program risks sinking without a trace. It remains high on the federal Liberal Party's hit list for either abolition or devolution. This does not mean that producing a history is a sign of community arts' imminent demise. The program warrants documentation because it has played a crucial role in supporting a vast field of cultural activity. This field is shaped by a number of different cultural practices: the amateur, the local, the political and the therapeutic. Behind all these various projects, organisations and cultural texts have been grants from the Community Arts Program. Many of these projects remain as lasting examples of the expressive and organising potential of culture. They sit next to a diverse array of other cultural developments from the 1970s to the 1990s, ranging from video access to public radio which signified the expansion of new forms of local and community-based culture.

For too long the significance of community-based cultural practice has been trivialised and devalued by both policy makers and cultural critics. In the interminable struggles to pin down national identity or to regulate import culture the pleasures of the local have been dismissed as purely parochial. Yet it is often here that the conditions necessary for democratic cultural production, for formal innovation and for expressions of ethnic, class or gender difference can most easily be established. Of course 'local' and 'community' are fluid categories continuously constituted in different sites and through different cultural practices. The intention here is not to oppose them as the authentic 'other' of the national or the international. Rather, it is to investigate how the Community Arts Program deployed these categories in the wider search for increased access to and participation in the arts.

Beyond the value of an historical record is the political impact of the Community Arts Program. As the program charged with extending the benefits of art to a more respresentative public it challenged some of the fundamental assumptions and practices underpinning arts funding. Assessing the nature of this challenge is a central aim of this inquiry. The creation of this program foregrounded questions of access and participation in arts policy. These 'new' objectives for the public support of art generated a series of tensions in the Australia Council around what could be considered a legitimate cultural activity and which audiences were being served by current funding practices and which were ignored or devalued. The Community Arts Program's various strategies for making arts funding more equitable signalled the entry of new constituencies and new discourses of value into the existing terrain of cultural policy.

However, while these achievements are important they must be situated within a wider context. Any appraisal of this program cannot avoid asking whether community arts represents the most effective strategy for radical reform of arts funding. This question challenges existing evaluations of the politics of community arts which have defended this program as automatically progressive in opposition to the supposedly inherent elitism of art. This rhetorical politics has been ever ready to dennounce the bourgeois excesses of opera and praise the authentic voice of oppressed experience manifest in the community arts project. Models for reform have involved increasing the status and funding of community arts at the expense of 'high' art; or privileging 'majority' culture over 'minority' culture.

This position is bankrupt because it leaves intact existing frameworks for arts funding and argues only for a rearrangement of priorities. The crucial issue for radical reform of arts policy in the 1990s is not how much money community arts gets in comparison to opera, but whether it is possible in a liberal democratic society to sustain a separate institutional and policy sphere for art. Although terms like cultural diversity and cultural pluralism have recently begun to feature in arts policies, funding patterns still privilege the 'high' arts and still effectively redistribute to the upper middle class. In this way arts policy functions as a crucial site for the hierarchical ranking of cultural forms and the differentiation of publics. As long as art signifies the top of an aesthetic hierarchy community arts will exist as the space where the multitude of other forms and publics excluded or devalued by this hierarchy are mopped up. And it is for this reason that a new politics of community arts must be established. One that asks that uncomfortable question: is community arts a cultural program whose moment has passed?

Note

1   In this history 'Community Arts Program' is used as a generic term covering the whole period under review, 1973 to 1991. Within the Australia Council the program has had changing official titles and status. Between 1973 and 1977 it was usually referred to as the Community Arts Committee (CAC); in 1978 it became a Board and its title changed to the Community Arts Board (CAB). In 1987 it became the Community Cultural Development Committee (CCDC).

Part I

Cultural policy and community arts

1
The politics of arts funding

With so many assumptions attendant upon 'community' and 'art' how is it possible to fix some boundaries around their multiple meanings? This is the task of Part I. Rather than survey the vast literature outlining the philosophical bases of art or sociological theories of community, the focus is on how these categories have been defined by the specific politics of arts funding. A politics that John Frow (1986) has succinctly described as involving the translation of aesthetic and social values into cash terms. Obviously ideologies of art and community are at work here. These terms are not neutral or empty. However, the immediate concern is to investigate how these ideologies are remade within the demands of administering and funding the arts.

This initial investigation of the structures underpinning state patronage of the arts poses three sets of questions. The first set concerns the history of arts funding institutions: what are the patterns of state intervention in the arts in Australia?, and what meanings have these institutions produced for 'the arts'? The second set of questions explores two of the central categories used to justify arts support: excellence and nation. How have these terms been invoked within arts policy? Why are they so crucial to the rhetoric of grants assessment? How are they used to distinguish various cultural forms, practices and audiences? What is their function within the discourses of value constituted by arts funding? The final set of questions investigates the political effects of these structuring influences: how equitable are they in terms of facilitating democratic access to and participation in the arts? Which audiences are being reached by these patterns of subsidy and which are being excluded? Which cultural forms and traditions are being supported and which are left to the market? Whose interests are legitimated and whose are ignored or devalued?

Community arts has to be seen as a product of these various political questions. Questions which surfaced when the fundamental elitism of arts funding could no longer be ignored, when the rhetoric of excellence and nation came under challenge with a counter rhetoric of access and participation. The Community Arts Program has been a significant force in contesting the structures of arts funding. When 'community' entered the discourses of arts policy previous assumptions were inevitably disrupted; what the ambiguity and apparent innocence of 'community' allowed was an onslaught of new forms, new constituencies, new methods of patronage and new purposes for art. It is only against an analysis of the dominant patterns and effects of arts funding that the story of the Community Arts Program can be told and that an evaluation of its political significance can be established. For this is the context that produced community arts and this is the context that was confronted as the program developed.

Defining the arts

Defining the arts is an activity central to the disbursement of subsidy. Without this it would be impossible to identify which activities are eligible for public support and which are not. Obviously this process of definition is never fixed; the practice of patronage continually produces meanings for 'art', in the same way that policy discourses are constitutive. However, within this shifting terrain certain meanings laid down in the past have persisted and their dominance reflects the power of ideologies about culture and value. It is for this reason that it is necessary to investigate key historical developments.

The problem with this task, however, is that histories of arts funding institutions in Australia are scarce and uneven. It was not until 1985, with the publication of Tim Rowse's *Arguing the Arts*, that there was any substantial documentation and analysis of the origins and work of the Australia Council. Although Rowse's history is schematic it sketched an influential model for others to fill in, modify or refute.

However, while this study marked a breakthrough this does not mean that assistance to the arts in general and the Australia Council's role in particular have never been scrutinised. On the contrary, they have been the focus of extensive controversy and debate. This debate has ranged across numerous themes, covering topics as diverse as regional patterns of grants distribution and the future of the Australia Council (see Ryan, 1981; Withers, 1981a; Davidson, 1981; Rowse, 1981a; Brett, 1982; Field, 1980; Macdonell, 1992; Roberts, 1983; Horne, 1988). In general, this public discussion has been both specific and polemical, often emerging in response to particular policy developments. Its value lies in the constant reminder of arts funding as a system of inclusion and exclusion in which the boundaries between subsidised and not subsidised are always open to challenge.

What has been missing in this literature, until recently, is sustained and critical analysis situating the arts and their funding within the broader field of cultural policy, cultural studies and cultural history. Lively debate and controversy are useful up to a point, if only to refute that tired but persistent idea that the arts are somehow above politics and the social, but they are no substitute for useful historical documentation and theoretically informed analysis. Without this, debates about the 'politics of the arts' in Australia have tended to be trapped in a rhetoric of reaction with the Australia Council in the centre of the target.

Two books stand out as making significant contributions to a more sophisticated analysis of arts funding. Rowse's (1985a) *Arguing the Arts*, as previously mentioned, and Geoff Mulgan and Ken Worpole's (1986) *Saturday Night or Sunday Morning? From Arts to Industry— New Forms of Cultural Policy*. Both these books are discursive and polemical. Their explicit intention is to intervene in current debates about cultural policy. However, underpinning their applied analysis is a commitment to historically informed argument and critical interpretation based on a thorough understanding of key debates in cultural theory.

Both books take as their broad area of investigation the scope of government's responsibility for culture. They scrutinise the effects of past and present policies specifically in terms of their democratic and undemocratic impacts. They also situate arts funding within this broader field and are able to investigate both its particular history and effects, as well as its relationships to other forms and developments from broadcasting to folk music. Both studies acknowledge the dualistic logic endemic within cultural policy: a logic that splits the cultural domain into subsidised art and commercial entertainment, a logic in which art is ideologically both separate and superior. Both are also in agreement when they argue that these divisions are the major barrier to progressive policy reform. So it is with Rowse and Mulgan and Worpole that an analysis of the politics of arts funding must begin, recognising however, that the concern here is not so much with the detail of historical developments as with an identification of the structuring influences on policy formation.

In the history of cultural policy that begins his book, Rowse traces the origins of cultural dualism. His narrative is organised into three distinct phases: voluntary entrepreneurship, statutory patronage and decentralised patronage. The first phase describes the period before any coherent government intervention. The distinguishing features of voluntary entrepreneurship were the efforts of a diverse group of self-appointed, altruistic cultural leaders who organised a range of cultural activities from the Australian Elizabethan Theatre Trust (AETT) to the Australian Film Institute, with very ad hoc Commonwealth government support (Rowse, 1985a: 10).

Rowse attributes to these entrepreneurs substantial influence in the establishment of more extensive state intervention from the late 1960s.

He identifies them as the architects of the second phase of policy development: statutory patronage. Their experience in cultural administration was not only rewarded with the acquisition of key posts in the new funding institutions; so too were their cultural values (Rowse, 1985a: 13). The emergence of government institutions to fund and develop the arts was the result of a number of diverse forces but one of the most important was the lobbying done by these voluntary entrepreneurs. Art warranted funding not simply because its value somehow commended itself but because it had powerful advocates. The arguments put to government urging more extensive and coordinated intervention carried weight because of who mouthed them. These cultural elites felt a deep obligation to the nation and its cultural needs, they had already demonstrated their commitment to filling the great Australian cultural lack, now it was time for government to take up this lead; to promote the cultural preferences of this upper middle class elite as exemplary (Rowse, 1985a: 117–18).

Rowse's history of the development of arts policy traces the play of political and cultural interests that produced increased Commonwealth responsibility for culture. In setting out this account he carefully avoids a crude class determinism that characterises so many left accounts of arts patronage. Although he documents the close relationship between certain cultural elites and government, he does not reduce this to an instance of 'ruling class hegemony' in which the state obediently becomes the agent of an economically or culturally powerful bourgeoisie. Instead he shows how the process of lobbying government to accept responsibility for art confirmed and consolidated the status of a cultural elite *and* reinforced the ideological distinctions between art and other cultural practices.

The value of this history is that it shows how the field of culture is mediated by classes and class fractions. So, while cultural distinctions must be read as evidence of class power this does not imply a neat fit between certain cultural formations and discrete class groups (Frow, 1986: 124). The crucial question, as Pierre Bourdieu (1980: 225) has pointed out, is not so much about the content of cultural distinctions— about football for the working class and ballet for the bourgeoisie—as about how they come to represent apparently natural hierarchies of value. How cultural distinctions are invoked by dominant groups to legitimate some cultural practices and not others; to credit some cultural forms with the status of taste, quality, aesthetics and Art; to win government subsidy for some cultures and not others.

The growth of government assistance to the arts, then, has produced an equation between subsidy and Art, with a very large capital 'A'. The connotations which surround arts funding are that what gets money, and therefore legitimation, are superior, high or fine cultural activities. This is enshrined in a multitude of different practices: from institutional structures based on aesthetic divisions between music, literature, theatre, visual arts or whatever, to the rhetoric of excellence which implies that only certain activities embody quality and national significance. Other implications flow from these: the arts that get subsidy are predominantly pre-twentieth century, live, non-commercial and appeal to minority audiences.

Of course, the separation of art from a range of related cultural practices is not unique to arts funding bodies. This process had been underway long before the state declared substantial responsibility for this area (see Williams, 1976; Pick, 1986; Walker, 1983). What is unique, however, is the particular role arts policies have played in perpetuating restricted meanings for art in the face of rapidly changing social and cultural relations. It is no coincidence that the establishment of official arts funding bodies in both Britain and Australia is a post–World War Two phenomenon, when developments in mass culture have been extensive. At the same time as the cultural field has dramatically expanded with new technologies, audiences and economics, art has been taken under the caring wing of the state and, to a certain extent, protected from these developments.

Art and mass culture

Statutory patronage, the second phase in Rowse's schema, saw the federal government accept responsibility for the funding and development of various cultural activities. This was the period when the ACFTA and the Australian Film Development Corporation were established (the Australia Council and the Australian Film Commission after 1975). The creation of these institutions changed the landscape of cultural policy in Australia dramatically. Not only were there official organisations in the centre of the picture but the emergence of the state as a patron meant that justifications for this intervention were now publicly debated. For Rowse (1985a: 14), the most significant aspect of these debates was how much they were shaped by already existing frameworks for cultural distribution, so that this new economics of subsidy both confirmed and entrenched previous meanings for art and previous patterns of support.

The major effect of expanded government support was that the separation between art and mass culture became a cornerstone of this new public cultural field. The formation of cultural policies in the late 1960s was predicated on a 'dual cultures' model: a persistent distinction manifest in most aspects of cultural administration between subsidised 'quality' and commercial 'entertainment'. In this way the relationship between certain cultural forms and certain methods of distribution was consolidated. The art that the state subsidised needed to be protected from the rigours of the marketplace; its integrity demanded live distribution. Commercial success was either an irrelevant or a dangerous measure of value (Rowse, 1985a: 59–64).

These are just a few of the many claims that were made about art in the process of establishing it as a field of public responsibility. What distinguished these arguments was the way in which they all depended on defining art *in relation to* mass cultural forms. Art was not simply different from television, radio, cinema or whatever, it was better. This distinction did not originate in arts funding institutions but rather reflected how arts policies negotiated the growth of technologies for mass communication.

What the expansion of the mass media after World War Two did was produce new sorts of audiences and cultural experiences that were the product of electronic rather than live distribution. This different process of audience formation did not simply challenge the authority of arts audiences through the sheer weight of numbers: it also raised questions about popularity and democracy. Mass culture was hardly exclusive, it was able to claim enormous appeal and reach and implicitly displace the cultural significance and exclusivity of live high cultural forms. This was a result not only of the inevitable competition that cinema and television represented but also of the increasing costs of live production. The rapid growth of mass forms marginalised art econom-ically and culturally (Mulgan and Worpole, 1986: 23).

Of course, one response to this could have been to use the mass media to distribute art further and wider. Drawing on the work of Walter Benjamin (1973b) Rowse argues that the mass media offered the chance to democratise high culture through technological means of distribution. However, rather than grab this opportunity the architects of arts policy dismissed it. Not only could the integrity of art have been threatened but mass audiences hardly had the skills to appreciate this democratic gesture!

This shows how the boundaries between subsidised and not sub-sidised were influenced by particular assumptions about the relation between audiences and forms. What advantaged art so much in this process was the fear that its advocates mobilised around the twin dangers of market forces and electronic distribution. Arts funding has generated a whole set of meanings for art based on the rejection of techniques for mass distribution and on the capabilities of mass audi-ences. This rejection is a product of more than just a concern to protect the cosy and exclusive atmosphere of the theatre crowd. It also reflects the idea that 'high' cultural forms demand more sophisticated skills on the part of the audience; that the competencies required for a night in front of television are trivial compared to the superior demands required for a visit to the art gallery. In this way arts audiences acquire greater cultural authority, through a series of distinctions that pose art as above entertainment, that represent the art lover as 'appreciating' while the entertainment lover merely consumes.

Both Rowse (1985a: 117) and Mulgan and Worpole (1986: 22) argue that in response to these new cultural relations arts funding emerged almost as a massive rescue operation, as an act of preservation. It had the effect of constructing new authority for art by giving it the golden touch of state subsidy:

> In showing that it could and would [support the arts] the Commonwealth also supported a tendency towards a duality in Australia's twentieth century culture. It not only preserved the Arts from their economic decline, it preserved their traditions of distribution and the social identities of their audiences. . . In the very economic necessity of subsidy lay one of the proofs of the Arts. Open-ended subsidy, a 'vote' for the Arts, demonstrated further the worth of both the Arts and those who voted. . . In every living room flashed the nightly evidence that the Arts were a necessary relief from the commercial, and Arts subsidies a necessary underwriting of that relief. (Rowse, 1985a: 117)

While the dual cultures framework may have protected art it also produced a series of ongoing administrative problems. Mulgan and Worpole describe the Arts Council of Great Britain as in a perpetual state of crisis over how to deal with new, or technologically based, forms: 'New cultural forms always seem to produce frenetic moral panics. . . By concentrating on pre-twentieth century forms the Arts Council has condemned itself to a semi-permanent crisis' (Mulgan and Worpole, 1986: 22–3). Raymond Williams' (1979: 163) evaluation is similar. He describes the dilemmas the Arts Council of Great Britain has faced over its definition of art as a relatively enclosed and continuing cultural canon. The arrival of 'new' forms like film, photography, performance art, community art and experimental art have all challenged these restricted meanings and the associated rhetoric about 'standards'. These discourses of value confer on art and 'high' culture immense aesthetic and social superiority and fix it as the anchoring point from which all else cultural is measured (Bennett, 1980: 22). In this situation, it is little wonder that the experimental, the local or the technological are all constituted as residual, lesser and negative. Nor is it any surprise to note the anxiety generated when these forms started clamouring at the door of arts funding bodies.

Although the cultural dualism argument represents an important analysis of arts policy, there are some dangers in its application. For example, when Mulgan and Worpole (1986: 116) argue that the cultural forms supported by the state are, by definition, those unable to survive in the market, the organisation of arts funding is reduced to economic determinism. Frow (1986) rejects this proposition by pointing out that much high culture is both fully commercial and electronically distributed. This makes it impossible to claim that the dual cultures framework is based on a fixed opposition between commercial versus non-commercial or live versus electronic.

Rowse's use of this concept is more sophisticated. In his discussion of the complex relation between subsidy and cultural status, cultural dualism is not defined in terms of simple oppositions. Instead, it is used to describe the shifting processes of differentiation that have established Art as a separate and special field of government responsibility. It is the ideological and aesthetic privilege that art occupies within cultural policy and how this is established specifically in relation to other cultural forms that is the real issue (Frow, 1986: 121). Cultural dualism shows how the dominant definitions established for art through the discourses and practices of subsidy have depended on a negative evaluation of mass forms and a sharp differentiation from them. Art was placed at the top of a universal scale of cultural forms, it was 'high' culture in opposition to the mass, the popular and the low.

Discourses of value: excellence

This broad scan of the historical patterns structuring arts funding has revealed how art came to occupy a privileged position in cultural policy. In this section the focus is on the specific discourses of value that have been produced through the practices of state patronage. What characterises these discourses is a rhetoric of accountability, a set of justifications for the public support of art that have the explicit function of explaining why it warrants special attention. Two categories are crucial to this process and their importance is evident in their repeated invocation in the charter of the Australia Council: excellence and nation. These terms are central to the ideologies of art constituted within arts funding which not only identify what art is but also, implicitly, who it is for. This reflects the fundamental function of discourses of value: the attribution of value to certain objects and also certain valuing subjects.

What needs to be investigated here is how excellence and nation are used to attribute value to art and to the audiences that recognise and appreciate it. Arts policy has to be read as a particular discourse of value, one which draws on certain aesthetic discourses and remakes them within a specific public institutional sphere. Bennett (1985: 36) argues that there is no necessary connection between the multiple discourses of value and aesthetic discourse; they usually operate in different registers. Aesthetic discourse is simply one of many discourses of value. However, it is when aesthetic discourse becomes hegemonic, when it is privileged in the identification of supposedly universal artistic practices that it needs to be scrutinised.

This tendency can be identified in arts policy, which invokes excellence and the nation in order to establish a distinct and special status for art. The effects of this hegemony are threefold: first, the social origins of aesthetic discourse are disguised; second, other discourses of value are devalued and excluded; and finally, those unable to recognise art, those outside the elite valuing community, are constructed as lacking. Excellence and nation are deeply interconnected categories within the field of arts policy: each implies the other. However, in this investigation each shall be considered in turn in order to situate the specific challenge of community. The discourses of value developed in the Community Arts Program disrupted certain assumptions about excellence and standards and also assumptions about the nation and cultural unity. These were distinct but related challenges that can only be understood with a detailed investigation of how discourses of excellence and the nation are mobilised in the practice of allocating cultural value and subsidy.

The promotion of excellence in the arts is one of the central emblems of the Australia Council and of most state arts institutions. It was an important justification for the establishment of the ACFTA and was reiterated in Whitlam's remodelling of this organisation into the Australia Council. Whitlam, however, added 'access and participation' to the platform and from the first official mention of these new objectives excellence and access have been represented as fundamentally antagonistic. In the first Annual Report of the ACFTA after the Labor victory, the Chair of the Council, Dr H. C. Coombs, declared:

> To some extent, of course, the arts are elitist. At their best they are the work of the exceptionally talented, and historically have been enjoyed by relatively few. Nevertheless the charter of the Council . . . clearly calls on it and the Boards to widen opportunities for the practice of the arts and to widen access to, and understanding, enjoyment and application of, the arts in the community generally. (ACFTA, AR, 1973: 16)

Here the sanctity of excellence was threatened by the spectre of access and the ongoing negotiation of this tension has been formative of community arts. It is for this reason that the dominant side of this opposition needs to be scrutinised.

Excellence is a category that arts funding bodies are keen to invoke but less keen to define. Its meanings are variable because it is a term around which a whole range of associations accumulate. If excellence is not used then terms like 'standards', 'quality' and 'professionalism' have the same effect. All these terms can be located in various aspects of the Australia Council's activities from the official charter to funding guidelines.

Rowse (1985a) offers a useful summary of the main components and effects of the discourse of excellence. First, there is the assumption that excellent art rests at the top of some single scale of aesthetic value. This representation depends on a utopian ideal of Australia as culturally homogeneous and therefore able to establish consensus on what this scale of values is. The second assumption is that excellence is intrinsic to objects, that the 'thing being valued commends itself' (Rowse,

1985a: 34). Here the arts are positioned above politics and economics, the act of funding is merely the necessary recognition of the object's inherent significance. The final effect of this discourse is the way in which it implies an audience with the skills and authority to make distinctions of quality and intelligence and 'to have these accepted as authoritative throughout the nation' (Rowse, 1985a: 33).

What Rowse does not explore is the relationship between the discourse of excellence and the broader field of aesthetics. Excellence has to be seen as a remaking of dominant discourses of art or the aesthetic within the specific context of a funding institution. Bennett's (1985) rejection of aesthetics as 'really useless knowledge' can be used to extend Rowse's account of excellence in several ways. Bennett develops a convincing argument against the viability of a theory of aesthetics in offering any useful conceptual tools for the concrete questions of cultural policy (1985: 29). However, one value of an understanding of philosophical accounts of aesthetics lies in the possibility of identifying the influences of these ideas on the discourse of excellence. Excellence implicitly refers to and reproduces certain assumptions which are embedded in the way aesthetics represent art.

Both excellence and aesthetics are discourses of transcendence where art always exceeds its determinations. According to Bennett, definitions of aesthetics, whether bourgeois or Marxist, are ultimately conceived in idealist, ahistorical and essentialist terms. This means that the distinction between art and non-art becomes dependent not on specific social or historical conditions but on formal properties or essences within objects (Bennett, 1985: 29).

Another parallel between excellence and aesthetics is the presumption of valuing subjects or audiences which recognise art from a position of disinterestedness (Bennett, 1985: 36). The idea of disinterestedness Bennett defines as 'that which pleases without regard to any interest of the subject' (1985: 42). Summarising Bourdieu (1984), Bennett points out that this is an attitude specific to those classes or class fractions most distanced from 'the practical need to secure the necessities of life. Indeed, it is a way of *displaying* that distance' (Bennett, 1985: 42) [emphasis in the original]. The effect of this is the legitimation of bourgeois taste as distinguished from others and as naturally superior and elite.

The primary function of discourses of value is social differentiation. What Bennett offers is a way of extending Rowse's discussion with an exploration of how aesthetic discourse is ideological, specifically in its production of subjects who recognise or fail to recognise art. And it is in this way that a place was cleared for community arts. Access and participation were represented almost as antidotes to the inevitable side effects of excellence. The elite valuing community constituted by the rhetoric of excellence also produced 'others' who were unable or unwilling to participate in this. Community arts claimed to represent those who did not recognise art, to rescue these 'others' and improve them. 'Community' then, was an extremely convenient category in which to group all those left out in the cold by the restricted and elitist definitions of value constituted by the discourse of excellence.

Nation and community

Like excellence, nation is a central category in public arguments for the arts. As previously mentioned, the rhetoric of excellence and nation are closely connected. Excellent art is represented as valuable to the whole nation; while its audience may be small its vicarious benefits for 'all Australians' are immense.

The pressure to justify government spending on culture in terms of the national interest is not peculiar to arts funding. Establishing the relationship between public cultural institutions and national identity is a recurring demand of cultural policies from film to television to the arts (cf. Rowse and Moran, 1984; Moran, 1982; Rohdie, 1983). Different cultural institutions invoke Australia in different ways according to the specificities of their economic and ideological organisation. Dermody and Jacka's (1987) work on film policy and institutions shows how the idea of 'Australian content', for example, has produced a particular set of definitions which serve the demands of administering grants, tax concessions and industry regulation. In his study of museum and heritage policy Bennett (1988b) explores another invocation of the nation. Here the state has a central role to play in constructing the national past, in 'organising the time-space co-ordinates of the nation' (Bennett, 1988b: 9). Museums are identified as having exceptional authority in demarcating both the past and the nation.

Cultural policy, then, is a rich site for exploring the idea that the nation is a construct, an 'imagined community' (Anderson, 1983). In public arts institutions such as the Australia Council, 'Australia' has been invoked in different ways at different times. Because the history of arts policy reveals a deep resistance to associations of art with money, claims about the national value of art have, until the 1980s, tended to be more ideological than economic. Like film policy, government intervention in the arts has been motivated by a certain degree of protectionism, by the representation of Australia as a relatively new and fragile cultural entity. But unlike that in film, protection has not taken the form of industry regulation and content guidelines; the production of art is more individual and artisanal than industrial. Instead, the system of direct subsidy to producers has privileged various ideas about the unique role of 'the artist' in making Australian culture.

This pattern of patronage was, of course, firmly entrenched with the establishment of the ACFTA and then the Australia Council. So too was the idea that the arts were a Commonwealth responsibility. The

establishment of the major arts support institution at the federal level
was not the result of any coordinated planning or negotiation with state
and local levels of government; the Commonwealth merely staked its
claim on the grounds that the national significance of the arts was
beyond question. Joan Rydon and Diane Mackay (1984) trace the
effects of this particular brand of federalism on the organisation of the
arts in Australia. Not only has it meant that Commonwealth discourses
and practices have strongly influenced the emergence of state government arts bureaucracies, but the dominance of national funding has
also forced federation on a whole range of previously state or local
arts bodies (Rydon and Mackay, 1984: 98).

Rowse describes how the earliest policies of the ACFTA had no
trouble claiming that the subsidisation of excellent performances or
objects benefited everyone in Australia (1985a: 37). The idea of the
arts as public goods, which provided external benefits to all and
therefore warranted collective payment, depended on the accompanying
argument that even those who did not attend reaped vicarious rewards
in the form of increased national pride and status (Rowse, 1985a:
38–9). These claims about the national benefits of arts funding represented Australia as an homogeneous culture with a single public able
to agree on what constituted the arts. Such claims have been increasingly under attack from many fronts since the late 1960s. The election
of Whitlam in 1972 can be read as symptomatic of these wider changes,
of new political mobilisations from the Vietnam moratorium to
women's liberation which refused the unity of the nation.

The invocation of community in arts policy can also be considered
in this context. It is a case study of the tensions involved in trying to
reconcile policies which address the nation as an undifferentiated whole
with those that seek to address specific groups that are represented as
'other', as outside the nation, as communities of difference.

The history of community in arts policy has to be analysed in terms
of how this category placed pressure on national discourses. At different moments in this history different pressures have surfaced. In some
instances 'community' produced a pluralist image of Australian culture
as the sum of smaller fractions; local cultural diversity was seen as
essential to the health of the national culture, as its source of renewal.
This is similar to the effects of the inclusion of local histories in
representations of the national heritage which Michael Bommes and
Patrick Wright (1982) describe. Here community projects entered the
public sphere as examples of the peoples' humble contribution to the
heritage of the nation; yet another example of the capacity of national
discourses to expand and include 'the people' (Bommes and Wright,
1982: 300).

In other instances pluralism did not give way to the integrative effects
of the nation, instead difference was asserted in more oppositional
terms. The idea of cultural rights was mobilised to argue for equal

funds for various cultural traditions and taste communities. In this configuration the role of arts funding was represented in terms of facilitating the identity and self-determination of all citizens. Community arts were not valued for their therapeutic effects but because they were a mechanism for maintaining collective identity or consciousness amongst different groups. They were a way of asserting and celebrating difference.

There is a third instance of the relationship between community and nation. Here the invocation of community has generated hostility and various threats to the security of the Community Arts Program within Commonwealth cultural policy. Throughout the history of the program this has most commonly taken the form of arguments for devolution, for the removal of community arts from the Australia Council on the grounds that it should really be the responsibility of local or state funding bodies. This exemplifies the idea that the nation cannot or should not be reduced to a series of communities, that this threatens the pursuit of excellence, that the local has no place in the national.

While the push for devolution is justified on the grounds of administrative efficiency, this is really a smokescreen. Stuart Cunningham (1992: 45–8) develops a convincing argument for the crucial role of a national cultural infrastructure in fostering policies and programs that reflect pluralism and diversity. In Australia national cultural policies have been the source of a vast array of innovative local, regional and community programs. These programs have not only been well resourced by national funding bodies but they have also made the category 'nation' problematic in important and productive ways. Not only has the idea of a single unified 'national culture' been contested but so too has the pervasive belief that the role of national cultural policies is to establish cultural unity. Community arts, public radio, access TV, Aboriginal and multicultural media programs are all products of cultural policies that represent national administration in terms of the management of diversity. There is little evidence to date that state or local governments have the political will or imagination to recognise and support cultural difference to this extent.

Conclusion

This chapter has explored three major issues in the framing of arts policy: how the arts have been defined; how the arts have been positioned in relation to mass culture; and the role of excellence and nation in policy discourses. Throughout the history of state support for the arts these issues have dominated. While they may have been given different inflections in various periods and policy debates there is no question about their role in shaping the political field of arts funding.

Many of the effects of these framing discourses have already been outlined. What they highlight is that the value of art is not intrinsic or fixed but ascribed. This process of valorising art, specifically through the winning of subsidies for it, has consolidated class differences and power. Arts funding has perpetuated ideologies of art as a superior cultural form and has also implied high status for those who appreciate it. Arts funding then, has to be seen as a field in which art and its audiences are continually constructed in relations of power and differentiation.

Restricted and elitist meanings for art have also made claims for funding from other cultural forms difficult to establish. These meanings have legitimated the tastes and pleasures of certain audiences and devalued those of others. Beyond this, state funding has effectively protected the arts from the rigours of the market and perpetuated the notion that commercial success or mass appeal equals cultural compromise. Excellence and nation have been used to make extraordinary claims about the special value of the arts and to effectively disguise the power relations behind these claims.

In summing up the net effect of the organisation of arts funding it is difficult to ignore Mulgan and Worpole's very blunt assessment. For them, arts funding functions as a form of redistribution to metropolitan elites. In subsidising the pleasures of upper middle class city dwellers arts funding effectively disenfranchises large sections of the citizenry whose cultural pleasures are either ignored or devalued by current mechanisms of support.

For many, Mulgan and Worpole's assessment is completely untenable. In desperate attempts to defend the arts against such attacks all sorts of counter claims are made: the era of economic rationalism is forcing the arts to pay their way; arts audiences are diverse and not class-based; touring programs have redressed geographical inequities; there are lots of arts shows on television; access and participation programs have made the arts far more popular. There is an element of truth in all these claims but they still cannot really undermine the fundamental point at stake: arts funding is not equitable.

In Australia community arts represents the single most important challenge so far to some of the more undemocratic aspects of arts funding. Tracing the history of the Community Arts Program, then, becomes a documentation of how 'community' was placed in relation to the dominant discourses structuring support for the arts. The intention here is not to argue that 'community' was automatically oppositional, far from it. Rather, it is to investigate how a space was cleared for community arts within arts policy and how this program was accommodated within the dominant practices and policies for funding the arts. Unlike other Boards of the Australia Council, community arts did not have a single artform that it was responsible for, nor did it have a definite constituency. Its purpose was not to service an aesthetic or a distinct social group. It had to construct a field of patronage over which it would preside, and crucial to this process was the establishment of different discourses of value which were able to legitimate a wide variety of cultural forms and constituencies.

However, before the story of the Community Arts Program can be told it is necessary to situate the challenge of 'community'. This does not mean fixing a definition for this extremely flexible category. Rather, it involves a critical evaluation of some of the assessments from the left of how 'community arts' are progressive. This 'left' discourse has had the effect of giving community arts a very specific set of political meanings, of structuring the terms in which it is evaluated as radical. Only when these terms are explored can they be dismissed or extended. This is the task of the next chapter.

2
The challenge of community

Identifying the institutional and policy contexts in which the Community Arts Program was constructed is a crucial step in any evaluation of its political impact. Unfortunately this has rarely been done. Most analyses of the 'politics of community arts' prefer, instead, to confer on community arts the status of a movement for cultural opposition. The idea of official invention is rejected in favour of assessments which represent community arts as part of a long history of radical cultural activism.

This left romanticism may be appealing but it is ultimately stultifying. Not only has it produced a lot of self-righteous rhetoric but it has also suppressed effective debate about the nature of community arts' challenge to mainstream art practice and policy. In this chapter left accounts of community arts will be assessed in order to see the terms in which they evaluate community arts as progressive. After this an alternative approach will be proposed. This alternative approach is based on a close understanding of the institutional origins of the Community Arts Program and its various aesthetic orientations. The primary question it seeks to answer is: how did the invocation of 'community' in arts funding contest dominant discourses of value and funding practices?

Left accounts of community arts

In this brief survey of the politics of community arts the intention is to set out the main themes rather than explore detailed arguments. In general, the eclectic and often polemical debates about community arts revolve around a central opposition: community and 'the people' are posed against Art and capitalism. A fundamental antagonism between community and Art becomes the rallying point for a variety of claims about the progressive impact of community arts.

Many of the arguments for community arts draw heavily on the

18

rhetoric of radical art criticism, community activism and Marxist accounts of the relationship between class and culture. Three main propositions dominate. First, there is a critique of bourgeois art as reflecting the wider problems of capitalism. Second, community is invoked as an antidote to contemporary alienation, and finally there is an insistence on cultural practice as an instrument for social change; on art that is 'socially engaged' (Dolk, 1983: 17).

The rejection of most contemporary art practice and objects is the starting point for many analyses seeking to establish the political value of community arts. Mainstream art is read as an effect of capitalist social order reflecting economic and class stuctures. Art, then, occupies a contradictory position. On the one hand it is removed from the majority of peoples' lives, rendering it an irrelevant cultural practice. At the same time, however, it is powerful and privileged because it has hegemonic effects on the definition of culture where Art is equated with Culture. The outcome of this is the marginalisation of an enormous range of other cultural forms and practices (Connell, 1983: 296). Art is simultaneously dismissed and deferred to by 'ordinary people'.

According to Connell, the focus of struggle against this hegemony has to be on the replacement of the category Culture with culture. This would ensure definitions for culture that were anthropological rather than evaluative and that were inclusive of the rich and varied activities of 'ordinary people'. This would also represent a major challenge to cultural distinctions such as high/low and elite/popular and their insidious political effects.

Other themes in this movement from the critique of art to the critique of capitalism focus not so much on the hegemonic effects of 'high culture' but on the stupefying effects of mass culture. The economic organisation of capitalism is held responsible for the 'erosion of traditional symbolism and ritual, and their replacement by Colonel Sanders' head, the Target bullseye and Kiss' (Hicks, 1982: 42). While the ruling class indulge in specialised, abstract cultural forms the masses are fed mindless mediocrity in the name of profit and social control. While this representation may caricature left discourses, it is not unfair. The missionary zeal expressed in some arguments for community arts reflects a more generalised left pessimism about mass culture and the need to rescue the working class from its dangerous effects.

If Art and capitalism are bad, then community and 'the people' are good; these categories are constructed in opposition. The use of ambiguous and inclusive terms like community and 'the people' allows for the mobilisation of a variety of critiques and programs for reform. The rhetoric of community that is privileged in left arguments for community arts shifts between two major emphases. One is a nostalgic invocation of an idealised past in which the community is the central point of social identity and organisation (Hicks, 1982: 42). The other draws on activist notions of community established during the radical welfare movements of the late 1960s and early 1970s in which community is something to be constructed as a weapon against the state, as the first step in winning back control.

Nostalgic invocations depend on an analysis of contemporary social life as a series of losses. Capitalism's emphasis on productive labour, on those who can generate profit, renders those considered unproductive as worthless. The old, the sick and those looking after children are, for example, considered scrapheap material, they are marginalised and disadvantaged. These people are denied a sense of personal worth and one area where this could be re-established is in collaborative artistic production in the form of community arts (Hicks, 1982: 42–3). People have lost their essential creativity, intimacy with neighbours, traditional symbols and sense of long-term origins and objectives. All these losses are expressed as components of the traditional community, which can be recovered and re-established via new forms of artistic practice.

Activist discourses of community emphasise the struggle for the decentralisation of power and self-determination. These struggles are organised around the community as the symbol of a new site of control, managed by and for locals or the people (Kelly, 1984: 48). Here the enemy is not some sort of generalised malaise such as modernity or contemporary society but the state:

> The domination of the centralised state, through the ideology it embodies and the programme it enacts, constitutes one of the major obstacles to achieving the kind of democratic and equitable access to the means of cultural production which community artists have claimed as their ultimate aim. The domination of the state . . . stands in opposition to the establishment of community, where community is understood as shared activities and goals. (Kelly, 1984: 49)

Community is not something to be magically recovered but a goal to be struggled for. It is not something to be manufactured by outside professionals but emerges out of collaboration and shared commitment and expression. Cultural work is an effective tool in the formation of community, it is a tool for activism. This definition does not see community in purely regional or geographic terms, it allows for the idea of communities of interest. It is also dynamic and accounts for the possibility of cultural practice being one of the processes whereby alliances form and cohere (Greenwood, 1983: 310).

In both these versions, the objective of cultural activity is to establish community. Art and capitalism are challenged in the same moment, the placement of community with art expresses this double opposition:

> Wide, deep, community practice of the arts is a precondition of a vigorous, self-identifying, self-expressive, truthful national people's culture. Such a national culture is one precondition of a successful resistance to imperialism and monopoly control. (Hicks, 1982: 43)

Here community cultural practice is represented as a weapon in the class struggle, successful community arts is that which serves broader political demands. Subversive art is not abstract or self-reflexive like the avant-garde (see Connell, 1983: 306), it is an instrument for radical social change.

Another element in the construction of community arts as oppositional is the identification of those who are opposing. While 'community' functions as a symbol of the organisational contestation of capitalism in general and the state in particular, 'the people' are posed against the ruling class. 'Ordinary people' are represented as the possessors of a rich and varied culture evident in anything from the hand-made wedding dress to oral history (Connell, 1983: 297). Hidden traditions are recovered and reasserted. A vibrant arena of everyday cultural production is pulled out from behind the wings of the rich and powerful's elitist definitions of culture. A majority culture is demanded, one that is both 'popular' and supported by dominant institutions and cultural policy.

'Ordinary people' serves as a handy, all-purpose category in this left discourse. Often its use reflects a certain class populism, implying little more than an alternative name for the working class. Similar slippages occur in the connection of cultural forms to audiences: while art is the preserve of the ruling class, popular culture is enjoyed by 'the people'. Definitions of popular culture are notoriously ambiguous; however, the meaning favoured in these discourses is one that implies folk culture. This culture emerges from 'below' in opposition to the imposition of mass culture or art from 'above'. For Bennett (1980: 23) the definition of popular culture as folk culture is ultimately romantic because it identifies the emergent cultures of oppressed groups or classes as *inherently* oppositional, as evidence of active cultural expression rather than passive cultural consumption.

The dangers of positing a neat correspondence between certain cultural forms and class groups have already been discussed. This tendency is endemic in left discourses of community arts, producing a series of crude oppositions that may serve rhetorical purposes but little else. To pose 'ordinary people' against the ruling class, majority culture against minority culture, democracy against elitism may appeal to a certain pleasure in slogans but ultimately this way of representing the political significance of community arts leads nowhere. These arguments persist only because categories like 'ordinary people' and popular culture are rarely defined. As Rowse so convincingly argues: 'it is easy to identify with a constituency called "ordinary people", only if the fantastic status of "ordinary people" remains unexamined' (Rowse, 1985b: 163).

These oppositions are inoperable, not only because they represent the cultural field as a set of fixed relations between forms and audiences but also because they offer little analytic assistance in the fundamental problem of democratic reform of cultural policy. This is however, a minor concern of many accounts of community arts. Rowse (1985b: 162) is correct in pointing out that in many arguments for cultural democracy the hardest questions of policy are generally unasked. 'Ordinary people' are presented as the constituency for a democratic cultural policy but they remain a monolithic mass, differentiated only in terms of being the opposite of 'the rich', 'the privileged' or the ruling class. Support of popular culture is held up as an egalitarian policy objective but the content of this culture is never defined: is popularity to be measured in quantitative or generic terms? (Rowse, 1985b: 166.) What would be the status of art in this reformed policy, would its privileged position as a supposedly central cultural tradition and canon be destroyed? Cultural distinctions such as high/popular are not analytical devices, instead their use has to be regarded as a cultural phenomenon in itself demanding investigation into how such distinctions are mobilised and to what effect.

The appropriation of community arts in the name of the class struggle, the age of Aquarius or whatever has produced essentialist and romantic arguments that refuse to acknowledge 'community arts' as an historically recent official invention. Instead it becomes an almost spontaneous cultural practice, a natural form of creativity cruelly suppressed by the growth of capitalism and class structure. There is little interest in assessing the specificities of community arts as a government arts funding program, in evaluating how well it actually represents the privileging of majority over minority culture or democracy over elitism. Community arts is merely the evidence displayed to reinforce a set of catchy but fundamentally flawed oppositions.

An alternative approach

Acknowledging the limitations of many of the existing evaluations of the politics of community arts is important for establishing the terms in which political impacts will be assessed throughout this study. The task here is to set down alternative methods of analysis, to develop an account of the Community Arts Program that puts into sharp relief the historical and institutional context in which it was constructed. This is not to discredit the wider cultural and political questions that the program raises, but it is to insist on an analysis that begins with a recognition of community arts as an official invention, as a relatively recent arts funding program. It is to insist on a view that situates community arts as one of several movements towards more democratic cultural policy. This approach is attentive to how the program contested the authority of dominant assumptions shaping state support of the arts.

Arts funding is a system of evaluation; the practice of patronage demands public criteria for assessment and selection. But it is important to realise that the terms in which these evaluations are made, the principles of selection, are open to contestation. The creation of the Community Arts Program signalled a shift in cultural policy. The introduction of the terms access and participation into the objectives of the Australia Council generated a series of tensions about what could be considered a cultural activity, about audiences whose interests were not acknowledged in existing funding practices, about different discourses of value and about different methods for disbursing grants.

Rather than fix an ideal definition of community and then measure policy developments against it the intention here is to explore how this term was mobilised, to trace the shifting interpretations the Community Arts Program gave to the objective of increased access and participation in the arts. The profound ambiguity of 'community' opened up a vast array of strategic possibilities; it was the term used to claim a new concern within arts funding for all those previously unrepresented 'others'. The central focus of the following account will be how community arts policy and practice has represented those others.

In contrast to left discourse, policy pronouncements did not use 'community' as a euphemism for 'ordinary people' or the working class. Policy meanings were far more specific, often referring to distinct social groups such as prisoners, children, trade union members, people living in the western suburbs, women and migrants. Community implied diversity, it was difficult to use this category in any monolithic sense. Instead, what the Community Arts Program generated was a proliferation of new constituencies; it fostered a pluralism that not only fractured the illusion of a singular public for the arts but also eventually forced a recognition of cultural difference.

John Clarke and Chas Critcher (1985: 132) argue that the creation of multiple target groups in community arts programs is little more than liberal pluralism, a way of including previously excluded groups by constructing them as discrete minorities distinguished by their special characteristics rather than their common class position. In their assessment, this pluralism dilutes the political challenge of community arts reducing it to therapy or welfare, to a technique for the integration of those constituted as disadvantaged.

This critique needs to be appraised. In assessing the political impact of the Community Arts Program the effects of this reluctance to unify different groups and cultures under the broader category of working class will be evaluated. In refusing to grant class the status of the most important axis of social difference, other divisions such as gender, race, age and region were given increased attention. What has to be answered is: did this attention to the various structures of difference foster a recognition of the heterogeneity of constituencies with grievances against arts funding? Or did it reduce these constituencies to the status of the 'culturally deprived' leaving the sanctity of art and its audiences intact?

Political evaluation is not just a matter of identifying who was funded through the Community Arts Program but how they were funded. Once again the ambiguity of 'community' was strategic. It facilitated the development of a range of different methods for disbursing grants and for assessing the value of various cultural forms and practices. Rowse's (1985a) argument about decentralised patronage is important here. This method of funding has the effect of displacing the authority of traditional cultural entrepreneurs by placing control in the hands of organisations closer to constituencies. Not only does it challenge the tendency within centralised patronage to privilege national flagship companies but it also involves the recognition of a more pluralist conception of the cultures which make up Australian society. The fundamental shift is from general to local criteria of evaluation (Rowse, 1985a: 27). Rowse's claims as to the radical impact of decentralised patronage are developed throughout his book:

> Decentralised patronage is a radical solution to the problem of making access and participation mean something because it offers to collapse the social distance between those who decide on the provision of a cultural item and those who are said to benefit from it. (Rowse, 1985a: 55)

Elsewhere, Rowse (1985b: 168) elaborates on the structural innovation that this form of patronage represented. What these various programs did was recognise a range of intermediary organisations as new patrons. Anything from an after-school centre to a trade union could request funding for an arts program on the basis that it had an established relationship with the constituency it was seeking to address.

New funding methods also demanded new criteria for assessment and here community took on other meanings. Decentralised patronage produced quite different discourses of value which privileged social criteria such as 'community need' or 'degree of community involvement' over and above notions of aesthetics or excellence. It was the process of cultural production, its impact on the sense of collaboration and community experienced by participants, that was valued. Instrumental meanings for culture were privileged with assessment based on how effective community arts projects were in expressing 'community'.

The significance of Rowse's analysis of community arts is that decentralised patronage is a far more insightful interpretive device than a category like 'cultural democracy'. It reflects a close understanding of the mechanics of arts funding and their political implications specifically in terms of how new patrons and constituencies were established. However, there are two flaws in this approach which limit its application here. For a start, in representing decentralised patronage as a third phase in a chronological account of arts funding there is a sense in which the history of patronage is represented as a progressive evolution towards increasingly more enlightened practices. Decentralised patronage becomes the pinnacle, the radical breakthrough in contrast to previous policies and patterns of funding. This tends to distort the 'success' of these developments and inflate their overall significance and impact within the Australia Council. In his review of *Arguing the Arts* Frow (1986: 120) points to the reality of the internal distribution of funds in the Australia Council, reminding Rowse of the persistent economic and ideological marginality of community arts, Aboriginal arts and crafts. Decentralised patronage still only represents a fraction of the Australia Council's budget; it also represents a continual source of tension and contestation. It is only through an analysis attentive to the micro-politics of the Australia Council and the Community Arts Program's continual struggle to claim a legitimate place in Commonwealth cultural policy that these claims about the success of decentralised patronage can be evaluated.

More serious, however, is the way in which Rowse displaces questions of formal value. The argument that decentralised patronage has allowed social groups to determine their own criteria of relevance is right, but this should not render analysis of the aesthetic outcomes of these decisions out of court. The limitations of the decentralised patronage thesis are that the analysis is weighted in favour of questions about who is funded and through what methods; what gets funded is rarely assessed. This avoidance fuels an almost patronising conception of all community arts projects as inherently wholesome. A useful political assessment of community arts has to be organised around three related questions: who gets the money, how is it disbursed, and what is produced with it. Without a consideration of the aesthetic outcomes of community arts projects there is the assumption that progressive methods of funding automatically produce progressive cultural forms.

Funding practices cannot be separated from what is funded. In this study funding guidelines and patterns will be documented as central to the formation of a set of knowledges about community arts. While Rowse's argument about decentralised patronage is useful, it will be extended with a consideration of how assumptions about who needed funds and how to fund them influenced the privileging of certain cultural forms. It is no coincidence that the most popular parody of community arts refers to 'festivals, face painting and murals'. Considering that one of the most persistent objectives of community arts policy has been collaborative cultural production in the interests of expressing 'community', it is little wonder that forms like festivals, face painting and murals occur often. For what these forms embody is a populist aesthetics, an aesthetics easily mobilised in the search for an almost instant representation of community.

Analyses of several community visual arts projects in Part III will consider how these projects were conceptualised in the application for funds and how, once funded, they negotiated the problem of how to represent. Questions about the politics of representation are central to the discussion of projects, for what distinguishes the forms produced with community arts funding is their claims to authenticity. Unlike official discourses which speak for and about 'others', the images produced in community arts projects are often hailed as the 'voice of the people'. It is in projects that these others are given a voice, that they are able to tell it like it is. The analysis of projects will scrutinise these claims to authenticity and document the devices used to give expression and authority to different social groups and cultures. While left discourses of community arts uncritically assume that anything produced in the community is inherently progressive, this inquiry will challenge this tendency with a discussion of projects attentive to their relationship with their funding source and their specific conditions of production and distribution. In this way questions about formal value are placed within the context of *how* these projects matter and to whom.

The Community Arts Program emerged out of the play of discourses and power within the Australia Council. This institutional context was both enabling and constraining. While Whitlam's commitment to access and participation saw a space created within the Australia Council where the unrepresented 'others' of arts funding could be addressed, this space was bounded by the powerful discourses of excellence and nation. The fundamental paradox of the Community Arts Program is that 'community' was a category that both contested and confirmed the structural exclusions performed by arts funding. On the one hand it was a space where the culturally disadvantaged could be reformed. On the other hand it was a space where cultural difference and diversity were recognised and affirmed.

The history of the Community Arts Program is a history of the tensions generated when questions about access and participation were asked of arts funding. The strategies that the program has produced to address the issue of equity have shifted between a concern to ameliorate cultural disadvantage and an alternative recognition of cultural pluralism. Tracing the formation and effects of these competing rationales for community arts is the central task of the rest of this book.

Part II

The story of the Community Arts Program

3
Finding the community: the Community
Arts Committee 1973–1975

This chapter explores the question of origins, not with the intention of pinning down exact beginnings but rather to trace the processes of official invention. It will investigate how a space was made for community arts within the ACFTA. Because the emphasis is on institutional and discursive contexts, as well as chronology, several intersecting themes will be explored.

The election of a Labor government in December 1972 is the starting point. Although reform of cultural policy had begun before this, this government gave massive increases in funds to this area and introduced a range of new initiatives. More important, however, was the particular inflection Labor gave to the terms 'access', 'participation' and 'community'. Generally, reforms to health, education and welfare are cited as evidence of Labor's experiment with social democracy. The Community Arts Program can also be considered in this way, as a case study in the invocation of social democratic ideology in the public administration of the arts.

Pre-existing institutional arrangements also influenced the establishment of the Community Arts Program. Since 1970 the ACFTA had had a Special Projects Fund (SPF) to support projects which fell outside existing guidelines. This fund was both an administrative solution to the problem of unclassifiable activities and a response to new arts developments. In 1973 this fund was converted into the Community Arts Committee (CAC). Reconciling the tensions between these original functions and the new objectives of access and participation was central to the formation of community arts. The role of the SPF in prefiguring community arts cannot be ignored.

While ALP policy and existing institutional patterns may have provided the impetus for the establishment of community arts, the real work was done when the money started to flow. Disbursing grants demanded guidelines and rules of inclusion and exclusion. What to fund and why was at the heart of the program's ongoing construction.

It was here that what was to be known as 'community arts' was prescribed.

Out of all this it is impossible to identify any simple model of determination; instead a picture of multiple influences emerges. It is only by tracing the chronology of events, the patterns of funding and decision making, the institutional power relations and the formation of a set of meanings, that it becomes possible to comprehend how community arts was invented.

Whitlam's first aid to the arts

> Among those involved in the arts, the situation after December 1972 had all the hallmarks of a cargo cult whose ship had actually arrived. Expectations, personal and corporate, ran riot. Every needy artist hoped for, and most expected, support; every group and organisation was sure that its project would now blossom; those interested in administration looked confidently for the elimination of the Old Guard and for the establishment of their own personal role and influence. Disappointments were inevitable. (Coombs, 1981: 252)

Reforms to the arts have been described as the Whitlam government's greatest achievement (Grant, 1986: 4). These reforms are assessed as having had the most enduring impact, not simply because many of them survived the cuts of the conservative Fraser government but also because they ended a long period of neglect and disorder with the establishment of new funds, strategies and institutions. In Whitlam's summation, developments in the arts signified 'national awakening' more forcibly than any other of his government's reforms (Whitlam, 1985: 589).

These sweeping claims as to the significance of the ALP's cultural policies are evidence of how easily and often Whitlam and his government are mythologised, and Whitlam's continuing role in this myth making. Whitlam has never been reticent in displaying his cultural capital. His pleasure in and commitment to the arts cannot be denied. Nor can the support he received from artists prior to the 1972 election. The cheers that still greet his appearances at the Sydney Film Festival or Opera in the Park are a continuing reminder of the middle class appeal of his arts policies. Despite all this adoration, a lack of critical analysis remains.

While histories of various cultural institutions and policies are now appearing, few offer a sustained evaluation of the Labor Party's policies on culture. In general, Whitlam is rather glibly assessed as offering more of the same only bigger and better. Rowse (1985a), Dermody and Jacka (1987) and Andrews (1982) all argue that key initiatives in cultural policy formation were well underway several years before the election of Whitlam. The impact of the Labor government is situated as part of a wider complex of institutional, economic and cultural changes. These accounts are in no danger of making Whitlamism seem larger than it was and in this way myths are contested. On the other hand, there is a certain reluctance to acknowledge the impact of massive increases in funds and to scrutinise the nuances of ALP arts policy, specifically those that opened up spaces for initiative and change.

The major themes of ALP policy for the arts in the campaign for the 1972 election were substantial increases in the level of public subsidy; a single statutory authority to administer this assistance; wider opportunities and rewards for artists; the promotion of excellence in the arts and the encouragement of a wider spread of interest and participation in the arts (Whitlam, Policy Speech, 13 November 1972). The difference in the Labor Party's policies certainly did not rest on a radically alternative, let alone socialist, approach to cultural administration. Instead, the attraction of Labor was established through a heady mix promising lots of money, increased government recognition of the arts and minor changes to existing institutional arrangements. Behind the rhetoric the 'new' policy reiterated established traditions. The firm commitment to excellence and the fostering of national identity through the arts sustained the principles of patronage already laid down by the AETT and the ACFTA. According to Rowse (1985a: 11), Whitlam merely fuelled a growth in state provision of culture that was already underway, he did not challenge existing frameworks for the production and distribution of cultural goods.

Whitlam's own account confirms this. For him, access to art and culture were democratic rights and active and equal participation in them was an indicator of a just society. Encouragement of the arts and the preservation of cultural and intellectual heritage were signs of a civilised community (Whitlam, 1985: 553). This was a rhetoric of democratising Culture, where the main solution to uneven participation was posed through new approaches to distribution. Culture had to be better disseminated. It had to move out of elite citadels and into everyday life. It had to be taken to 'where the people were'. It was an Opera in the Park or Shakespeare in the Suburbs model of cultural reform. This confidence in the benefits of art and culture meant that what actually constituted these categories was rarely examined. There was nothing radical in this position—the touring policies of the Council for the Enjoyment of Music and the Arts and of the AETT in the 1950s were based on the same assumption: that Culture was inherently civilising and better distribution was one way to spread its benefits.

Some sections of the Labor Party had reservations about this approach to cultural administration. In responding to attacks that the policy was fundamentally elitist, Whitlam challenged his critics to explain why:

The poor, the under-educated and the socially disadvantaged, while presumably entitled to greater material security and better health care and education, should somehow be expected to tolerate inferior standards in the arts and to resent all efforts to improve their access to them. (Whitlam, 1985: 588)

This was the classic social democratic response and an important indicator of the broader political context in which Labor's arts policy was implemented. While critics of this policy were correct in identifying its maintenance of entrenched patterns of privilege it cannot be denied that the increased commitment to access and participation was a shift that opened up new possiblities in arts funding.

Central to the Whitlam government's experiment with social democracy was the category 'community'. This category was used extensively in various federal government programs aimed at improving participation rates in public services. State and local governments were side-stepped in a vision of direct support from central government to the 'community'. Community was an invaluable device in arguments for centralism, getting around the problems of too many competing authorities impeding reform. It was also a way of establishing national concern for and contact with 'ordinary Australians'. 'Community' was represented as the most democratic organisational base for this process of secondary distribution, for the generation of improved access.

Related to this was an attempt to explain who needed access and why. Whitlam's version of social democracy relied less on the identification of class as the central axis of inequality and more on a generalised concept of disadvantage. The significance of this shift was that, in pushing masculine labourism slightly to the side, Whitlam initiatives recognised and supported emergent mobilisations around gender, ethnicity and race. This interpretation of access represented the disadvantaged largely in terms of their inability to participate in dominant institutions. While, within social democratic ideology, major institutions were often criticised for structurally excluding sections of the population, the central argument focused on the characteristics of the disadvantaged. They were typically constituted as lacking, as victims of their own failure to participate.

The terms access, participation, community and disadvantage were crucial to Whitlam's version of social democracy; they were the basis of his rationale for reform. While the Labor Party's major concern for the arts may have been the provision of urgent financial first aid, increasing access and participation were also avowed objectives. In the institutional upheaval of the ACFTA that followed Whitlam's election, this new policy emphasis had to be turned into programs and practice, the rhetoric had to be converted into strategy.

Remaking the Special Projects Fund

Prior to the 1972 election Whitlam had commissioned from Dr Jean Battersby (Executive Officer of the ACFTA) and Dr H. C. (Nugget) Coombs (Chairman of the ACFTA) a paper on the future of arts administration in Australia. This paper conformed to Whitlam's request for a statutory authority structure, drawing on British and Canadian models. The four broad objectives of the transformed Council were:

> to encourage excellence in the arts, to foster a wider spread of interest and participation, to help develop a national identity through artistic expression and to project Australia's image in other countries. (ACFTA, AR, 1973: 9)

During the first half of 1973 the new organisation of the ACFTA, to be known later as the Australia Council when legislation was in place, was established. There was to be a thirteen-member Council overseeing policy development, liaison with government and provision of common services. Seven Boards were also set up and, with the exception of the Aboriginal Arts Board, these, were defined on the basis of artforms: Theatre, Music, Literature, Visual Arts, Crafts, and Film and Television. Although the establishment of Boards was built upon the previous structure of the ACFTA of advisory committees dealing with separate artforms, the 1973 rearrangements were more than just tinkering. The changes were institutionally and economically dramatic and they owe more to the work and beliefs of Battersby and Coombs than they do to the vision of Whitlam. Battersby and Coombs were both the managers and intellectuals of the ACFTA. Their models for reform exemplified the creative role of middle class professionals in policy and institutional change.

These reforms represented a complex mix of consolidation and innovation. First, they gave recognition to artforms marginalised or ignored by previous systems of state patronage. The scope of the remodelled ACFTA was enlarged to encompass the functions of the Art, Literary and Composers funds (ACFTA, AR, 1973: 12). The new Board structure also recognised crafts. The hegemony of the performing arts, which the ACFTA had inherited from the AETT, was challenged with an administrative structure committed to servicing all the arts under one roof and with common objectives.

The second effect of the Board model was to reinforce the idea of art as a series of distinct and special aesthetic forms and to structure assistance around the financial and institutional needs of these artforms. Only the Aboriginal Arts Board had a focus on constituencies as well as forms. In the other Boards questions about distribution and audiences were much lower on the agenda; supporting cultural production and producers were the primary objectives.

In its coordinating role, the organisation's Council had responsibility for a grab bag of activities that were not artform-specific and had across-Board significance. A series of Council committees was established to administer the areas of International Cultural Exchanges, Entrepreneurial Activities, Publicity and Information, Research, and Community Arts (ACFTA, AR, 1973: 17). As in other developments, these committees reflected both consolidation and innovation. Most were a continuation of previous activities but with the addition of new projects, increased budgets and extended rationales.

The Community Arts Committee (CAC) was a result of the conversion of the Special Projects Fund (SPF) (ACFTA, AR, 1973: 20). This fund had been set up in early 1970 to deal with four areas that were outside the ambit of the artform committees (SPF, *Minutes*, 19-2-70: 2):

- activities in the arts other than establishment activities;
- stimulating new talent;
- assisting Council's objectives of attracting young people to the arts;
- assisting experimental and professional work including visits by international figures in the arts.

The SPF was both a response to the limitations of the artform committee structure and an indicator of cultural developments at the time. It reflected the problems inherent in funding procedures organised around the needs of separate aesthetics. The eclectic array of functions listed here shows that the ACFTA's solution to the problem of unclassifiable applications was to establish a residual fund, that could mop up a vast assortment of disparate activities. Each of these functions alludes to a complex of organisational and ideological dilemmas. The terms 'other than establishment' and 'experimental' hinted at the perennial problem of what constituted art. These categories implied a challenge to 'establishment art' from two different directions, the amateur and the avant-garde. The creation of new audiences, specifically 'young people', reflected the problems of winning and maintaining support for what were largely pre–twentieth century forms. The desire to stimulate 'new talent' indicated how much the artform committees were trapped in obligations to traditional cultural organisations and how much these obligations limited their potential for risk-taking.

The institutional upheaval in the ACFTA, after the change of government, saw the first half of 1973 devoted to the design and establishment of the revamped organisation. Although the encouragement of access and participation was represented as a central principle of Labor's approach to arts support, the immediate problem for the ACFTA's management was how best to establish a visible commitment to this.

In this atmosphere of rapid reorganisation the SPF, like most other activities of the ACFTA, was scrutinised (Hull, 1983: 316). Its history made it particularly appealing as a solution to the dilemma of where to put access and participation. While these terms had not been prominent in the organising rhetoric of the SPF, the functions of this program were ambiguous enough to be adapted in any number of possible directions. Also, its role as a residual funding category was identified as still necessary in the new Board-dominated institution (Hull, 1983: 16).

However, converting the SPF into a program explicitly committed to access and participation in the arts was not a straightforward task. The name change was no problem: 'community arts' had already been one of the funding categories of the SPF; 'community' was an increasingly popular word in a variety of other Whitlam-funded sites; and 'community art' programs were already being funded in England (see Kelly, 1984: 12). The difficult part was to devise a set of meanings and funding guidelines for community arts which would establish a distinct field of patronage over which the CAC could preside.

The crucial difference between the proposed CAC and the Boards was the way in which it had to construct its constituency. The Boards were justified primarily on the basis of artforms and organisations and their financial needs. The CAC was justified on the basis of a policy problem: uneven participation in the arts. In the Boards, patronage was organised around the support of cultural production. In the CAC the aim of patronage was to increase the cultural consumption of certain groups. In this way, access and participation were established as the proprietary interest of the CAC. This was the field of administration which legitimated its existence and power.

Cultural disadvantage

Internal debate and discussion preceding the creation of the CAC focused on the identification of a constituency. This process was dominated by an investigation of the nature of cultural disadvantage. It was obvious that the arts were a minority activity that had 'historically ... been enjoyed by the relatively few' (ACFTA, AR, 1973: 16). Some people were more cultural than others and once those others, those less cultural, were found, then strategies for involving them in the arts could begin. This search for a constituency was difficult, for the culturally disadvantaged were both silent and invisible:

> It is of primary importance for the Council to respond not only to the needs of the community as they are articulated by the people with the volatility, motivation, resources and position in the community to do so, but to tap the unspoken but insistent need of those sections of the community without the sophistication or capacity for organisation to become pressure groups on their own behalf. In other words, the Council ought to seek out clients who may, for various reasons, not be able to come forward themselves. When it moves into this area it is very necessary to do so humbly in the recognition that one is not extending 'charity' or behaving paternalistically

but simply attempting to devise methods for people to avail themselves of the Council's resources in situations where the orthodox relationship of Council and applicant cannot be formed. (Morgan, 1977: 6–7)

The disorganisation of the culturally disadvantaged made them difficult to both name and reach. One solution was to poach 'clients' from other bodies; in this way their identity was alluded to:

. . . this committee would see its main clients as being social welfare organisations, city councils and municipal authorities, regional and community festival organisations, trade union and employee organisations, prison authorities, migrant and community organisations, service clubs and societies. (SPF, *Minutes*, 18-4-73: 4)

Here the ambiguity of community was strategic. It allowed for the identification of multiple constituencies. The focus on local government emphasised community as a regional or geographically coded space. The mention of prisons targeted captive inhabitants in anything from hospitals to schools. The welfare rhetoric opened up that vast field, the disadvantaged and 'migrant and community organisations' allowed for communities of common interest or experience. Constituencies could be constructed around several axes: spatial, institutional and economic. Community was a shifting site, a classificatory and organisational space where micro-populations presented 'problems' for the CAC to administer.

What unified these various communities was their common lack, their cultural deprivation. Communities were not only 'found' but also endowed with unmet cultural needs. In explaining the causes of this cultural lack and need, biological factors were reluctantly rejected in favour of those old standbys, poor upbringing combined with social, economic and educational disadvantage.

The dilemma facing the designers of the CAC was that those who lacked the arts were not clamouring for access and participation. They were not demanding their cultural rights. This silence was read as more evidence of lack, it heightened the need for state intervention. The problem was how? If demand was not forthcoming how could the culturally disadvantaged be made aware of the benefits of the arts and of the money available within the ACFTA to spread these benefits? Implicit here was a recognition of the need to develop different systems of patronage that would reach the culturally deprived. Existing patronage, organised around the support of cultural production, privileged both art and the cultural elites that enjoyed it. It was more difficult to support cultural production for those without culture. What had to be developed were new mechanisms for patronage that took art to people who currently showed little interest in coming to it. A combination of cultural missionaries and de-institutionalistion was proposed (see ACFTA, AR, 1973: 25).

The earliest discourses of community arts invoked unrepresented 'others'; imaginary communities who were spoken about and for. This was a discourse on behalf of the silent and the invisible, and one of its effects was to fix boundaries around those considered in need of access and participation. There could be no mistaking the target groups for community arts; they may have been various but they were also only certain sections of the population. The search for the culturally disadvantaged implied the culturally advantaged. To identify prisoners or migrants or children or those living in the western suburbs or welfare recipients or the aged was to reinforce the ideal of bourgeois pleasure in and appreciation of art.

If the 'problem' of access and participation justified the establishment of the CAC then the production of a discourse on cultural disadvantage identified constituencies for the program. Within this discourse on disadvantage there was a tension between the idea of community and the idea of audience. Strategies for extending involvement in the arts are implicitly about audiences and how they are formed. The debates preceeding the establishment of the CAC skirted around this issue. Rarely were the groups requiring access and participation referred to as either potential or neglected audiences. Instead, they were communities of need, characterised by their common cultural deprivation. 'Audience' implied cultural competency and skills in appreciation. Prisoners, children, the aged et cetera were denied this status. Their cultural lack meant that for them art was primarily a form of therapy, a hands-on activity, an aid to self-expression and identity. Communities participated, audiences appreciated.

The formation of a discourse on cultural disadvantage was crucial to the establishment of a rationale and agenda for the CAC but this did more than demarcate a space for the program within the ACFTA. It also worked to affirm the hegemony of art within this institution. The concept of cultural disadvantage was operative only on the terrain of high culture (Frow, 1987: 65). The Community Arts Program was constructed within this framework, which assumed that all Australians could become interested in the cultural activities subsidised by the state if they were given special programs and assistance. While the rhetoric of access and participation had all the hallmarks of social democracy, implicitly it was a rhetoric of legitimation which established the cultural preferences of the upper middle class as the standard from which all else was measured. Culture was to be shared, the 'more cultural' were now the generous custodians of excellence for the 'less cultural', and community arts was to be one of the main mechanisms for their cultural improvement (Rowse, 1989: 14).

From other audiences to other art

In bureaucratic terms, the CAC inherited the functions and funds of the SPF. Special Projects had given out grants to an extraordinary assortment of cultural activities (see ACFTA, AR, 1973: 20) and when the policy and guidelines for the CAC were being designed many aspects of the SPF were easily accommodated within the new objectives. The funding of prison arts programs, creative activities for children and local government, for example, had been going on since 1970. With the emergence of the CAC new meanings were imposed on these projects. They were re-presented as evidence of broader participation in the arts and their constituencies became the culturally disadvantaged. However, other activities funded by the SPF were not so easily converted from 'special' to 'community'.

The establishment of the ACFTA in 1968 had ensured that art was constituted as a relatively enclosed and continuing cultural canon. However, the security of tradition was continually undermined by the arrival of 'new' forms. The problem was how to deal with these other activities, how to recognise innovation, how to give the appearance of responsiveness without threatening the mainstream areas. As an institution for cultural legitimation the ACFTA had to appear as more than just an economic prop to the proven. It also had to appear as a stimulator. It had to sustain an image of tolerance and innovation. The SPF had been established to meet this demand. Terms such as 'fringe', 'experimental' and 'other than establishment' were part of its organising rhetoric. As the 'fund for everything else' Special Projects had supported heterogenous activities from the amateur to the avant-garde and while the amateur were easily re-presented as community arts, this was not the case with the avant-garde.

The pressure on the ACFTA to accommodate requests for funds from these other arts was a sign of the times. The late 1960s were a period of social change and liberalisation. Movements such as the counter culture, women's liberation, Aboriginal land rights and the Vietnam moratorium were expressions of burgeoning political activism and opposition. There was also a growth in radical cultural activity, evident in the proliferation of diverse and innovative cultural practices and organisations that mushroomed in this atmosphere of dissent. Developments like the La Mama theatre, conceptual art, Pram Factory, filmmakers' co-operatives and Inhibodress Gallery, to name a few, formed part of the political and cultural context for the invention of community arts.

Insider's accounts of the origins of community arts identify three main influences from the social changes of this period. The first was the emergence of artists intent on contesting elitist art practices. These artists were questioning the role of art, the interests it served and the responsibilities of artists to society. The second was the growth of political activism organised around local or community groups. Small local meetings of Women's Liberation and resident action groups exemplified a philosophy of community control and opposition. Finally, there was the push for alternative lifestyles based on a rejection of materialist society. In the age of Aquarius simple was best (see Kelly, 1984: 11 and Robertson, 1982: 19).

Ideas about radical art, community activism and alternative lifestyles surfaced in the earliest policies of the CAC but their enunciation in the field of arts funding gave them new meanings. These heterogeneous discourses were not simply incorporated into the policies and practices of the CAC, they were recreated and reformed in this new arena. They were put to work in different ways and with different effects.

One of the explicit justifications for the creation of the SPF had been to mop up requests for funding from 'other than establishment' arts. In the conversion of this fund into the CAC this role was retained. So the CAC inherited the problem of administering the meaning of 'other arts'. In the official announcement of the CAC's functions 'other arts' were renamed 'multi-arts' and support of these activities became a parallel responsibility to the encouragement of access and participation.

Multi-arts was an ambiguous category, implying activities that were both administratively and aesthetically problematic. Two meanings dominated: projects dealing with several artforms, such as festivals, and innovative work that was difficult to classify. Multi-arts was not only outside the Boards' single artform boundaries but also outside traditional definitions of art:

> The evidence at present suggests that the Boards, at first sceptical as to the need for a special fund, have become increasingly aware not only of the peculiarly demanding nature of the work in this area but of the *convenience* of having a multi-media, all purpose fringe arena, into which exploratory (and even questionable) propositions can be sent for investigation. The Community Arts Fund and its small staff are seen as a useful supplementary program through which the Boards can expect flexible types of assistance. (ACFTA, AR, 1973: 26) [emphasis added]

The tension between the administrative and aesthetic justifications for multi-arts was striking. What the above quote reveals is how the principle of supporting innovative cultural practice could not stand alone. It had to be tempered with the convenience of having a place that could function as a dumping ground for the Boards.

The multi-arts category addressed an institutional dilemma. It also maintained a space for various experimental and alternative cultural groups and practices proliferating at the time. More than any other aspect of the CAC, multi-arts reflected the continuity of the SPF's heterogenous funding practices. However, as the rhetoric of access and participation began to dominate, the relationship between these two areas had to be explained: how did the support of programs to encourage wider participation and the support of multi-arts add up to 'community arts'? There was a pressure to present the CAC as a unified and internally coherent program in order to sell it within the ACFTA, in order to convince sceptical Boards that it was not only necessary but viable.

Debates surrounding the formation of the CAC grappled with the problem of how to reconcile these apparently disparate functions. In this process the place of the avant-garde and innovation within community arts was scrutinised. The evaluations were generally hostile. In the search for new constituencies new art was definitely not considered the drawcard:

> The avant-garde does not necessarily belong with audiences encountering the arts for the first time, and it will be self-defeating and paternalistic to think of factory workers, for example, as guinea pigs to be exposed to a theatre experience which may be challenging to the conventional expectations of even the habitual theatregoer. In our experience, quality work in traditional forms has in the short term been a rewarding introduction to the arts, but again, this is not to pre-judge the capacity of any audience to enjoy and assimilate innovative work. (Morgan, 1977: 8)

The support of avant-garde or experimental work within the CAC was hardly central or secure. These activities were regarded as counterproductive to the delicate process of extending access and participation. Despite this marginality, the issues that these new arts raised could not be dismissed and they simmered away within the CAC. Questions about new audiences could not be separated from questions about new art. The emphasis on collective cultural production and participation made the role of the artist as individual creator problematic. The emphasis on de-institutionalising the arts, in taking art to the people, echoed the conceptual art movement's concern to move out of the gallery and onto the street. The emphasis on making art relevant and accessible meant that questions about form could not be avoided. In this way, debates from the cultural fringes infiltrated the funding program. Once there, however, they were played out between different people, with different terminology and with different institutional and discursive effects.

Giving out the grants

The first meeting of the Community Arts and Development Committee was held on 27 June 1973. The chairperson was Betty Burstall, one of the founders of the Melbourne experimental theatre, La Mama. As a member of Council she was given the task of overseeing this committee. Other membership consisted of representatives of each of the Boards, a member of the SPF for the sake of continuity, and a consultant on community arts. At the first meeting discussion focused on the need to develop a definition of community arts and clear policy objectives (CAC, *Minutes*, 27-6-73: 1). However, detailed policy formulation proved to be a luxury. In the pressure to disburse funds and deal with a backlog of applications grant-giving soon began to dominate the committee's activities.

This produced frustration. Grant administration was regarded as detracting from the real work of policy formulation. But, in the process of assessing applications and giving out money, policy was implicitly devised. Funding practices were crucial to the constitution of community arts. The formulation of guidelines and categories, the lists of successful applications, all prescribed this new field of patronage to the extent that *what* was funded was more often used to explain community arts than why. The pressure to give out money was also exacerbated by the rapid increases in funds which followed the election of the Labor government. In 1973 the Community Arts Program's budget was $225 204, in 1974 it jumped to $437 448 in 1974–75 to $952 384 (ACFTA, ARs, 1973,74,75). The ideal of making policy prior to the assessment of grants was quickly recognised as an impossible fantasy. 'Policy' was made on the run, in the dialectical relationship between the assessment procedures and funding requests.

The two broad objectives of the CAC, encouraging wider participation and support for multi-arts, produced a distinct set of funding categories. In the pursuit of increased arts participation funding was organised either around specific populations such as children, youth, ethnic groups and senior citizens or around specific institutions such as trade unions, gaols, hospitals and local government. The multi-arts objective was dominated by festivals. During the first few years of funding these categories shifted but the main tendencies did not fundamentally alter.

Grants for activities with children consistently received the highest proportion of funds. As table 3.1 shows, the category Children, Youth and Multi-Arts Workshops received 57 per cent of the 1974–75 budget. This reflected the proliferation of after-school programs and community centres, which were fuelled not only by arts money but also by a range of other Whitlam initiatives such as the Australian Assistance Plan and the Children's Commission. Grants for children and youth were easily justified under the rubric of increased participation. Children were represented as having a natural affinity for the arts, an intrinsic creativity. Early access to and involvement in the arts was seen as a way of preventing the cultural deprivation caused by television, poverty or regional disadvantage (ACFTA, AR, 1973: 16).

The SPF had made the occasional grant to Trade Unions but the CAC expanded this area of assistance. In 1974–75 it made four grants, representing 2.1 per cent of the budget. Lunchtime workshops and concerts dominated these grants. Patronage was based on two related assumptions: workers lacked culture and, in order to remedy this, the arts needed to be de-institutionalised and taken to these disadvantaged populations. Projects in prisons and hospitals reflected similar assumptions. Captive communities, whether they were patients, prisoners or

Table 3.1 Distribution of Community Arts Committee funds 1974–75

Funding Category	Amount ($)	% of Total CAC Budget
Trade Unions	19 700	2.1
Institutions and Prisons	13 560	1.4
Ethnic Projects	44 682	4.5
Senior Citizens	1 477	0.2
Children, Youth and Multi-Arts Workshops	542 655	57.0
Training and Communication	35 431	3.7
Fieldwork and Consultants	52 000	5.4
Local Government	54 230	5.7
Festivals	188 649	20.0
Total CAC Funding	952 384	100.0

Source: Compiled from grants list of the CAC, AC; AR, 1974–75.

process workers, were offered culture packaged and transported to them. The emphasis on concerts and arts workshops implied that, in these contexts, passive observation or appreciation could not stand alone but had to be accompanied with hands-on involvement. For these special groups, access to the arts meant doing it not just watching it. In these programs for increased participation, art in the community was not an end in itself but an instrument for therapy, rehabilitation, or education. This rhetoric drew on discourses about recreation which represented art as something that was 'good' for people because it encouraged productive leisure. Art for captive communities was definitely not defined by individual talent, special locations or precious objects.

In 1972 major arts festivals in Adelaide and Perth were being supported by the ACFTA as well as a range of smaller local celebrations. After the election of the Labor government the administration of festival grants was transferred to the CAC. Here they were made a separate funding category and although they appeared quintessentially multi-arts they fostered a long-running debate about their status as community arts. While all festivals were accepted as a conglomeration of many artforms, it was much harder to argue that all festivals exemplified the principles of access and participation. Adelaide and Perth festivals were big unashamed celebrations of high culture committed to attracting prestigious overseas acts. The emphasis on imported content was not only evidence of cultural deference but also an open rejection of local concerns and relevance.

Alongside these showcase festivals was a plethora of smaller, locally based 'community celebrations'. The most notorious of these was the Aquarius Festival at Nimbin in 1973. Soaking up a significant proportion of the budget, it signified some of the more startling impacts of

Whitlam's first aid to the arts. In the 1973 Annual Report Nimbin was justified as 'an experiment, an exercise in togetherness and the simple pleasures of arts and crafts activities' (ACFTA, AR, 1973: 22). Nimbin was the antithesis of the high culture binges at Perth and Adelaide; its hippie ethos equated the festival with the recovery of an organic, pre-industrial community.

The Perth and Adelaide festivals were fairly quickly passed onto the Entrepreneurial Committee when their community credentials could not be established (CAC, *Minutes*, 25-6-74: 3). But the majority of festivals stayed with the CAC and the debate about whether they were multi-arts or community arts continued. The multi-arts function of the CAC worked to marginalise other roles and meanings. It represented a straightforward administrative justification for the committee's existence which most Boards easily understood. In this context it was difficult to assert a different and more political justification for community arts, specifically the need for greater access and participation. Festivals highlighted this contest, and the struggle to claim that not all of them were automatically the responsibility of the CAC was the struggle to establish the necessity for a political justification for community arts rather than an administrative one.

The funding categories in operation from 1974 such as children, ethnics, trade unions, festivals and senior citizens reflected the legacies of the SPF days and the tendency to respond to *expressed* demand. The problem with this was that demand was uneven. The target groups, or the 'culturally disadvantaged', were often unaware of the existence of the CAC. As Mulgan and Worpole point out, 'where little provision has existed before, it is very difficult to suddenly stimulate a revolution in demand' (Mulgan and Worpole, 1986: 76). The development of the Field Officers Program was an attempt to redress this imbalance. This program was intended to make the committee proactive rather than reactive. More specifically, it was to establish models for outreach work. Field Officers carried out surveys of existing cultural facilities in regions and municipalities, worked with local government and generally disseminated information about the CAC and the Australia Council. Their task was not simply promotion but also liaison with potential 'clients' to assist them in identifying their latent cultural needs (CAC, *Minutes*, 12-10-73: 2).

Conclusion

Tracing the earliest patterns of grant giving shows how money and meanings circulated in the formation of the Community Arts Program. It shows how notions invoked in the debates preceding the establishment of the CAC were transformed into specific funding practices and assessment procedures. Central here was the idea of cultural disadvantage. The 'problem' of cultural disadvantage had justified the creation of the CAC, and when the money started to flow so too did the strategies for remediating the disadvantaged.

The funding categories used during 1973, 1974 and 1975 implied two different meanings for disadvantage. The first emphasised geographic disadvantage. Those who lived in remote regions or who were locked away in hospitals, prisons and workplaces were physically unable to attend the arts, a very literal interpretation of access! New systems of distribution were the remedy here. In the 1973 Annual Report a group of artists who covered thousands of miles touring remote regions were congratulated for their 'pioneer spirit' (ACFTA, AR, 1973: 25). Whether people were captured by institutions or distance, this interpretation of disadvantage did not question the nature of art but merely the ways in which it circulated. A frontier mentality echoed throughout much of the early rhetoric: 'festivals also carried the arts into distant communities . . . [w]ider dissemination of the arts in Australia involves communication and encouragement over vast distances' (ACFTA, AR, 1974: 22).

The second meaning for disadvantage referred to those groups not physically captive but captured by their age, ethnicity or socio-economic status. These groups were culturally disadvantaged because they were either unaware of or uninterested in the arts. For them, strategies focused not simply on education about the arts but on access to art as a form of therapy or recreation. The right to culture was based on the right to be helped through art. Disadvantage did not imply cultural difference or political and economic exclusion but cultural lack. Both these meanings for disadvantage produced funding practices organised around cultural missions or cultural charity.

If community arts was to be successful as a form of cultural charity then new systems of patronage had to be established. Wider distribution of the arts and different purposes for art demanded the use of non-art organisations. Within the CAC there was little recognition of the significance of this form of patronage. It was rather innocently presented as the only way to take art where it had never been before. Yet, as Rowse (1985a: 27) argues, it had important implications. Decentralised patronage not only devolved patronage decisions onto a vast array of 'non-culture' organisations, it also displaced the hegemony of excellence and standards as the main criteria for arts support. It was one of the major forces behind the emergence of alternative discourses of value.

When community centres or trade unions or hospitals devised arts programs their approach to art was instrumental, as a means to an end. By mid-1974 the assessment criteria for community arts projects had established that 'community support and involvement' were the essential elements of a valuable project. In assessing grants, the CAC looked for projects that had been initiated by community groups, projects whose purpose was involvement rather than spectatorship, and projects that encouraged the *development* of artistic activity rather than professionalism or excellence (CAC, *Minutes*, 25-6-74: 4). In this way art or the aesthetic outcome of the project was pushed to the margins. The cultural outcome of a good community arts project was described in this way: 'It may not in fact be excellent in terms of either material or performance, but it is *engaging* in the true sense as community groups are concerned.' (CAC, *Minutes*, 25-6-74: 4)[emphasis added]

The worth of community arts projects lay, not in the quality of the art, but in the experiences of their constituencies. The tension between excellence and access produced a defensive commitment to art that was 'engaging'. The assumptions underpinning excellence were not explicitly challenged, rather a space was created for community arts that existed outside of aesthetic discourses of value.

The dismissal of aesthetics, however, could never be complete. The valuing of community support and involvement meant that certain forms were privileged. If art was an instrument for collective expression then, inevitably, the festival loomed large. If raising self-esteem or therapy was the explicit intention of a project, the workshop— in anything from drama to face painting—often dominated. The funding of cultural forms that were transient, that emphasised process rather than product, that had little concern with the production of a lasting commodity or repeatable performance, characterised the grants disbursed during the first few years of the CAC. In this context, the distribution of forms was also of little importance. One-off performances, murals, festivals and workshops were devised to speak to specific constituencies. They rarely circulated beyond their original site of production. These were forms that often spoke only to themselves, their content being profoundly local. The value of culture in and for 'the community' was measured in terms of how something was produced rather than what was produced.

This strong emphasis on the conditions of production signalled the materiality of art and its social context. In the formation of the Community Arts Program the flexibility of the term 'community' was strategic. It could be invoked to mean different constituencies or different sites or different uses for art: art *for* the community, art *in* the community, art to *express* community. As the CAC grappled with the work of formulating policy, disbursing grants and justifying its role within the Australia Council the broad boundaries of the community arts field were laid down. Out of this process of official invention art and community were aligned in an awkward and insecure marriage.

4

Creating a Board: the struggle for survival 1975–1979

During its early years the establishment of the Community Arts Program had to be continually justified. Not only in public documents such as Annual Reports but also within the Council. There was constant pressure from the Boards to explain the need for and functions of this new program and, in an atmosphere of rapid institutional growth and change, this was not always easy. Most of the other Boards were dismissive and derisive about the objectives and activities of the Community Arts Program. Michael FitzGerald, Project Officer with the Theatre Board at the time, summarised the general attitude in this way:

> The perception was that community arts was all amateur and we didn't want to be in that, we'd left it all behind. If amateurs wanted to do it fine, they could do it for the love and the fun but not on money. There was a fair degree of patronisation [sic] from the Theatre Board and other Boards about community arts. It was funding face painting in the park, drawing on buildings and what's all this really got to do with high arts? (FitzGerald, *Interview*, 16-11-87)

Part of this early hostility can be explained in terms of internal struggles over resources. The steady increases in funds to the Community Arts Program, culminating in substantial growth in the 1975–76 budget, outraged the Boards that had not experienced such rapid growth. However, tensions were also a product of competing discourses about art. The Community Arts Program supported cultural practices that many of the Boards were determined to dismiss in this period of new nationalism. The amateur, the regional and the accessible were both embarrassing and irrelevant. They signified the erosion of 'standards' and the demise of excellence.

After two and a half years of operation the Community Arts Program occupied a marginal position within the Australia Council (the ACFTA's successor, established as a statutory authority in March 1975). The

46

program's objectives and work were not widely understood let alone accepted within the organisation. While other Boards were happy to enjoy the increased funds and support provided by the Labor government they were far less willing to adopt its policies for extending involvement in the arts. Resistance to the principles of access and participation was not the only barrier to institutional acceptance for the Community Arts Program. General confusion about what 'community arts' were was also a contributing factor. The idea of community arts as the dumping ground, the too-hard basket, the 'ministry for everything else', persisted.

These internal tensions escalated during 1975. So too did media attacks on the Australia Council which was singled out as a prime example of the Whitlam government's excessive spending and policy chaos. Andrea Hull (1983: 318), a Project Officer for the CAC during this period, describes 1976 and 1977 as the 'black years' of the Community Arts Program. The election of a Liberal government in December 1975 brought an end to Labor's largesse. However, although Prime Minister Fraser proved to be an enemy of a vast array of Labor initiatives, he was not the major threat to the survival of community arts. Most of the attacks on the program came from within the Australia Council, and the departure of Whitlam provided the perfect opportunity for their escalation. In this chapter the focus is on the micro-politics of the Australia Council. It is only through a close understanding of the battles that raged within this institution during the mid-1970s that it is possible to understand the paradox of how the Community Arts Program improved its status under a conservative government, with its conversion into a fully fledged Board.

The Fraser government and the McKinsey Report

In October 1975 the management consultants McKinsey and Company began an inquiry into the administration of the Australia Council (AC, AR, 1975–76: 13). This inquiry was initiated by the Council in response to a series of problems. Since the election of the Labor government its arts policies had been under almost continual fire. Most of these attacks focused on the remodelling of the ACFTA into the Australia Council. The massive increase in funds, rapid growth in the organisation and flurry of new grants all generated intense public debate and criticism.

Media attacks took several forms. First there was criticism about the excessive centralism of the new body: it had failed to appoint state government representatives to the Council; it had not engaged in any systematic consultation with the states and their cultural departments; and it was dominating the cultural life of Australia (*Sydney Morning Herald*, 25-3-74). Then there were the administrative costs of the Australia Council: the wastage of staff who indulged in too much travel and too many luxury lunches and the excessive costs of flying Board members all over the country for meetings (*West Australian*, 7-6-75). Rapid growth without adequate policy was also a common attack. The Australia Council was accused of having confused and contradictory objectives:

> The current confusion about ends and means is, ironically, a result of vastly increased funds. 'The pursuit of excellence' is submerged by other considerations. There is the artist's prosperity. . . There is a vague hankering for cultural democracy ('taking the arts to the people'). There is the veneration of youth and experiment (i.e. untested talents and works). The result is the subordination of 'excellence' to 'activity'. (*Sydney Morning Herald*, 20-6-75)

The subtext of these attacks was becoming all too familiar: Labor's reforms were simply 'too much too soon'. But with the arts this theme took on a particular inflection. Increases in cultural spending were fostering a proliferation of aesthetic fiascos which posed a threat to the 'standards' so assiduously maintained in the past. Nowhere was the 'subordination of excellence to activity' more evident than in the Community Arts Program. Although the commitment to 'democratising the arts' represented only a small percentage of the Australia Council's budget it provoked the most intense criticism. A $500 grant from the CAC to the Eaglehawk Dahlia and Arts Festival in Bendigo was picked up by the media and used to signify all that was frivolous and excessive about arts funding. Whitlam himself defended this grant:

> It's part of our policy to give encouragement and expression to diverse and off-beat activities if they can enrich the lives of our citizens. It doesn't cost much but the returns are great. . . We ought to guard against mean-spirited people who resent the idea of games and pleasure for communities which lack decent facilities. (Whitlam quoted in the *Melbourne Sun*, 4-8-75)

Apart from continual media attacks the Australia Council was also experiencing internal dilemmas and these were the second reason for initiating the McKinsey inquiry. Rapid growth had generated what was perceived as excessive bureaucracy with a proliferation of committees and rising administrative costs. The Council felt that its operations were becoming unwieldy and that this was threatening effectiveness, engendering bad feelings among artistic communities and fuelling media and political criticism.

McKinsey's report was presented in March 1976, after the demise of the Labor government and in the context of the Liberal government's drive to cut public expenditure and dismantle many Labor initiatives. The Australia Council had to respond simultaneously to a change of government and a report critical of its organisation and practices. Inevitably, these two developments became connected. The McKinsey report was read by a new government keen to justify institutional changes and cuts.

McKinsey's recommendations covered three main areas: streamlining administrative structures, including the abolition of all committees; devolution of small grants to state or local organisations; and a reduction in the size and frequency of Council and Board meetings (AC, AR, 1975–75: 13). These recommendations had serious implications for the Community Arts Program, which manifested most of the examples of administrative inefficiency identified by Mckinsey. Not only was it part of the plethora of Council committees, it was also one of the main sources of small grants. With the completion of the McKinsey report the Community Arts Program faced its first serious threat.

The idea of devolution was central to McKinsey's appraisal of 'access activities'. In arguing that support for these activities should be handed over to other organisations, the report acknowledged their value but, at the same time, insisted that they had no place in arts policies at the federal level. The devolution theme established by McKinsey exploited the anxieties about excessive federalism that had surrounded the Labor government, and it also sharpened the tension between the idea of the nation and the idea of community. The logic of devolution seemed abundantly clear: the small, the local, the amateur could claim no impacts on the 'nation' and therefore could not make a legitimate claim to federal money. 'Community' could not escape connotations of parochial. In contrast, the idea of 'national significance' went unexamined; like excellence it was a category often invoked but rarely defined.

Although the McKinsey report was structured around a review of management, its recommendations had profound policy implications. McKinsey's notions of management efficiency explicitly endorsed an Australia Council committed to the support of large cultural organisations with national significance. The national functions of the Australia Council had to be reasserted, its national goals and programs clearly identified (McKinsey and Co., 1976, Section 1: 2). This insistence on national programs was also, implicitly, a privileging of excellence over access. Excellence and nation are categories whose genealogy is deeply interconnected in the formation of arts policy. The McKinsey report made these two categories synonymous. The tension, or 'goal conflict' as McKinsey referred to it, between excellence and access that was built into the original charter and structure of the Australia Council was to be resolved by cutting back on access activities and consolidating the search for excellence. The Australia Council needed to get 'back to basics' and eliminate worthy but peripheral activities. In this report the diversity and confusion characterised by the Community Arts Program were equated with management inefficiency.

During the first half of 1976 the CAC awaited Council's response to the McKinsey report. The impact of the Liberal government was evident immediately in significant reductions in funds given to the

Australia Council and in the imposition of stringent staff ceilings. The 1976–77 budget represented a 12.7 per cent reduction in real terms for the arts (AC, AR, 1976–77: 12). Institutional changes were also implemented. Some of these were a direct response to McKinsey, such as reductions in Council and Board membership and the promotion of other sources of funding for the arts ranging from state governments to business.

Fraser's changes were praised by a media that had thrived on hysterical attacks on Labor's initiatives. The *Sydney Morning Herald* advised Fraser to:

> rid the Council of the pressures of philanthropy, social justice and 'social therapy' and let it concentrate on what should always have been its main concern—the fostering of artistic excellence for its own sake. Of course . . . there are underprivileged communities. But it is at the local and community levels that their needs can best be judged and met. (*Sydney Morning Herald*, 7-6-76)

The commitment to access and participation was represented as a momentary aberration in the operations of a national arts policy. The support of excellence was the proper role of subsidy and a conservative government the proper custodian of such a policy.

The Australia Council, beleagured almost since its inception, now faced a new range of threats: internal reorganisation, substantial cuts and political attacks. In this atmosphere the CAC was particularly vulnerable. In the middle of 1976 the Prime Minister advised Council on his response to the McKinsey report. Despite the report's recommendation to eliminate all committees, the Community Arts Program was given a temporary reprieve. It was allowed to continue while its future was assessed.

However, this reluctant and temporary reprieve for the Community Arts Program did not protect it from internal attack and reorganisation. In the 1976–77 budget the CAC's funds were reduced from $1.4 million to $851 775 (AC, AR, 1976–77: 17). While the CAC lost funds the Boards gained; they were now responsible for 'community projects' in their particular artform. McKinsey's idea of giving responsibility for community arts to other bodies was beginning to be realised. Devolution was the justification here, even if it was initially implemented only within the Australia Council. The role of the CAC was now constructed as assisting other Boards to realise community objectives.

With many of its functions and some of its money now devolved to the Boards the CAC meetings were dominated by discussions about the survival of the program and the inability of the Boards to adequately assess community arts projects. Previous experience had highlighted the Boards' varying knowledge of and commitment to community arts. News that the Music Board had used community arts funds to support the Melbourne Choral Society confirmed the CAC's worst fears. It was obvious that in a lot of instances funds for community projects were being used by the Boards to offset the impact of Fraser's cuts (CAC, *Minutes*, 22-11-76: 3).

There was little the CAC could do about the perceived misuse by the Boards of money for community arts projects. The status of the committee was at an all-time low and there were few within the Australia Council who were prepared to fight for its survival. In fact, the McKinsey report and the election of Fraser provided great opportunities for those who were hostile to community arts. For these people, the reassertion of excellence and national significance was a welcome return to 'normal'.

During 1976 and 1977 the future of the Community Arts Program hung in the balance. The legacy of Whitlam had been the enshrining of excellence and access in the statutory charter of the Australia Council, but no sooner had this been achieved than a cost-cutting government fighting inflation and 'Labor's excesses' was elected. Combined with this was the McKinsey report with its recommendations for a leaner Australia Council committed to clear national objectives. The responses of the Council to these changes were varied. Some involved direct attacks on the status and functions of the Community Arts Program, while others involved a more generalised retreat from questions of equity and access.

The direct attacks on the Community Arts Program were both organisational and ideological. Stripping the program of funds and devolving many of its functions to the Boards was an effective mechanism for exacerbating its already marginal status. But so too was the Council decision to respond to the loss of revenue by giving priority to the most expensive and privileged cultural forms. As Rowse (1985a: 21–2) points out, the Theatre and Music Boards gained a greater proportion of the Australia Council budget under Fraser, while the more innovative Boards such as Crafts and Aboriginal Arts lost out. This was an implicit endorsement of the significance of 'excellence' over equity. Another threat came from McKinsey's devolution rhetoric. All these factors provided plenty of ammunition for those within the Australia Council keen to eradicate the irritating and embarrassing presence of community arts.

The constituency fights back

While the battle raged inside the Australia Council, outside it those who had benefited from grants from the Community Arts Program began to sense that their source of funding was under threat. Letters in support of the Community Arts Program had been arriving at the Australia Council since the devolution of some of its funds and functions to the Boards. Grant applicants found the new arrangements confusing and disturbing and could get little clarification from CAC staff who were equally disoriented. The 1976–77 Annual Report acknowledged the anxiety that this caused:

> Substantial changes occurred in the method of funding Community Arts in 1976–77, and most such grants were dispersed directly by the Boards. Through this shift of responsibility, some applicants were uncertain which section of the Council was handling their requests. The shortage of Council's funds led to apprehension about the extent of Council's commitment to the Community Arts Program. (AC, AR, 1976-77: 17)

At the Second National Community Arts Conference in March 1977 in South Australia an organised campaign in defence of the Community Arts Program was established. Recipients of community arts grants and people with an interest in 'arts in the community' had met before. In 1973 Ros Bower, a consultant to the ACFTA with an interest in youth arts and community arts, had organised a small meeting in Melbourne. But the first substantial conference, or 'Compost' as it was referred to, was organised by Andrea Hull in August 1974. Hull described those who attended in this way:

> There were artists in community arts centres wanting to develop new ways of working. There were also a whole series of community-based workers that had come into being because of the Whitlam principles of self-determination, Australian Assistance Plan workers, community education and health workers. There was a whole range of people who shared the same principles although the medium might have been different. . . The base was arts centres, the arts councils movement, various community-based workers who saw the use of the arts as a way to achieve their ends. There were artists who felt more politically comfortable with this way of working. . . People were already bustling away on things, the CAC gave them a renewed financial base and it also established connections between those people that had not been there before. (Hull, *Interview*, 11-9-87)

In this account the diversity of the participants is striking. So too is the role of funding from the CAC in constituting this group around the rhetoric and practice of community arts. In 1974 this was not a political movement with specific objectives, demanding state funds and programs. It was a group of disparate people, some with community concerns and some with aesthetic concerns, attracted to a source of funds with guidelines that were ambiguous enough to accommodate an extraordinarily eclectic range of demands.

The other significant feature of the 'community arts field', as it became known, was that it was not made up of those special populations identified in policy discourse as 'in need'. Conference attendance was not dominated by the aged, those living in the western suburbs, migrants or trade unionists. Those who received grants, attended conferences and promoted community arts as a new cultural practice spoke on behalf of the participants and audiences for projects, the culturally disadvantaged. Community arts practitioners represented these groups, they wrote the grant submissions, they initiated the projects, they spoke for and about these 'others'.

In this way two constituencies were produced in the discursive formation of community arts. In the sphere of policy the culturally deprived were identified as the targets of special programs and assistance. The administration of their cultural 'needs' was a constant theme in Annual Reports—whilst in the sphere of grants disbursement and conferences it was the interests and needs of the community arts practitioner that dominated. Obviously, these two constituencies were connected in a web of often difficult and ambiguous relations. Like the 'white advisor' class that has developed around various Aboriginal communities, community arts practitioners were often middle class professionals employed to serve various 'clients'.

These community arts practitioners met at a second Compost in 1977 but this time discussion was dominated by the threats to the CAC. Rumours about the imminent abolition of the Community Arts Program galvanised the conference participants into organising a National Community Arts Co-operative (NCAC) to campaign for the survival of the program. It was quickly decided to go for an ambit bid and demand that the CAC be converted into a Board. This was regarded as the only possible source of real security for community arts. The NCAC, made up of representatives from each state, began a vigorous campaign. The main strategy was a massive letter-writing effort. The key targets were: Tony Staley, Minister Assisting the Prime Minister in the Arts; Prime Minister Fraser; members of the Council of the Australia Council; and the media.

The rhetoric of the NCAC was a rhetoric of defence. It was a lobby group established not simply to argue for the principle of state support for community arts but also to protect a bureaucracy that had constructed and sustained community arts practitioners. Many of the claims of the NCAC focused on the administrative structures of current and future patronage. At the same time as the NCAC expressed its full support for the staff and committee of the CAC it also demanded that its members be regularly consulted about community arts policies and that they should be represented on the Board, if it was established. The demand was not only for the money to continue but also for the constituency's right to have a say in how it was given out. Community arts practitioners had been constituted in relation to the funding body and could only conceptualise their role within this field. The language and categories of the NCAC were those of the CAC, and this was one of the main effects of a battle organised around the preservation of funding.

The campaign also produced new categories. The 'community arts movement' was the most significant because it so effectively blurred the boundaries between the bureaucrats, whose job was to administer community arts grants, and the recipients of this money. All were represented as equally committed to the promotion and practice of community arts. This alliance was strategic, it highlighted the complex power relations between the funders and the funded. The illusion that all power lay in the hands of the state or the bureaucrats was quickly shattered. For community arts practitioners the threat to the CAC was enabling, it mobilised them into an organised force which claimed the authority to demand continued funding. The relations between the CAC and its constituency were not fixed, they shifted within a field of mutual expectations and obligations. Each constituted the other. All the conferences to organise those interested or working in community arts had been initiated and run by staff of the CAC. The first meeting of the New South Wales branch of the NCAC, a lobby group set up to fight the Australia Council, was organised on Australia Council phones thanks to the assistance of a staff member of the CAC.

The final battle to establish a Board was fought at the Council meetings. By early 1977 Fraser's reprieve was running out. Council had to make a decision in order to incorporate any changes into the 1977–78 budget. The April 1977 Council meeting was dominated by debate about the future of the Community Arts Program. Most of the Board chairpersons were hostile. The internal fights over territory and resources, that had been going on since the election of the Liberal government and the release of the McKinsey report, had fostered a deep antagonism towards the CAC. The committee had come to signify administrative inefficiency and an ideological threat. Joan Campbell, deputy chair of the CAC and an artist member of Council, maintained a spirited defence in the face of immense hostility. She was supported by Ken McKinnon, deputy chair of the Australia Council and head of the Schools Commission, who had persistently argued for the program, by Doreen Warburton from the Q Theatre and by Wally Curran, a trade union representative (Campbell, *Interview*, 23-2-88). The meeting was also being lobbied from outside. Apart from the swarms of letters sent to all Council members, a telegram from eighty NCAC members arrived on the first day of the Council meeting. After two days of fierce debate, where personalities and ideologies battled it out over the future of the Community Arts Program, a decision was made. Council resolved that: 'Government be requested to establish a Community Arts Board' (AC, *Minutes*, 15-4-77).

The decision was far from unanimous. The Theatre Board dissented from the resolution on the grounds that it ignored 'the Minister's wishes and Council's earlier resolution in respect of small grants' (AC, *Minutes*, 15-4-77: 7). So too did the Crafts Board, on the grounds that the Community Arts Committee or Board should not be responsible for community arts activities initiated by the Crafts Board (AC, *Minutes*, 15-4-77: 7).

On 4 September 1977 Prime Minister Fraser announced the establishment of the Community Arts Board (CAB) in the Australia Council, with the same powers and status as the other Boards. The decision of a conservative government to preserve and enlarge the Community Arts Program was not as ironic as it first appears. Rydon and Mackay (1984: 93) point out that, in his first parliamentary statement on the arts after his election, Fraser argued that devolution was to be the Australia Council's most important and urgent task. However, even though the McKinsey report offered the Liberal government the perfect blueprint for rationalisation of the Australia Council, the opportunities for dramatic reorganisation and restructuring were not taken up. A General Manager was appointed, the Film, Radio and Television Board was banished, the Australian Opera and Australian Ballet companies were funded directly from federal cabinet, and savage revenue cuts were made. However, substantial devolution of funds and functions to state and local governments never took place, despite all the rhetoric about new federalism and small government.

This was one of the reasons for the Community Arts Program's survival. Another could have been the ambiguity of the category 'community'. Although this term took off under Whitlam, its appeal was not exclusive to those committed to progressive reform. 'Community' had the capacity to convey different but favourable meanings to all sides of politics; it posed no threat to liberal ideals. If community arts meant increased participation in the arts then the Liberals were for it, for they, like their Labor colleagues, believed in the civilising benefits of culture.

Creating a Board

Five years ago the concept was still suspect. Community arts were seen as largely amateur, second rate and of dubious relevance to the future of the arts in general. Even three years ago some newspapers could criticise the Australia Council for granting $500 to the Eaglehawk Dahlia and Arts Festival. Britain, Canada and the United States are still sharply divided over the official recognition and funding of community arts. In this country we allowed doubts to be outweighed by the conviction that, in the long term, widening participation in the arts was necessary if they were to flourish overall. The Australia Council largely pioneered this form of support. (AC, AR, 1977–78: 8)

With this self-congratulatory rhetoric the Australia Council announced the establishment of the CAB. In this official representation the CAB was held up as evidence of the Council's capacity for innovation. Although it was acknowledged that more participation was essential if the arts were to 'flourish overall', the cautious references to amateurs, second-rate products and the ubiquitous Eaglehawk Dahlia and Arts Festival echoed previous tensions. The apologetic subtext of this offical announcement hinted at a certain ambivalence and anxiety about the commitment to community arts.

While the Australia Council was busy priding itself on pioneering this new form of arts support, it remained silent on the significant institutional changes that the creation of a Board represented. There was no official discussion of the background of the Board members, the budget or the implications of a new Board both within the Australia Council and for recipients of community arts grants. The shift from Council program to Board was represented as a smooth continuum, little more than a name change. This official silence denied the extent of the conflict that had preceded the establishment of a Board.

Acquisition of Board status was contradictory. In administrative terms Council programs had always functioned along similar lines to the Boards. They had reasonable autonomy to disburse funds and their own policies and programs to pursue. However, they were still committees of Council and lacked the independence of Boards especially in terms of membership. The CAC had always been made up of representatives of other Boards with a Council member as chairperson. It suffered from both constant changes in membership and the occasional member who had been coerced into attending and had little interest in or knowledge of the area. Unlike the Boards, committees were not able to operate a system of peer review of grants. Outside members representing the field were only occasionally nominated and were always a marginal minority.

The other problem with Council committees was their vulnerability. The McKinsey report had shown how easy it was to target them in any claims for rationalisation. Board status diminished these institutional weaknesses. It meant the opportunity to appoint an outside chairperson and board members and increased staff. It placed community arts alongside the other Boards and this was often represented as the Community Arts Program's symbolic acquisition of adulthood within the Council. Andrea Hull likened it to turning 21 (*Interview*, 11-9-87).

Soon after the announcement of the establishment of the CAB Ros Bower was appointed as Director. She had been acting in this position since early 1977 (CAC, *Minutes*, 8-2-77: 1). Employed as a consultant to the ACFTA in 1969 she had remained on staff and worked on many of the Australia Council's programs including the SPF, education and the arts, young people and the arts, ethnic arts, and the CAC (*Artforce* 27, 1980: 1). Bower had credibility and clout within the Australia Council, probably because she had never been permanently attached to the community arts area. While she had produced many of the early policy documents and justifications for the community arts program, she was not identified as purely community arts but rather as a generalist with knowledge of a wide range of arts development issues (Hull, *Interview*, 11-9-87). Bower's influence on the earliest constructions of community arts was substantial and her appointment as director of the Board gave her the opportunity to consolidate these initial developments, to shape the CAB in the interests of these earliest formations.

Selection of an appropriate chairperson for the Board was crucial. While staff of the Board were able to make suggestions, the final decision was the Minister's. For staff the most important criterion for a chairperson was the capacity to represent community arts effectively at Council meetings, especially in the face of several extremely hostile Council members (Hull, *Interview*, 11-9-87). In February 1978 Dr Peter Botsman took up the position of chairperson of the CAB. At the time he was Principal of Kelvin Grove Teachers College in Brisbane. Prior to this Botsman had been Associate Professor in Community Service Education at Cornell University, where he had been involved in a range of extension programs. In Brisbane he was involved in several arts organisations in a voluntary capacity. He was also committed to encouraging more cultural life on campus. Botsman's initial response to the offer from Staley to chair the CAB was surprise: 'What's community arts? I really was not au fait with the vernacular as it had developed in Australia'. (Botsman, *Interview*, 19-11-87.)

Despite this initial ignorance, Botsman accepted the appointment and in early 1978 began a tour of Australia interviewing prospective Board members. The first Board represented a compromise reached between a director and staff keen to recognise and reward key members from the field and a chairperson without any current knowledge of or contacts with the community arts movement but keen to assert his own influence and philosophy. June Jeremy, Ken Conway and Susie Roux were all community arts practitioners with extensive involvement with the CAC and the campaign to save community arts. Ted Greenwood and Paul Barron were outside the movement and reflected Botsman's desire to have internal diversity within the Board and to prevent a ghetto mentality.

The Board began work in an atmosphere of renewed energy and status. The backlog of grant administration that had built up over 1977 meant that initial meetings offered little time to discuss policies or the significance of Board status especially in relation to the rest of the Australia Council or the field. Assessing grant applications was very demanding and there was not much opportunity for the Board to collectively establish guidelines. Board members with no previous experience of community arts policy or funding categories had to develop an understanding via the grants assessment process. Initial impressions were interesting:

> Community arts officers, community arts centres, women's refuges, craft for married women at home, festivals, face painting . . . like party activities. It sounded as though they were concerned with amateur activities and they wanted these to be legitimised. That there was a creativity that needed to

be recognised. That the arts were in the hands of a minority. (Greenwood, *Interview*, 14-11-87)

New status and new members did not mean a dramatic change of direction. In this context the influence of the director and staff was crucial. They provided continuity, especially Bower and Hull who had long institutional histories and whose experience was deferred to (Botsman, *Interview*, 19-11-87 and Greenwood, *Interview*, 14-11-87). The relationship between Board and staff was remarkably democratic, each recognising the value of the other's contribution. The staff were particularly glad of the presence of a Board which provided legitimacy and institutional support.

By the end of its first five years the Community Arts Program had achieved Board status after a long campaign. The threats to its survival had come, not from the election of a conservative government, but from within the Australia Council. The space established for community arts within this institution had always been on the periphery. It was a marginal funding program supporting marginal constituencies and cultural forms. The victory of Board status was a tribute to both the mobilisation of community arts practitioners, who organised a massive campaign to protect the bureaucracy that had constructed them, and a collection of committed staff, Board and Council members who defended the program long and hard at Council meetings. This victory highlighted the contradiction of Fraser's policies for the arts. The areas that did best out of his government were the Music Board, Theatre Board and community arts. In a period of cost cutting and inflation their funding increased. The ambiguity of 'community' had proved of strategic value in the campaign to save one of Whitlam's innovations from the conservatives' razor.

5
Funding the community: 1980–1985

The work of consolidation and review during the first years as a Board was crucial in establishing a more confident and assertive presence for the CAB within the Australia Council. By 1980 evaluations of several major funding areas such as Community Arts Centres and Community Arts Officers were either completed or underway. This signalled the emergence of a distinctive set of cultural practices and organisations which prescribed community arts. Previous confusion about the definition of community arts diminished as certain patterns of funding became entrenched. The shift away from funding categories targeting specific populations towards the funding of particular cultural organisations and workers meant that the search for those unrepresented 'others' without access to the arts no longer dominated policy discourse. Questions about the nature of cultural deprivation, who suffered it and why were pushed to the sidelines. While the problem of cultural disadvantage was still central, the emphasis was now on the relative merits of different methods for working 'in the community'.

The disbursement of grants produced a constituency, not the one identified in the earliest policy discourses as 'in need', but a constituency of cultural workers who received grants, ran projects, managed community arts centres, organised rural tours and such. Funding constructed the 'community arts practitioner' and the increasing presence and organisation of this constituency was one of the forces that shifted policy and practice. The preoccupation with finding the community had been a product of the pressure to justify the Community Arts Program and demarcate its field of responsibility. By the 1980s this process of legitimation was no longer as determinant. The CAB began to speak more to its constituency and less to its critics.

By 1980 funds for the CAB had reached $2 050 000 which represented 8 per cent of the Australia Council's 'support for the arts' budget. This made the CAB the biggest of the smaller Boards which included Visual Arts, Crafts, Literature and Aboriginal Arts. In terms of funding and staffing levels the Community Arts Program could no

Table 5.1 Distribution of Community Arts Board funds 1980–81

Funding Category	Amount ($)	% of Total CAB Budget
Community Arts Organisations	210 000	10.0
Community Arts Centres	227 000	11.0
Community Arts Officers and Field Officers	168 000	8.0
Festivals, Celebrations and Happenings	209 000	10.0
Ethnic, Folk and Traditional Arts	115 000	6.0
Fellowships and Training	36 286	1.8
Communications	38 076	1.9
Ethnic Programs	101 000	5.0
Pilot Projects	221 925	10.8
Arts Council of Australia	719 274	35.0
Other	5 738	0.5
Total CAB Funding	2 051 299	100.0

Source: Compiled from grants list of the CAB, AC; AR, 1980–81

longer claim marginal institutional status. At the centre of the Australia Council were the Music and Theatre Boards which continued to swallow up 51 per cent of the budget (AC, AR, 1980–81: 10).

Table 5.1 sets out the CAB's funding categories for 1980–81 and their share of its total budget. In each of these funding programs different meanings for community arts were established and different cultural practices were privileged. While the Arts Councils were busy touring culture to the country, Community Arts Officers were using cultural activities to develop community identity. Even within each category there was immense variety.

This funding diversity was symptomatic of the flexibility of the term 'community'; no single meaning dominated, instead it signified a fluid field of cultural practices and forms loosely unified by a sense of being alternative to both 'high' culture and mass culture. At this stage the oppositional inflection given to 'community arts' came from its representation as a more authentic cultural practice than either high or mass culture. Community-based cultural activity was small, intimate and bonding:

> Shared enjoyment or participation in the arts is one form of community bonding. The word 'community' clearly does not apply to a metropolitan theatre audience where the juxtaposition of individuals is largely accidental and no inter-personal relations are created, nor to casual attendance at an art gallery. The sense of community involves communication and a degree of regular and continuous association. This can occur at a small community theatre where neighbours inevitably meet; it can occur at the corner store but not in Myers. (Bower, 1981b: 6)

Because of the diversity of programs within the CAB it is difficult to summarise the patterns and effects of funding. Each program was the product of a specific history and discourse. Rather than give a superficial sweep over all the funding areas it is more useful to consider two in detail. In this way it is possible to explore the role of funding practices in the formation of community arts during the 1980s. Pilot Projects and Communications have been selected because they manifest distinctive but equally significant aspects of funding as a discursive practice. Within each of these categories it is possible to trace (a) how heterogeneous discourses about anything from radical art to community development were utilised and transformed in the rationales for community arts, and (b) how the process of assessment and disbursement of grants involved the negotiation of power relations both internally, between the CAB and other Boards, and externally, between the CAB and its constituency. The assessment of grant applications was at the heart of the CAB's ongoing formation, for this was the place where both money and meanings were administered.

Pilot Projects: managing experimentation

Pilot Projects was one of the new funding categories established with the creation of the Board. It was envisaged as a fund that would support innovative projects in conjunction with other Boards. Within the CAB, Pilot Projects represented an attempt to respond to two administrative dilemmas. First, there was a need to keep some funds available for projects which fell outside the guidelines of the fixed categories, enabling the CAB to respond to new developments and innovations. A flexible category was the only way to guarantee a balance between funding guidelines that were prescriptive and others that were broad enough to attract unorthodox projects.

The second motivation behind the Pilot Projects category was the ongoing problem of the CAB's relationship with the other Boards. This fund was an attempt to confront inter-board hostilities from a new angle. The CAB was still funding a vast array of single artform projects ranging from community theatre companies to murals. This practice was a result of the other Boards' resistance to community arts and their continual refusal to accept responsibility for projects with even a hint of community about them. The existence of the CAB provided the perfect escape clause. According to the Theatre Board, for example, 'community theatre' was more community than theatre (FitzGerald, *Interview*, 6-11-87). This ambiguity was frustrating for the CAB. Single artform community projects extended the scope and meaning of *both* community arts and theatre, music, painting or whatever. As long as the CAB continued to provide almost exclusive support for them the challenge which these activities posed to mainstream cultural production and practice could be evaded.

The Boards' reluctance to support community arts projects was an effect of both ideology and economics. Many of the Boards were locked into funding patterns which were difficult to change and which offered little scope for innovation or flexibility. The Theatre Board had responsibility for many big companies which had a virtual mortgage over funds. Smaller companies or groups found it difficult to get a fair hearing. The Music Board was in a similar position; it too was virtually captured by its clients. There was a sense in which certain long-standing obligations were not negotiable. The Visual Arts Board was trapped not so much by the economic demands of big companies but by its own discourses of art. It was extremely elitist and nowhere was this more visible than in its hostility to the CAB. Visual artists with an interest in or commitment to community-based work were given little, if any, recognition. In fact, a commitment to community was seen as evidence that you were definitely not an artist (see Hull, 1982: 35).

Another contributing factor in the development of Pilot Projects was the effect of repeated cuts to the Australia Council's budget. Between 1975 and 1982 total Australia Council funds declined by 20 per cent in real terms (AC, AR, 1981–82: 13). It was difficult to encourage Boards to fund community arts projects in their specific artform in an atmosphere of funding constraints. In this context the CAB adopted responsibility for maintaining a space for innovation within the Australia Council.

The guidelines for Pilot Projects allowed for new ideas, whether multi-arts or single artform, to get funding provided they were in a 'community context'. Initial funds were to come from the CAB but, after a year, joint funding with the relevant Board was expected. Close consultation with other Boards was promised during the pre-submission period in order to encourage eventual joint funding or devolution (Hull, 1981a: 2).

Policy and funding guidelines for Pilot Projects had to tread the difficult ground of definition. In trying to fix boundaries around the idea of a 'pilot project' the CAB openly rejected projects which were committed only to aesthetic innovation:

> Proposals must be related to a known community context and, whilst experimental, *should relate to a new application of the arts or a new artistic experience for the people, rather than experimentation for arts' sake.* (Hull, 1981a: 2) [emphasis added]

This policy statement echoed previous tensions. In the discursive formation of community arts, responsibility for activities outside the mainstream had been a recurring theme. From the SPF of 1970 to the creation of Pilot Projects in 1978 community arts had been identified with the cultural fringes. 'Community' signified forms and practices that were institutionally and aesthetically on the margins. However, within this space questions about the purpose of cultural innovation remained problematic. The guidelines for Pilot Projects reiterated earlier fears about 'experimentation for its own sake'. For community arts the cultural margins were not places where questions about art and its meaning were explored, but rather places where communities without access to the arts could be enticed into participation. Experimentation in community arts meant the development of arts that would provide new experiences 'for the people' and relate to a 'community context'. Without these instrumental objectives experimentation was automatically elitist, abstracted and reflexive.

This reluctance to articulate experimentation in terms laid down by the political avant-garde was an effect of the overwhelming deference to 'community'. In most radical cultural movements questions of text and context have been given equal attention. The development of new sites for the production and distribution of art has not been separated from the development of new forms. However, in the history of community arts there was fear of aesthetics. Concern with the formal outcomes of projects and their qualities was regarded as a sign of creeping elitism. This disregard for 'art' was also manifest in the repeated emphasis on participation, community-based culture and hands-on activities. These terms prescribed community arts as a 'new' rather than a radical cultural practice committed to making the arts more appealing and accessible and committed to taking the arts to the community. The cultural experience was more important than the cultural product. This silence about formal outcomes produced a sharp separation between text and context, fuelling criticisms of community arts as an aesthetically irrelevant leisure activity.

Despite the refusal to prescribe formal criteria as a measure of success in community arts projects the Pilot Projects fund did provide a crucial space for the development of a number of aesthetically innovative projects. It was the source of funds for many projects which were to become celebrated as exemplary for both the way they were produced and what was produced. Although the organising rhetoric of Pilot Projects emphasised new cultural contexts and practice as the source of innovation, questions of aesthetics could not be ignored; new contexts meant new texts. The other major achievement of Pilot Projects was the progress it made in generating support from the other Boards for community arts projects in their particular artform. It was one of the major forces in breaking down some of the resistance to community arts policy and practice across the Council. The incentive of joint funding and the careful work done by CAB staff in consulting with other Boards about proposals for pilot projects was crucial in cutting through this resistance (Hull, *Interview*, 11-9-87 and FitzGerald, *Interview*, 6-11-87).

Responses from the Boards to participate in the Pilot Projects program varied. Some had already incorporated elements of community arts policy and practice into their programs. The Crafts Board was the leader in this area. It had invoked 'community' in several of its programs since the mid-1970s. In 1976–77 it had supported a community craft project, the *National Rug Event*, and in 1978 it had launched *Crafts in Gear*, a project jointly funded with the CAB (AC, AR, 1979–80: 38). However, these developments did not diminish the competition and hostility between the CAB and Crafts Board; if anything they fuelled it. It was not until the Pilot Projects fund that relations began to thaw. Pilot Projects provided money for a variety of community-based crafts projects which encouraged the Crafts Board's growing commitment to participatory craft production. Two of the most distinctive projects to emerge from this alliance were Viv Binns' *Mothers' Memories Others' Memories*, an Artist-in-Community project celebrating womens' domestic culture, and Cedar Prest's stained glass window project based at the Parks Community Centre in Adelaide.

The Visual Arts Board had made few concessions to the Community Arts Program prior to the establishment of the Pilot Projects fund. It had always supported an Artist-in-Residence program but this was based on a model of professional artists located in educational institutions for short periods. Its Public Art program involved 'bringing the community into contact with significant works of contemporary Australian art' (VAB, 1978: 13) and was designed to move 'high' culture out of the gallery and into civic centres, parks, schools and plazas for the public's edification and enjoyment. Both these programs privileged professional artists and elite artforms.

The Visual Arts Board's involvement in the Pilot Projects fund challenged these tendencies in several ways. In 1980–81 the Visual Arts Board agreed to jointly fund two Artists-in-Residence at the South Coast Trades and Labour Council. This was the beginning of Redback Graphics, one of the most important new poster workshops to emerge in the 1980s (Hall, 1989). It was also the beginning of the Visual Arts Board's acceptance of a vast range of community organisations as appropriate sites for the placement of artists. The idea of the university as the best and only site for residencies was no longer tenable. Artists residing in community organisations, whether they were trade unions, libraries or whatever, could not sit back quietly and create: they had to be 'useful', they had work with and for a community rather than simply display their skills to them.

The Visual Arts Board also provided funds jointly with the CAB for several mural groups including the Prospect Mural Group, Addison Rd Community Centre, Brunswick Images and Wolloomooloo Billboards (Hull, 1981a). Support for murals stretched the Visual Arts Board's category of public art to include images painted on walls, often with overt political messages and often with extensive community participation. This forced a recognition of public art as more than just fountains and sculpture, and it also meant that the CAB was at last able to offload some of its funding for murals now that the Visual Arts Board had finally acknowledged that images on walls could be visual art.

The Theatre Board had expressed token commitment to community theatre since the late 1970s. It was included in its funding guidelines as an acceptable category. Despite this official recognition, in practice the Theatre Board had granted very little money to community theatre over the years (see AC, ARs, 1975 to 1980). It did have a tradition of funding youth theatre, theatre in education, puppetry and regional theatre but none of these categories completely embraced the work of community theatre companies, who were continually left out in the cold. Many community theatre groups sought funds through the CAB after unsuccessful approaches to the Theatre Board (FitzGerald, *Interview*, 6-11-87 and Hull, *Interview*, 11-9-87). The Pilot Projects fund allowed the CAB to nurture new community theatre groups and also begin to erode the Theatre Board's resistance in this area. The Theatre Board participated in this fund with joint funding of the Mill Community Theatre based at Deakin University in Victoria, the Murray River Performing Group, West Community Theatre and Sidetrack Theatre (Hull, 1981a).

Each of these companies had a strong commitment to theatre which emerged from communities and functioned to express their interests. Local participation was central to their cultural practice; this was theatre committed to collapsing the social barriers between audience and performers. Each of these companies produced work noted for both quality of production and powerful content. The Pilot Projects fund was one of the key forces behind the Theatre Board's gradual acceptance of the significance of community theatre and its responsibility to support it. By the early 1980s the Theatre Board had assumed major responsibilty for community theatre companies (AC, AR, 1979–80: 144–5) and the CAB's role had diminished. This significant shift was also assisted by the development of a well-organised and articulate community theatre lobby group which had been putting pressure on the Theatre Board for several years (Laurie, 1984: 83).

The example of community theatre indicates the way in which the CAB used the incentive of joint funding to involve other Boards in community arts projects. This involvement inevitably generated a confrontation of previous resistance and offered the possibility of cautious participation before complete responsibility was assumed. Pilot Projects forced a reluctant acceptance of some aspects of community arts policy and systems of patronage across the Australia Council. While most of the Boards had already invoked 'community' in some form prior to the development of Pilot Projects, it was this fund that produced substantial change.

The other effect of the Pilot Projects fund was its support for innovative community arts projects signalling new aesthetic languages and new ways for artists to work. Despite the reluctance to encourage experimentation 'for its own sake' this funding category, of all those within the CAB, produced some of the most seminal community art works. Most of the projects mentioned in this brief account were celebrated as evidence of the potential of community arts to create original, powerful and aesthetically innovative forms. Mothers' Memories, Redback Graphics, the Prospect Murals and Sidetrack Theatre were all held up as evidence of the cultural and social significance of community arts (see CAB *Caper* 8, 11, 20; Binns 1980; Burke, 1981). Discussed and promoted both outside and inside the Australia Council, these projects were praised for their methods of production, for indicating new possibilities for collaborative creativity and new roles for artists. Other Boards had to reluctantly accept the quality and impact of these projects as evidence of community arts' growing authority.

Communications, Training and Resources: managing the field

These three funding categories appear throughout the history of the Community Arts Program, sometimes grouped together and at other times clustered with related categories like Fellowships or Documentation. Although the funds allocated in these areas represented only a small percentage of the budget of the Community Arts Program, how these funds were spent was significant. Under these various headings the Community Arts Program supported activities like the promotion of community arts, national conferences, training for community arts practitioners and the publication of newsletters (cf. AC, AR, 1974–75: 34–5). Grants in this area were based on the pursuit of two different but related objectives. They either funded activities geared to the development of a higher profile for the Community Arts Program outside the realm of the official policy statement or Annual Report, or they supported activities which addressed and developed the field. More than any other area of the CAB's funding programs, the pursuit of these two objectives was influenced by the shifting relations between the CAB and its constituency and this is the significance of this loose assortment of categories.

The role of the CAB in promoting community arts outside the Australia Council had been a recurring agenda item during 1978 and 1979. Improved promotion was needed in order to solve two related 'problems'. First, the widespread confusion and lack of understanding about the nature and value of community arts. And second, the need to educate the field. The well-worn theme about community arts' novelty was trotted out again: people did not understand the area because it was so 'new'. Even community arts practitioners, those legions of cultural workers out there 'doing it', suffered from ignorance; they lacked relevant training and information and it was the CAB's duty to become both advocate and educator.

The CAB's decision to adopt the role of advocate for community arts outside the Australia Council was significant. Here was the funding body claiming the authority to speak for and about community arts as its main representative. This paternalistic gesture reinforced the dependency of the constituency. Community arts practitioners were represented as not only ignorant but disorganised and unable to speak for themselves. This defence of the CAB's role as 'leader' of a new cultural movement not only denied the possibility of other voices speaking from outside the Australia Council, it also completely ignored the recent display of effective organisation during the campaign by community arts workers to establish a Board. This campaign had consolidated relationships between community arts workers in several states. In 1980 state networks established during the struggle for a Board were still operating and attracting new members in New South Wales, South Australia and Victoria.

The push for better promotion of community arts and education of the field also depended on the invocation of an unproblematic unity between CAB staff and Board members and those in receipt of grants. The years of struggle and defence were held up as evidence of the common purpose between the bureaucracy and its constituency. The establishment of the Board was a glittering prize for all. In this rhetoric community arts acquired the status of a quest, something that everyone involved with it was equally striving for:

> Ros [Bower] and I were the continuants throughout the 1970s. Neither of us saw ourselves as public servants, we were both fuelled by a vision. We saw ourselves as part and parcel of the community arts movement, it was just that our position happened to be in this building and not in the field. We strongly identified with the field. That's how we felt; of course how the field saw it might have been different, we were highly visible in the field. (Hull, *Interview*, 11-9-87)

The commitment of the Board and staff members to moving out of the bureaucracy was impressive. The desire to know the field, to understand its experiences and perceptions of community arts, even to be seen as part of it, was often perceived as an indicator of the CAB's democratic attitude to and relationship with its constituency. In comparison with other Boards the CAB did have a strong sense of engagement with and obligation to those it funded. Dialogue with the field was central to many of the CAB's activities ranging from the organisation of national conferences to the development of friendships between staff and community art workers (Hull, *Interview*, 11-9-87).

However, the repeated representation of the CAB as just another arm of the 'community arts movement' glossed over the different positions which the funders and the funded occupied and the shifting web of power relations which structured their interactions. As the analysis of the struggle for a Board has shown, power was not aggregated within the CAB, it was elaborated and transformed in relations of mutual deference and dependency between the CAB and those it funded. In the early days the work of the funding institution in producing policy and grant assessment guidelines was central to the determination of a set of knowledges about community arts. However, during the campaign to create a Board the constituency was enabled. This was a period in which the power and authority of the funded dominated. As practitioners they claimed the right to define and defend community arts. After the acquisition of Board status the constituency's role diminished as institutional security fuelled the bureaucracy's confidence. Relations between the CAB and the field were realigned. The expanded commitment to promotion and training positioned the constituency as children and the CAB as concerned parents, watching over them and concerned to nurture their full potential.

The development in mid-1979 of *Caper*, a bulletin published by the CAB for the circulation of ideas and information about community arts, was evidence of the Board's growing advocacy role and sense of responsibility to its constituency. *Caper* was promoted as a mechanism for the Board to share its knowledge with the field. However, the content of the first issue was dominated by reprints of two articles from state community arts newsletters. At the same moment as the field was establishing its own networks of writing and debate about community arts, *Caper* was introduced as the solution to the 'absence of information'. Although the development of a journal with national distribution was an important mechanism for the promotion of community arts, the field's ability to circulate information and organise its own exchange of ideas was barely acknowledged.

The growth of community arts networks in several states was another issue in the increasingly complex relationship between the Board and its constituents. Membership of the networks grew during the early 1980s, partly as a result of the expansion of several programs. Notable among these was the Community Arts Officer program, which generated an increased number of jobs in the community arts field. In 1981 several of the networks requested funds from the CAB to establish paid organiser/administrator positions (CAB, *Minutes*, 15-12-81). These requests met with a hostile response from some Board members, who did not see it as the role of the CAB to support state-based advocacy groups especially if they could become potential critics of the Board. At this stage the CAB's paternalism towards the field did not extend to the possibility of self-determination. This position was gradually eroded with the counter argument that the networks were performing crucial functions that the Board could not carry out, such as lobbying for community arts funds from state and local government and organising regional links between community art workers. In 1981 the CAB handed over responsibility for the organisation of national conferences to the state networks and agreed to fund them to carry out the necessary administrative work. During 1982 the pressure on the CAB to fund the networks increased.

CAB support for state organisations of community arts practitioners was a crucial test case in relations between the Board and the field. The demand for substantial funding of 'independent' lobbying and promotional bodies was a sign that the field could no longer be constituted simply in terms of its relationship to the funding body. It was now a vast complex characterised by the emergence of state-based seminars, newsletters, funding and regional preoccupations. In 1983 the networks were funded (AC, AR, 1982–83: 110), and the CAB acknowledged the fundamental shift this signalled in its relationship with its constituency. The children nurtured by this 'bureaucratic invention' had reached adulthood:

> The last two years in particular have seen a burgeoning of analysis, dialogue and documentation in the field. This has led to more effective arts activity and also the growth of independent and articulate groups able to voice their communities' demands. No longer can it be claimed that the community arts are a bureaucratic invention. The movement has a life of its own that extends far beyond the ambit of the Community Arts Board. (AC, AR, 1982–83: 38–9)

Despite this recognition that the 'community arts movement' was no longer contained by the relations of deference and dependency created by federal funding, the CAB claimed a proprietorial role over the state networks. The Board's justification for funding them was based on their potential role in national policy development and promotion; the networks were legitimated as the official site for the management of Board/field relations.

The increased focus on the field which began in the early 1980s was often referred to as the 'professionalisation of community arts'. Concern for questions of training, the conditions of art workers, state organisations and the production of glossy information materials like *Caper* was regarded, in some quarters, as a threat to the simplicity of earlier days, to the 'integrity of community arts'. These reservations invoked the rhetoric of the counter culture and its suspicion of bureaucracy. They also indicated a reluctance to consider the Board's relationship to its constituency in industrial terms, to recognise its role as a de facto job creator. 'Professionalisation' was not imposed on the field, but resulted from various historical contingencies.

Until 1983 the relationship between the CAB and those it funded was marked by a deep paternalism. Most often it was the CAB that set the agenda, that financially and ideologically nurtured the 'children' its funds had created. The effect of this, according to Heks (1985b), has been a field that defines the 'politics' of community arts in terms of the processes of survival with government. The funding of state networks in 1983 signalled an important shift in this relationship, as an infrastructure was established that organised community arts practitioners around other issues apart from their common dependency on the CAB.

Shifting status

The changes in each of the funding programs analysed contributed to improved status for the CAB within the Australia Council. Pilot Projects, *Caper*, state networks all gave the CAB credibility as a distinctive cultural practice. The pleas for a definition of community arts could now be answered by pointing to an array of cultural activities all created with CAB money. However, the work on consolidation and expansion during the early 1980s did not eradicate all opposition to the CAB within the Australia Council. It was still ideologically marginal. While other Boards were beginning to accept responsibility for some community arts projects in their artform and were incorporating elements of community arts rhetoric in their policies, questions about access, equity and participation had not dislodged the support of excellence from top position on their agendas. Acceptance of community arts seemed to be based on the grudging recognition that it was here to stay.

Another contributing factor to the changing status of the CAB was the advocacy work of Peter Botsman at Council meetings. As first chairperson of the CAB he identified his most important role as challenging the hostility to community arts within Council. Committees were Botsman's playground; while he may not have known much about community arts he knew a lot about lobbying, deals and strategy. With these skills Botsman was able to fight for the CAB within Council, and he gave the program an institutional clout it had never had (Botsman, *Interview*, 19-11-87 and Hull, *Interview*, 11-9-87). Botsman's influence in the Australia Council grew rapidly. In 1980 he was one of the main instigators of a Policy Working Party aimed at addressing the purposes and objectives of the Australia Council. This interest in the broader functions of the Australia Council and in the formation of cultural policy was justified by Botsman on two counts. First, there was a need to review the policies of the Australia Council as this was rarely done. Second, there was the desire to see community arts principles embraced across the Council rather than restricted to an individual Board (Botsman, *Interview*, 19-11-87).

The Policy Working Party was one of the first steps towards a period of institutional analysis and reorganisation within the Australia Council which culminated in the appointment of Timothy Pascoe (former Federal Director of the Liberal Party) as the first full-time Council chairperson in September 1981 (AC, AR, 1981–82: 13). Pascoe's appointment produced anxiety in some sections of the community arts field where his conservative political credentials and previous work organising corporate sponsorship for the arts were seen as a sure sign of another attack on the CAB.

These fears were not realised. On the contrary, Pascoe became an advocate for aspects of the CAB's work within Council and was able to both consolidate and expand the developmental work begun by Botsman. At the end of 1982 he presented a Policy Priorities Paper to Council entitled 'Setting Priorities for the Second Decade'. The most significant feature of this paper was the extent to which it endorsed some of the principles of community arts and proposed these as important issues for the whole of the Council. Pascoe's vision argued for a major reorientation of the Australia Council in three key areas: tightening the criteria for the support of excellence; a differential increase in support for artists and innovative organisations; and similar preference for programs that reintegrated the work of artists and the arts with community life (Pascoe, 1983: 8).

In opposition to the entrenched deference to excellence Pascoe held up the Australia Council's alternative programs, or what he referred to as 'Council's other children', as evidence of progress and innovation. Most of the areas deemed alternative were those initiated within the CAB. Pascoe offered unequivocal support for community arts:

> Community arts—as a means to de-institutionalise artists and foster community artistic expression—is one of the Council's great national and international achievements. But, it is still not well enough accepted in Council or elsewhere. (Pascoe, 1983: 9)

This degree of institutional recognition of the CAB's philosophies and programs was remarkable. While the Australia Council had no option but to promote community arts in the official display of Annual Reports, few attempts had been made by either senior management or Council members to promote it to the other Boards, or to push in other ways for greater internal acceptance. The presence of Botsman at Council meetings had begun to change this and Pascoe's paper gave an added push to this advocacy work. In holding up community arts as an alternative to the obsession with excellence, which seemed to grip so many of the other Boards, this program was now praised as the source of innovation and progress for the whole Council.

Response to Pascoe's paper from the CAB was wary. Enthusiastic praise for community arts from the conservative chair of Council triggered a concern for the program's radical credentials and anxiety about the symbolic loss of marginal status. Concerns were expressed within the CAB about the need to maintain a vanguard role.

From early 1983 the CAB began rewriting much of its policy and funding guidelines, not to outsmart Pascoe but in response to a variety of forces which had impacted on the program. A changeover of staff and Board members at the end of 1982 had introduced several members with histories of radical cultural work. The most notable of these was Jon Hawkes who took over as director of the Board after Andrea Hull. Hawkes was a founding member of Circus Oz with a long history of involvement with various alternative cultural organisations. His appointment signalled a break with the tradition of female career-bureaucrat directors who, in some ways, reinforced the welfare connotations of community arts.

The 'discovery' of community arts by a range of progressive artists also meant a challenge to aspects of community arts doctrine. There was now evidence of a distinctive community arts aesthetic manifest in a proliferation of projects documenting political issues and signalling a concern for 'social problems'. Some cultural expressions from the field were speaking back to the funding body in a more agitational voice. The state networks were getting more articulate in their demands for funds and had begun a campaign for improved conditions for art workers. Finally, there was the creation of Incentive Funds. These funds were designed as Council-level programs that would offer each Board funding incentives (50 per cent matching grants) to develop programs in areas that were considered of priority. Incentive Funds were established at the end of 1982 in three areas: Art and Working Life, Multicultural Arts, and Youth Arts (AC, AR, 1982–83: 23).

This combination of events triggered a process of review within the CAB. It did not mean a sudden break with previous discourses but rather a gradual reframing of certain concepts within a more explicitly political and oppositional context. The commitment to access and participation was not abandoned, nor was the emphasis on community development. These objectives were firmly entrenched. Rather, a space was created where questions about culture and politics could be explored. Between 1983 and 1985 a discourse on cultural difference was formulated. While this had always been the subtext of the earliest rationales for the Community Arts Program it was now foregrounded. However, what emerged in this realignment was an explanation of difference in terms of cultural pluralism rather than cultural lack.

Culture: politics and difference

At the end of 1985 a new Programs of Assistance booklet was completed outlining the CAB's policies, activities and funding procedures. This was its most extensive official publication to date, devoting a lot of space to an introductory section on definitions, aims and objectives (CAB, 1986: 9–14). This document can be read as the culmination of the shifts in policy and funding practices that escalated from 1983 onwards and for this reason it deserves close analysis. This key text was shaped by two interconnected themes: recognition of plural cultures and the social objectives of cultural practice. It balanced an argument for cultural diversity with the demand that culture be put to work in the interests of fostering critical awareness and a 'sense of community'.

Despite the anonymous plain English of the statutory authority this booklet appeared as a manifesto for community arts. Gone was the cautious and confused language of the 1970s. There was now a set of definitions for key terms, presented with the explicit intention of fixing meanings once and for all. The three terms that the Programs of Assistance booklet defined were culture, art and community. While these were not foreign categories in community arts discourse, they had been differentially invoked. While community was incessantly foregrounded in most policy formulations, art and culture generally remained on the sidelines. The fear of aesthetics and the distancing of community arts from both high and mass culture made them almost too hot to handle. Art and culture implied discourses of value predicated on notions of excellence and standards, and this was something the Community Arts Program sought not so much to reject as to avoid.

Although the Programs of Assistance booklet brought art and culture in from the margins questions about aesthetic value were still sidestepped. Earlier policies for community arts produced two related meanings for culture. Community arts was a new term for an essentialist popular creativity and a panacea for the dangerous effects of mass culture. It was *both* something people had always done and something people needed to take up in order to be saved from the manipulation and mediocrity of mass culture. The moral evaluation implicit in this rhetoric, which equated folk, popular and amateur with good and 'mass' with bad was discarded in 1983. Rather than placing community arts somewhere on a mythical scale of cultural values, it was now placed in relationship to 'Australian culture'. This representation asserted the significance of community cultural activity for the nation. It challenged the idea of a unified single culture structuring 'Australia' and defined the role of community arts as both recognising and recovering those activities which were excluded from dominant definitions of national identity:

> Arts development at the community level is an integral part of the maintenance and growth of a vital Australian culture. . . A live culture is in a constant state of metamorphosis, particularly in Australia where geographical isolation, combined with a large proportion of recent arrivals amongst the population and a unique natural environment, all create conditions for the development of a culture quite specific to this continent. Video, fashion, popular music, graphic design, community radio are but a few activities which exemplify the constantly changing nature of arts practice. Other activities, ranging from the experimental or innovative edges of the arts to a great deal of apparently mundane activity, long ignored (even despised)

and denied the credibility of belonging to the genus 'Art', are equally disadvantaged because they do not fall into recognised categories. Quite often the ignorance and denial of these activities has its roots in class, gender and race—in attitudes which effectively maintain the status quo. (AC, AR, 1982–83: 38–9).

Two themes were overlaid in this text. First there was the idea of culture as an immense variety of expressive activities. Culture was not a pantheon of great artefacts, it was 'live' and inclusive, it was anything from 'mundane activity' to fashion. Into this extended definition art was placed, not at the top of all these creativities but as one of many. The equation of Art with Culture was challenged with a realignment that located art as a subset of culture. This was an important development because it confronted head-on the restricted and exclusive meanings for art that were dominant in the Australia Council. In pointing to the everyday nature of cultural production and pleasure the institutionalised boundaries of art were exposed. Beyond the confines of the theatre and the gallery was a rich variety of 'other' forms and expressions.

The second theme connected processes of cultural distinction with power relations. The maintenance of art at the top of a cultural hierarchy 'has its roots in class, gender and race'. However, despite the invocation of the classic left triumvirate, the actual processes of cultural distinction were not explained. Culture was simply identified as a site where power differentials were either maintained or contested.

In 1985 these ideas were rearticulated. An anthropological definition for culture was established which emphasised social processes rather than the variety of expressive forms beyond art. Culture was now the mechanism for 'communicating with each other, interacting with our environment and organising ourselves' (CAB, 1986: 9). This definition was inclusive and non-evaluative to the point where everything was culture. However, despite its democratic intent, without the identification of clear boundaries around what was and what was not eligible for subsidy it was of little use in disbursing grants. This was the policy problem that an anthropological meaning for culture produced.

Several 'solutions' were proposed. The first focused on a consideration of power relations. The idea of a dominant culture was contested with an argument for pluralism:

> If we act as if there is only one culture (the prevailing one), then those that can't or don't operate within it are discriminated against. What's more, we miss out on the surprises that diversity always brings. New and unexpected connections can be made that will be to everyone's benefit. (CAB, 1986: 9)

This was a very feeble plea for cultural pluralism, meekly pointing to the problem of 'discrimination' and justifying a recognition of difference on the grounds of liberal tolerance; the value of diversity was primarily as a guard against boredom. This plea was also opportunist in its crude populism: 'everyone benefits' from a bit of variety. The hard political questions were evaded. While the acknowledgement of plural cultures was crucial in contesting evaluative policies based on aesthetics and a single national culture, the problem remained: how could a policy based on the recognition of cultural pluralism be translated into equitable systems of patronage? If multiple cultural constituencies were accepted how then were they to be funded fairly? What rules of selection would apply and what was the purpose of public support? These questions highlighted the fundamental political dilemma that the Community Arts Program had faced since its inception: was it possible to establish funding strategies for non-art activities in an arts funding body?

In the past that old standby 'community' had offered a partial solution to these dilemmas. It was dragged out yet again, only slightly remodelled. The strategic value of 'community' lay in its profound ambiguity. Communities were invoked as the ultimate producers, consumers and assessors of community arts. Representing their interests and meeting their cultural 'needs' was the primary objective of funding. The benefits of cultural activity for communities were social rather than aesthetic. Artefacts were largely irrelevant:

> The work we promote is designed to assist communities develop their own expression; to control their own arts practice from the starting idea through to the distribution of the final product (*if there is one*). (CAB, 1986: 11) [emphasis added]

The idea that communities were the real patrons of community arts was not new. Decentralised methods of patronage using community-based organisations or intermediaries had been utilised by the Community Arts Program since its inception. What was new was the explicit refusal of this method of patronage as a technique for the cultural improvement of certain populations or regions. The patronising rationales of the past were revoked:

> Community arts is not a tool for increasing arts appreciation, audiences or purchases of arts products. These may be by-products of a community arts program. But it is a community's active intervention in its own cultural destiny, not a way to increase consumption of other peoples' culture. (CAB, 1986: 10)

These invocations of 'community control' did not completely usurp the Board. Its task in assessing grant applicaions was now based on measuring the suitability and commitment of the community to the cultural project proposed. Communities had to prove that they were worthy candidates for cultural self-determination. Submissions had to show evidence of community participation in the design of the project, projects had to emerge from the community's needs and interests, the community had to be actively involved in the creative process (CAB, 1986: 34).

These requests were central to the constitution of the CAB's distinctive discourse of value. In the rejection of aesthetic criteria other standards were established. These 'non-aesthetic' discourses of value focused not on artefacts, institutions and excellence but on the social and political relations that community-based cultural practice produced. Cultural practice was a way of linking people through collective expression, it was a way of fostering a 'sense of community'; this was its value (CAB, 1986: 11).

However, although the replacement of aesthetic criteria with social criteria was an important counter to the hegemony of art and excellence it created other problems. 'Community need and benefit' were, in many ways, equally vague measures of value. Not only were they extremely difficult to assess but they also implied that harmony and integration were the fundamental purpose of good community arts. The welfarist connotations of 'community' were difficult to shake off. Generating or reviving 'community' through cultural practice implied isolated enclaves that were both different and worthy. The radical potential of alliances based on common locality or interest was marginalised by the overwhelmingly nostalgic search for 'community'. While community arts policy recognised the value of giving expression to difference and diversity it was burdened by the identification of community as the site where this would take place. 'Community' was represented as the ultimate sign of pluralism: it was the site where difference was accommodated. It was the site where common identity was formed; where conflict and antagonism were denied.

Another unresolved problem with the use of non-aesthetic discourses of value was the status of art. Although the 1985 'manifesto' devoted a lot of space to defining culture, in an attempt to broaden the scope and objectives of arts funding, art would still not go away. The Community Arts Program persistently refused to impose general aesthetic standards and this left it open to accusations of cultural condescension: 'anything will do for the community'. Formal diversity was read as an absence of standards, as aesthetic deregulation. There is substance in these attacks. Rather than avoiding art the program should have articulated other standards and languages of critical evaluation in which the aesthetic was situated in its conditions of production and reception.

Although community arts discourse in the mid-1980s recognised plural constituencies and cultures it was unable to explain the relationship between the two. It was unable to explain the specificity of most arts whose origins and impacts are firmly rooted within particular times and within particular constituencies. The solution to this problem was not to impose general aesthetic criteria such as 'excellence' but to clearly argue that the meaning and value of all texts is socially anchored; to insist on the diversity of different cultural values and tastes and their social origins.

The shift towards cultural pluralism from 1983 onwards dislodged notions of cultural disadvantage and deprivation. However, in order to solve the problems created by an anthropological meaning for culture, social rather than aesthetic objectives for funding had to be identified. 'Community' was the central category in this process. It was both the pretext for and the outcome of cultural practice. This produced a fundamental contradiction. On the one hand the policies of the mid-1980s were progressive in their stress on collaboration, self-determination and participation in cultural production. But on the other hand the emphasis on community development meant that the most important objective of projects was to make 'community' rather than art. The effect of this was a persistent silence in policy about the aesthetic outcomes of funding. While the commitment to social objectives was crucial to the recognition of different constituencies it was less effective in giving recognition to different forms. The obsession with the social often worked to devalue or dismiss the cultural or aesthetic results of community arts projects. Yet what many projects revealed, especially those funded through Pilot Projects, was the multiplicity of arts and creativities outside the restricted and formalised meanings dominant in the rest of the Australia Council.

6

From community arts to cultural development: 1986–1991

During the late 1980s the Community Arts Program underwent a series of transformations on several fronts. In July 1987, after nearly ten years as a Board, the program was converted into the Community Cultural Development Committee (CDCC). This change was part of a major reorganisation of the Australia Council in response to the 1986 Report of the Inquiry into Commonwealth Assistance to the Arts (the McLeay Report). This institutional shift from Board back to Committee triggered changes in philosophy and direction. While the fundamental principle of recognition of cultural diversity remained, new strategies for supporting this were developed. The key to understanding the changes of this period lies in the replacement of 'community arts' with 'community cultural development'. Getting rid of art allowed the program to emphasise community 'empowerment' and organisation as the primary objective of funding.

This chapter explores the nature of these changes, their context and effects. Central to this process is an assessment of the McLeay Report. This government inquiry followed in the tradition of earlier investigations of the Australia Council, especially the McKinsey Report (1976). Under the guise of ensuring management efficiency and effective spending of public money a series of attacks were launched on various Council policies and programs. The McLeay Report was the Hawke Labor government's most dramatic intervention into arts funding, and its impacts during the late 1980s on the Australia Council in general and the Community Arts Program in particular were substantial.

Another important factor during the period under review was the influence of Donald Horne, who was chairperson of the Council between 1985 and 1991. Horne was an active and articulate chairperson whose commitment to cultural pluralism and cultural rights provided important ideological and institutional support for the work of the Community Arts Program. Horne's support also reached well beyond the confines of the Australia Council. As an advocate for the principles of cultural democracy he not only extended justifications for arts funding but also initiated several forums which sought to make connections between community arts and other cultural organisations. The rise of community development involved the privileging of a radical welfare rhetoric that had always been part of community arts policy. The key terms in this rhetoric were 'empowerment' and 'strategic partnerships'. In seeking to shed some of community arts' excess baggage, the CCDC embarked on an aggressive campaign of promotion and networking with a diverse range of organisations from local government to various social movements. The purpose of this strategy was to put cultural issues on the agenda of generally non-cultural organisations. In this way it would be possible not only to broaden the funding base for community cultural expressions but also to highlight issues of cultural diversity. Several areas were given special attention in this process. A survey of the development of two of these priority areas, local government and multiculturalism, will document the formation of new meanings and purposes for community arts.

The McLeay Report and community arts

Tim Rowse (1986: 3) has described the McLeay Report as an exercise in marginalising and humiliating the Australia Council. This is a fair assessment. Although the Sub-Committee of the House of Representatives Standing Committee on Expenditure was charged with the task of reviewing all areas of Commonwealth assistance to the arts, the operations of the Australia Council were the major focus. The report recommended a 'streamlined' Council with fewer Boards, staff and functions. This was not only in the interests of establishing greater devolution of some responsibilities to the state arts ministries and other relevant bodies but also in order to break the Council's supposed capture by its clients. Advocating for better conditions for artists, for example, was not considered the role of a national funding body.

However, it was over the question of access that the report revealed its true colours. Although the first recommendation urged 'the democratisation of culture' in order to ensure wide community access to a diversity of cultural experiences, this was a very token gesture. The real beneficiaries of many of the recommendations were the flagship companies. As Rowse points out, they were placed beyond the demands of access and their requests for greater funding security were deferred to. It was recommended that they be given triennial funding and that a Major Companies Program be established within the Australia Council free from too much interference from the Boards. While the report contained the standard Labor Party jibes about the flagships' irrelevance to Australian culture, their drain on limited public funds and their dubious record in financial management, ultimately the committee responded to them like a group of 'working class Tories' (Rowse, 1986: 4). They were simultaneously contemptuous and deferential. The dismissal of access was most evident in the report's demand for a restructured Australia Council. The request to reduce the number of Boards was not simply an exercise in administrative efficiency but an implicit attack on the central role of the Boards in formulating policy and liaising with clients. The Community Arts Board was particularly strong in both these areas. It had played a major role in the production of innovative policies and had also devised a wide range of strategies for reaching new constituencies. By the mid-1980s the impacts of the Community Arts Program were evident across the Council. The rhetoric of cultural diversity and cultural rights was no longer exclusive to community arts. It was also becoming central to mainstream arguments for the arts. For some in the arts community these changes in philosophy were disturbing. Reasserting the power of the Council and the Minister was represented as the best way to contain the threat of recalcitrant Boards. The McLeay Report's recommendations endorsed this belief.

The Australia Council's response to the McLeay Report was cautious and conservative. It did not challenge the dismissal of access or the privileging of the flagship companies. Although there was internal dissent within the Council over this apparent acquiesence, especially from the CAB, this had little impact on the Council's negotiations with government. Rowse summarised the Council's response in this way:

> The Council has apparently made the political judgement that the public support that it draws as a patron of major companies is more valuable than any support it might get by publicly endorsing the smaller Boards and their philosophies. (Rowse, 1986: 7)

On 1 July 1987 the restructured Australia Council came into being. The number of Boards was reduced from eight to five and these Boards had fewer members. The Music and Theatre Boards were combined (forming the Performing Arts Board) as were the Visual Arts and Crafts Boards. The Community Arts Board became the Community Cultural Development Committee and, as in the first years of the Community Arts Program, it was now accountable to the Council. Its membership comprised Board chairs and six nominated representatives. The chair of the new CCDC was the chairperson of the Australia Council, Donald Horne.

The conversion of the Community Arts Board into the Community Cultural Development Committee could be read as an attempt to protect and extend the Australia Council's commitment to access in the face of the McLeay Report's disinterest in it. The name change meant a chance to shed the lingering confusion generated by the term community arts. 'Community cultural development' gave the committee a wider brief by establishing culture rather than art as the focus. But defining culture proved to be as tricky as defining art.

The change in the program's institutional position and membership meant that recognition of cultural diversity was no longer quarantined within a separate Board, letting the other Boards off the hook. It was now represented as a Council-wide program. The appointment of the Board chairs to the CCDC was an old strategy, first tried in the early 1970s. The aim was to encourage them, through participation in the CCDC, to embrace the principles of community cultural development. As in the past, their erratic attendance signalled resistance to this strategy. After a few years membership of the CCDC reverted to Ministerial nominations. The appointment of the chairperson of the Australia Council to chair the CCDC was more successful. Donald Horne was an articulate advocate of Australia as a culturally pluralistic society and was keen to both consolidate and extend the focus and activities of the CCDC.

Donald Horne: philosopher and arts administrator

The appointment of Donald Horne as part-time chairperson of the Australia Council was an interesting choice on the part of the Hawke Labor government. Horne came to the position with a reputation as an iconoclastic writer and cultural critic. He certainly did not regard chairing the Australia Council as a quiet sinecure. Instead, he relished the opportunity to give cultural policy and the role of the arts in society a higher profile.

Horne's introductory essays in the Annual Reports of the Australia Council were intellectual and often polemical. Sycophantic praises of artists and government were definitely not his style. In many ways he reasserted the independence of the Australia Council by using the Annual Reports and other public forums to counter attacks on the organisation, especially the comparatively low levels of government funding for the arts. An ongoing theme was the administrative efficiency of the Australia Council, especially when compared to other government bodies. His parting shot in his final Annual Report outlined how much money he and other senior officers had saved by refusing to use their entitlement to fly first class (AC, AR, 1989–90: 3).

However, compared to his other concerns administration costs were a minor theme. Horne played a key role in the emergence of wider debate and analysis of the relations between government and culture in Australia. His contribution to the emergent field of cultural policy studies remains significant, particularly because he spoke from several different positions. As an intellectual and author he produced a series of influential studies during the 1980s which explored the relationship between cultural theory and social organisation (Horne, 1986; Horne,

1984). As an arts administrator and advocate he gave cultural policy a much needed dose of ideas and argument.

Central to Horne's proposed reforms of arts policy was his avowed commitment to both republicanism and social democracy. In seeking to justify arts funding in the national interest he rejected the rhetoric of the 1970s. Arts funding was not good for the nation because the support of 'excellence' was spiritually and morally uplifting. The arts were not a tool for civilising the uncultured masses. Rather, they were a necessary component of a mature post-colonial society. Art was an important form of social criticism and an essential contributor to identity and creativity (Horne, 1988: 4). Apart from this, art was big business with significant economic multiplier effects (AC, AR, 1986–87: 3).

Of course, economic arguments for the arts had been around within the Australia Council before the arrival of Horne. They had been developed to counter the creeping spread of economic rationalism. While it was acknowledged that the arts were good for the economy not just the soul, Horne gave this argument much greater force and impact. He foregrounded the connections between the arts and the economy in various public forums and played a major role in changing perceptions of subsidy. According to Horne, arts funding was not a form of protection but an investment and a necessary part of cultural research and development (Horne, 1988: 5).

However, it was in the development of a renewed social democratic rationale for arts funding that Horne's impact was most widely felt. And it is here that his ideas were closely aligned with the discourses of community arts. Two interconnected terms were central to his arguments for the arts: citizenship and cultural rights. Unlike the social democratic rhetoric of the Whitlam era Horne's philosophy was not structured around a deficit model of cultural participation. Cultural disadvantage did not feature at all. It was superseded by the concept of rights. Access no longer only meant access to high culture but access to a wide field of creativity, meaning and symbolic expression:

> In a democratic society there should be potential for individuals to extend their levels of creative experience and there should also be an extension of choice both in work and leisure. Just as citizens have political rights, economic rights, social rights and civil rights, they can also be thought of as having cultural rights. These cultural rights, which are a legitimate concern of the state, consist of rights of access to our common cultural heritage and to use it as we wish, a right to new art and a right for citizens to participate in their own art making. It is by the assertion of rights such as these that we can offset the monopolistic claims of public culture. (Horne, 1988: 5)

Within the political field of arts funding this charter for cultural rights represented a major achievement. It signified the symbolic exhaustion of the idea that high culture had a unique value. While high culture's role in the formation of a 'common cultural heritage' was acknowledged it was not privileged over and above new cultural forms or those emerging from community-based cultural practice. Horne realigned cultural relations with his refusal to grant the 'high' superior status. These ideas also challenged aesthetic discourses of value. The role of the state was not to support certain cultural forms because they were inherently valuable but to secure citizens' legitimate cultural rights.

Horne's charter reiterated the discourses of cultural difference and pluralism that had been developed within the Community Arts Program. He did not demand token recognition of the cultural margins but began from the premise of a culturally pluralistic society. In many ways, his arguments *depended* on the policies of the Community Arts Program. During the early 1980s these policies prefigured his approach to the democratic reform of arts funding. Within the Australia Council, community arts policies had begun to contest the hegemony of excellence and to establish non-aesthetic discourses of value. Both these principles were implicit in Horne's vision of reform.

The legacies of community arts were most evident in his recognition of the 'right for citizens to participate in their own art making'. Horne acknowledged the progressive potential of cultural participation, and he foregrounded this in his charter by placing it on an equal footing with support for the high and the new. However, this wholesale endorsement of community arts was occasionally reminiscent of the earliest invocations of 'community' in cultural policy. According to Horne (1986: 234) the objective of community-based cultural practice was to restore 'art to life'. This demand was deeply nostalgic, harking back to an imaginary pre-modern period when everybody was an artist busy with the pleasures of an authentic folk culture.

Despite Horne's occasionally romantic representations of community arts, his work in the Australia Council produced a higher profile for the program than it had ever experienced before. His main achievement was to establish connections between community arts and a variety of other organisations ranging from museums and galleries to the Boards. Horne was a constant defender of the CCDC and his active promotion of the program contributed to its growing status and credibility. He not only provided encouragement for the work of the CCDC but extended its philosophies with the concept of cultural rights. Although Rowse (1989: 21) has criticised Horne's charter as lacking any programmatic content it is possible to cite the work of the CCDC as one place where concrete strategies were developed to address the cultural rights of particular constituencies.

Strategic partnerships: local government

During 1989 and 1990 staff of the Community Cultural Development

Unit (CCDU) embarked on a process of review. This was prompted by several factors. First, there were the long-term effects of cuts to the Australia Council's administration budget. Staff cuts in particular had meant that the CCDU had to do more with less for several years. Then there was the declining value of the grants dollar and increased demand. Finally there was a sense that the program needed to develop more allies: that it was time to make connections with a wider range of organisations than the established constituency. The outcome of this review was the development of a strategic framework aimed at focusing the work of the CCDU on six priority areas:

- arts for a multicultural Australia;
- art and working life;
- local government;
- urban growth centres;
- community environment art and design (CEAD);
- rural and remote communities.

In each of these areas different approaches were adopted according to their specific history and organisation. However, there was one common link: the disbursement of grants was not privileged as the dominant mode of intervention. A broader range of strategies was developed ranging from joint projects with state ministries to seeking representation on a variety of peak bodies. This was more than a public relations exercise: it was an attempt to bring community cultural development in from the margins and put it on the agenda of mainstream organisations, to establish partnerships rather than systems of patronage. Or, as Deborah Mills, Director of the CCDU at the time, called it: 'courting the establishment' (Mills, 1992: 3).

The significance of this change in direction is most evident in the area of local government. Since the beginning of the Community Arts Program local government had been targeted as an important site for arts development. The standard approach had been the funding of Community Arts Officers who worked in local government initiating various cultural projects. By the late 1980s the limitations of the CAO program had become apparent. Most CAOs worked in the Community Services departments of councils where welfare and recreation programs were administered. This environment meant that community arts were often incorporated as an arm of the welfare program offering cultural integration and therapy to various constituencies (Heks, 1985a: 51). Working for councils also placed pressure on CAOs to generate cultural representations of the municipality as one great big happy family. Local festivals, history projects, Mayor's art prizes and the like were often the forms privileged in this attempt to facilitate municipal pride.

In 1989 the CCDU's relationship with local government was remodelled. Rather than just dealing with individual councils in a patronage relationship a series of moves were made to establish links with various peak national and state local-government bodies. The objective was to promote the principles and benefits of cultural development to local government through their existing organisations. In 1990 a Local Government and the Arts Task Force was established as a joint program between the Australia Council and the federal Office of Local Government. This task force reported to the Cultural Ministers' Council and the Local Government Ministers' Council. An extensive national promotion campaign was implemented to sell culture to councils (see Local Government and Arts Task Force, 1991).

This strategy signalled the ultimate triumph of cultural development over community arts. In the courting of local government the CCDU sidelined references to cultural difference and diversity. The aim of local cultural development was not so much to address the cultural 'needs' of particular social groups in the interests of access and equity, as to use culture as a *resource* in anything from economic development to urban renewal. Council involvement in arts and culture was sold as a mechanism for generating jobs, tourism, new industries and improved local identity (Local Government and Arts Task Force, 1991: 7). The CCDU spoke a language that was familiar to local government and that situated culture within their current concerns.

The term 'cultural planning' was deployed to assist in the local government campaign. This was a term borrowed from various British and American urban planning organisations. It referred to the integration of cultural concerns into the overall planning process. Councils were urged to recognise the benefits of cultural resources from arts centres to street life and to establish links between economic, social and cultural policies.

The promotion of cultural planning by the CCDU did raise the cultural consciousness of peak local government bodies. At the level of individual councils there were also signs of change. Numerous municipalities around Australia embarked on programs ranging from community design projects to the development of cultural plans for new urban releases. Despite these achievements there were serious limitations in the CCDU's cultural planning model that reflected its origins within an arts funding program.

The first problem was the overemphasis on aesthetic definitions of successful cultural planning. Many of the examples used by the CCDU to 'educate' local government privileged art over and above culture. Public sculptures, main streets painted in heritage colours, artist-designed parks all reflected middle class notions of urban amenity. Related to this was the failure to acknowledge the central role of commercial culture from leagues clubs to pub rock in meeting most people's cultural needs. The CCDU's definitions of culture were generally blind to the questions of economics and the market. Ultimately, the rhetoric of cultural planning functioned to deny the extraordinary diversity of urban popular culture.

The second problem with the cultural planning push was that it was predicated on the assumption that local government knew nothing about culture. This was a rather naive belief. All over Australia councils were grappling with development applications for anything from large-scale shopping malls to tourist resorts. These developments had both economic and cultural impacts, transforming urban form and the everyday cultural practices of locals. What was missing in the arguments for cultural planning was any analysis of the forces restructuring local economies and the cultural consequences of these changes. There was little if any recognition that councils were already doing cultural 'planning' often unwittingly and by default.

Despite these limitations the strategic partnership between the CCDC and peak local government bodies represented a sophisticated strategy for the promotion of community cultural development. It signalled the development of a viable alternative to the federally controlled patronage or project-based model of intervention. National advocacy, applied research and effective promotion all had significant impacts. They were based on the astute assessment that in order for local government to become effectively involved in local cultural funding and development they needed education and assistance. While the role of community cultural participation was still valued this was no longer privileged as a compulsory component of local government arts projects. Councils were offered a variety of techniques for exploiting and developing cultural resources.

Arts for a multicultural Australia

Throughout its history multicultural arts had been a major responsibility of the Community Arts Program. Of course this area had not always had the label 'multicultural'. In the first years of funding it was referred to as 'ethnic arts' and the focus was almost exclusively on support for the folk or traditional arts activities of non-English-speaking groups. In the days of the CAC the discourse of ethnic arts invoked tradition in a way that restricted the possibility of connections with other artforms and practices. It implied that migrants were essentially cultured and that their cultural expressions were pure and original. The effect of this was the production of a narrow cultural ghetto for migrants within the Community Arts Program.

From 1978 the limitations of the ethnic arts model were realised and attempts were begun by the CAB to both extend the focus of the area and extend responsibility for it across the whole of the Australia Council. The commitment of the Fraser Liberal government to multiculturalism assisted in this push. In 1982, in response to the Review of Post-Arrival Programs and Services to Migrants (the Galbally Report), the Australia Council created a Multicultural Arts Incentive Fund and a position for a Multicultural Arts Officer. Both these developments were attempts to establish Council-wide support and involvement in the area. They met with limited success. There was entrenched resistance within sections of the Australia Council to the idea of migrant arts, artists and audiences receiving special attention. Underlying this resistance was the belief that migrants and their cultural difference were the CAB's problem. They had nurtured them, they could keep them.

The main challenge to this resistance came from the development of a new policy during 1988–1990. The Arts for a Multicultural Australia policy signalled the end of the ethnic arts/multicultural arts era which had inevitably represented migrants as special and separate. The new policy posed a fundamentally different question: how should arts funding be organised in a multicultural society? The fact of cultural diversity could no longer be ignored. Nor could the need for Council-wide involvement. After all, the focus was now on the obligations of funding bodies rather than the special needs of a constituency.

The programmatic content of this policy focused on standard techniques for affirmative action: increasing the representation of people of non-English-speaking background (NESB) on Council Boards and Committees; improving the promotion of Council programs to NESB organisations and communities; holding internal forums to raise staff awareness; and ensuring that all Boards and Committees developed policies and projects to target NESB artists and communities (Dimech, no date: 3). Another significant feature of the new policy was the recognition of the need to fund Anglo–Australian companies whose work reflected multicultural Australia (AC, AR, 1990–91: 12).

In different ways these strategies ended the idea that money spent in this area should flow exclusively to targeted constituencies. Explorations of the nature of multicultural society and the education of funding bureaucrats were equally important strategies.

The CCDU's involvement in multiculturalism was extended with the production of the new policy. Several staff had been active in its development and had played a key role in supporting and promoting it to the other Boards. After all, cultural diversity was familiar currency to them. Similar to the approach developed in the Art and Working Life Program, cultural maintenance was the focus of the CCDC's specific multicultural policy. Migrant communities needed resources so that their cultural identity could be expressed and developed. Beyond this was a more militant demand for marginalised cultures to be 'sufficiently powerful to negotiate their inclusion in the dominant culture, on equal terms' (Mills, 1992: 6). The exact nature of the dominant culture's dominance was not explained.

Strategies to achieve these goals reflected the strategic partnerships approach. Links were set up between peak national migrant organisations and the National Multicultural Arts Network in the interests of getting cultural policy issues onto the agenda of national NESB advocacy bodies. Work was also begun establishing a national network of multicultural arts officers. Beyond this the CCDC continued its commitment to funding projects involving NESB artists and communities. Within the Australia Council the CCDU maintained the highest levels of funding to this area.

Throughout its history the Community Arts Program had always been far more involved with issues of difference and multiculturalism than any other program in the Australia Council. While it is possible to argue that this was its 'natural' territory, the shifts in multicultural arts policy from 1973 to 1991 are a case study in the relationship between organisational structure and systematic institutional exclusion. Most of the attempts to make multiculturalism a Council-wide responsibility were initiated by staff of the Community Arts Program. The hostility to these attempts from certain sections of the Australia Council could have been a result not only of racism but also of the desire to keep the 'difficult' issues contained within community arts. It was hard to alter the perception of the Community Arts Program as the 'ministry for everything else', as the convenient dumping ground for problem areas that the other Boards did not want to confront. It is for this reason that the Arts for a Multicultural Australia policy represented a significant achievement that owes a lot to the persistence of the staff of the Community Arts Program. This policy and program finally ended the 'ghettoisation' of multiculturalism in community arts, and it posed a substantial challenge to the authority of excellence and the nation by forcing the Australia Council, as a whole, to recognise and represent previously unrepresented 'others'.

Part III

Practising community arts: from policy to projects

7

Art and Working Life: class, culture and tradition

In this Part the focus shifts from historical narrative to case studies of key issues in the formation of community arts. The issues selected are: art and working life, practising community arts, and the aesthetics of affirmation. Central to these case studies is the consideration of several community arts projects. Obviously the funding institution is not the sum of community arts: beyond the production of policy and the disbursement of grants is a vast complex of cultural activities, organisations and workers. Patronage is, after all, enabling. It is for this reason that projects are accorded an important place in this account. A focus only on administrative arrangements and policy discourses would exclude a consideration of the effects of the Community Arts Program outside the micro-politics of the Australia Council.

The first case study explores the relationship between Art and Working Life (AWL) policy and a project funded through this program. AWL was one of three Incentive Funds established at the end of 1982; the other two were Multicultural Arts and Youth Arts. The Incentive Funds were administered as Council-level programs and were designed to provide matching grants to Boards which funded projects in these areas. These priority groups, workers, migrants and youth, for so long regarded as typically community arts, now became the focus of special 'incentives' or cultural affirmative action for the whole Council.

Official justifications for this initiative acknowledged two related issues: first, the central place of access and participation in the charter of the Australia Council and, second, the problem of getting some of the Boards to accept adequate responsibility for this. Strategies for generating more opportunities for 'Australians to enjoy the arts' (AC, AR, 1983–84: 19) could no longer be the burden of the CAB alone. The institutional structure of artform Boards, which contributed to this separation of duties, was challenged. Incentive funds were designed to coerce reluctant Boards into accepting a more conscientious commitment to special populations in particular, and access and participation in general. They shifted some of the work of lobbying for these issues away from the CAB and onto the Council, which had to promote them internally and externally.

The significance of Incentives was their explanation of cultural disadvantage in terms of the unequal distribution of subsidy rather than in terms of the cultural lack or ignorance of specific populations. The causes of disadvantage were now located in institutions rather than individuals. As Rowse argues, Incentives highlighted the political weakness of certain cultural traditions which had been either neglected or dismissed by government as unworthy of support (1985a: 26). Incentives must be seen as an attempt to confront entrenched institutional resistance.

In the formation of the Community Arts Program, AWL is an important case study for several reasons. First, of all the Incentives it had the closest relationship with the CAB. AWL was initiated by the CAB and the campaign to gain support for it, both within Council and externally, was run by CAB Project Officer, Deborah Mills. Second, AWL provides an important example of how one arts support program represented and addressed a constituency, in this instance 'workers and their families'. Third, in the discursive formation of AWL the categories 'working class', 'culture' and 'tradition' were central. The mobilisation of these terms established a strong link between AWL and earlier forms of trade union culture and also connected questions of cultural difference to class structure.

These tendencies in AWL policy distinguish the program from community arts in several important ways. While community arts policy and practice were represented as cultural innovations, the AWL program was written into the history of union culture as evidence of resurgence and recovery. AWL policy was also differentiated from community arts through its references to class. In the formation of community arts class was not privileged as the most important axis of social differentiation; instead 'community' functioned as a sign for various divisions from gender to income to age to region to ethnicity. In AWL the recognition and support of working class culture was the main policy objective; when 'community' was invoked it was as a sign of class difference and solidarity. This provoked claims that the AWL program was 'more political' than community arts on the basis that it had a coherent political philosophy and polemic.

In the first section of this chapter the major discursive themes of AWL policy will be assessed in terms of how they represent working class culture and establish mechanisms for its public support. The main question behind this reading of policy is: which cultural forms, practices and audiences were legitimated through the AWL program? In the second section one AWL photo project, *Retrenchment—Denying Skills*, will be considered in detail. What this structure facilitates is a consideration of the policy and project representations of AWL in terms of how each constitutes a set of meanings about class, culture and tradition. These meanings reflect the relationship between funding bodies and the funded and also the very different fields in which institutional and project representations of 'art and working life' are produced.

Reading Art and Working Life policy

Probably the most definitive document produced about the AWL program was the joint CAB/ACTU publication *Art and Working Life: Cultural activities in the Australian trade union movement 1983 (Caper 18*, 1983). This publication had two sections. The first was a long essay outlining the rationale for the program and situating it within the history of trade union culture. This essay was commissioned by the CAB from Ian Burn, ex-lecturer in Fine Arts and owner of Union Media Services, a graphic arts service for trade unions. In the second section Deborah Mills outlined the origins of the program and its policy objectives. While Mills has been referrred to as 'the architect of AWL' (Stephen, 1987; T. Smith, 1984; Burn, 1985) Burn could be described as its ideologue. *Caper 18* was circulated widely to trade unions, artists and arts organisations. This document functioned not only to announce the arrival of AWL but also to articulate its central philosophies. It was a crucial text, constituting AWL around several interrelated themes: the long tradition of cultural activity within the union movement; the role of trade union practices in expressing working class culture; and a critique of artists and elitist notions of creativity. Other documents produced after this reiterated these themes, remaking AWL within the discursive framework laid down in *Caper 18.*

A close reading of this text allows for an assessment of AWL's objectives. If the purpose of AWL was to legitimate 'working class cultural traditions' how was this realised? What forms did this legitimation take at the level of policy (where working class culture was defined) and at the level of funding (where subsidy was distributed to particular cultural forms and practices)?

Official justifications for AWL anchored it firmly within history. The program was not hailed as an innovation. Instead, it was presented as the continuation of a long tradition of cultural activity within the trade union movement:

> A union which has lost a sense of its culture loses an essential relation to its own history and the understanding which that gives in current struggles. It is important then that the Art and Working Life programme should develop in ways which not only embody an understanding of labour movement history and its culture but are also able to contribute to the sense of its significance. *The traditions are there to be built on, revitalised and transformed in that process.* (*Caper 18*, 1983: 5) [emphasis in the original]

Labour history was identified as the authentic source of contemporary

union cultural programs. Related to this was the insistence on maintaining cultural traditions within trade unions as mechanisms for both
celebration and struggle. This emphasis on tradition created a very
strong sense of the past in AWL policy. In fact, throughout the development of the program, this historical context has remained as a central
point of reference. Unlike the early rhetoric of community arts which
constituted this cultural practice as new, a 'world first', without pre-
cedent, AWL policy looked backwards for its inspiration and direction.

Eric Hobsbawm's argument about the invention of tradition is relevant here. His exploration of the various forms of tradition and their
functions identifies a recurring device: invented traditions all depend
on reference to the past specifically through the repetition of certain
practices and values which imply continuity (1983a: 1). In the formation of AWL several of the tendencies Hobsbawm identified can be
traced. The use of tradition in AWL established a relationship between
contemporary policy and past union culture. The cultural traditions of
the labour movement were represented as fragile and their episodic
history read as evidence of the need for urgent attention. Public
patronage was justified on the grounds that these traditions needed to
be not simply recognised but recovered and revived; subsidy was one
mechanism for facilitating their continuation. For Mills, Australia
Council funding was the main source of a 'renaissance' in cultural
production in the labour movement (1985: 6).

How history was used to justify AWL warrants close scrutiny. This
does not mean an evaluation of the 'truth' of the past invoked in policy.
Rather, it means a consideration of the contradictory effects of the
invocation of history and tradition to establish a rationale for AWL.
Because the past is a site of contested meanings and shifting discourses
the focus must be on how historical contexts are connected to the
concerns of the present.

In the early days of the Community Arts Program support for trade
union cultural activities was situated within the general sweep of
community arts policy. This was simply another program for one of
many targeted communities. The formation of AWL removed trade
union arts and trade unionists from this generously inclusive context
and gave them a distinctive cultural identity and past. The evidence of
tradition was central to the establishment of a break with previous
policy discourses which had placed workers and workplaces out there
in the mythical cultural desert. The constituency for AWL—trade
unionists and their families—was not represented as in need of culture.
Nor was the program justified as a form of cultural outreach work.
References to the past enabled a significant political reorientation. They
established the cultural authority of trade unions as legitimate producers and patrons of culture and they justified subsidy on the grounds of
pluralism and equity, not on the grounds of cultural welfare.

The assertion of a strong cultural past within the union movement was also used strategically to counter resistance within the Australia Council. History was a powerful weapon, especially when used to claim the presence of alternative cultural values and to confront accusations of cultural lack or disadvantage. References to tradition were equally important in marketing the program to the unions, who could hardly reject what was presented to them as their own past.

These instances highlight how the production of an historical context for AWL had positive consequences. History was mobilised to win support for the program and to identify its constituency as a culturally distinctive group. However, other effects of this discourse were more problematic. The documents announcing the arrival of AWL were undeniably exhortatory in their tone. The past was not simply presented as a resource for contemporary action but also idealised as a period of unity and effective struggle.

The desire to recreate the golden days of union power and organisation led to the valorisation of certain cultural forms and practices as exemplary. One consequence of this orientation to the past was the identification of a very distinct aesthetic field of reference for the projects funded. Nowhere was this more evident than in the discussion of trade union banners in *Caper 18*. *Caper 18* accorded banners a very special place in the iconography of union culture. They were hailed as the archetypal expression of the past. The restoration of old banners and the production of new ones was evidence of 'tradition' at work:

> Even in these days of advanced communications technology, the most traditional form, the trade union banner, can be revitalised to retain its practical importance. . . A contemporary banner should be 'read' quickly and be flexible in its use—and at the same time must still be seen to be asserting an entire history of union organisation and struggle. (*Caper 18*, 1983: 10)

The problems with this tendency to look backwards are complex. While the value of reviving dormant cultural traditions cannot be denied the dilemma remains of how to align present practices to those from the past. In *Caper 18* the demand that modern banners must 'assert an entire history of union organisation and struggle' was excessive, unrealistic and profoundly nostalgic. It fixed the past as the source of the most correct aesthetic and cultural practice, fostering what Bennett has described as 'rear-view mirrorism', a process of 'walking backwards into the future by rediscovering historically superseded forms of "the popular" and offering these as a guide for action in the present' (Bennett, 1983: 11).

In his essay 'A Blue Plaque for the Labour Movement?' Patrick Wright develops this theme. He describes these nostalgic past–present relationships as 'the marching proletariat alignment'. Historical development is represented as a continuous process of struggle through which the working class 'wins' the present (1985: 153). Wright goes on to argue that this tendency experienced a revival in the 1980s, just at the time when the forward march of labour appeared to be faltering. Looking backwards became a way of avoiding both the present and the future. While the context of Wright's observations was England under the conservative government of Margaret Thatcher, his analysis of trade union culture remains invaluable for the interpretation of AWL policy. Wright pinpoints the essential contradiction in nostalgic invocations of the past. On the one hand they are immensely pleasurable because they affirm real and important historical consciousness and attachments. But on the other hand nostalgia has little political effectivity if it is unable to move beyond sentimentality and the shallow resonances of historical style.

Apart from fuelling anti-labour sentiments, references to the great days of solidarity have other serious consequences. For a start they tend both to romanticise and to reproduce the limited definitions of the working class which characterised these earlier forms. The very issues which are a source of contemporary alienation and disaffection with the union movement are uncritically revived and celebrated. The groups previously either ignored or marginalised remain as such. Women, migrants, Aborigines, non-unionised workers all become problems in contemporary representations precisely because in earlier forms 'worker' generally meant male manual labourer.

This tendency was evident in AWL policy where the celebration of past visual traditions limited the initial application of the program. Many of the projects funded in the first years reflected a rather uncritical revival of previous forms, whether it was the production of a banner, an oral history project or the recording of folk songs about work (AC, AR, 1983–84: 20; AC, AR, 1985–86: 30). While there was a vast field of historical imagery available of the archetypal heroic male worker, this was of limited use in documenting the diversity of contemporary workers and labour processes. An over-reliance on traditional designs and forms was a constraining influence, restricting the variety of projects and the aesthetic languages deployed in them.

Assessment of AWL's historical discourse is difficult because its effects were contradictory. While 'history' was used strategically to win support for the program it also had a conservative influence, fostering a creeping nostalgia in the early years of funding. AWL's argument for cultural plurality and its insistence that trade unions were legitimate patrons of culture represented a significant shift in how access could be interpreted, and there is no doubt that the impact of this shift was progressive. But this has to be balanced against an orientation to the past that fixed AWL in a state of deference and obligation to tradition; that privileged forms and practices that were difficult to adapt to the complex contemporary realities of work and workers.

Class and culture

The second discursive theme in AWL policy was the identification of a constituency. While 'workers' or 'the working class' were targeted some boundaries had to be established around this heterogeneous and shifting social formation. Trade unions provided the answer. The 'working class' that AWL would address was that represented through union organisation and practices. Trade unions were identified as the most important institutional and expressive base of working class interests and culture. In tracing the discourse on a constituency this relationship between unions, class and culture has to be unravelled.

Caper 18 developed a clear argument about the role of the trade union movement in supporting the program. Previous forms of subsidy were criticised as tokenistic because they did not generate the substantial involvement of trade unions:

> The way beyond this impasse is for more initiatives to develop within unions themselves in response to their own and members' needs and values. The projects must be seen to contribute to the activities of unions, not rival or distract from their work. The continuing threat of rising unemployment, the fight to maintain real wage levels . . . these are the issues absorbing the energies of trade unionists and the Art and Working Life programme can and should contribute to those struggles. (*Caper 18*, 1983: 6)

In this instance AWL was marketed to unions as a cultural program that they could mobilise for trade union campaigns. Here was an explicit address to trade unions to claim the program in their own interests, to make it serve the cultural and political needs of the labour movement. This thinly disguised plea to trade unions seems designed to counter resistance and lack of interest. It also highlights the complexities of decentralised patronage. The formation of policy recognising trade unions as suitable patrons of culture was only the first step. Guaranteeing that unions would take up the offer was the next and more difficult one. *Caper 18* did not constitute unions as the passive recipients of AWL, but placed the control of the program in their hands. The success of AWL was to be determined by the extent of union involvement and initiative (*Caper 18*, 1983: 14).

However, while the identification of trade unions as the organisational base for the program was relatively straightforward, defining the working class was more difficult. In AWL policy the working class was more than just the membership of trade unions. It was also the possessor of a distinctive culture. The rationale for the program depended on a cultural definition of class; this was how the constituency was defined as both different and worthy of subsidy. In arguing for the recognition of plural cultures it was important to establish that the bourgeoisie were not the only ones who were cultured.

In *Caper 18* two articulations of 'working class culture' were developed. In the first, tradition was used to establish working class culture as an enclave of certain forms, rituals and associations. The historical context for AWL documented a rich cultural legacy that was valorised for expressing working class identity. Banners, May Day, collectivity, social realism; this was working class culture. References to the past pointed to a loosely identified period when unions played an important role in organising the working class as a political and cultural formation. Unions were one of an array of institutions that had helped maintain the working class as a socially cohesive and identifiable group.

The second articulation of working class culture focused on contemporary forms. It was much less definitive, for obvious reasons. The foregrounding of other social divisions from gender to ethnicity and the emergence of new social movements have dislodged class from its privileged vanguard position in struggles for social change. More significant, however, has been the development of mass cultural forms with their enormous reach and vast and heterogeneous audiences. In this context arguments about class and culture have to be handled with care. *Caper 18* got around this problem by differentiating 'working class culture' from both bourgeois and mass culture. Cultural distinctions were mobilised not simply to declare diversity but to position working class culture in an oppositional relationship to mass and bourgeois cultural forms. The working class were represented as struggling against imposed and alienating bourgeois forms: 'if unionists aren't interested in culture, it's because culture often isn't very interesting' (*Caper 18*, 1983: 13). They were also under threat from the homogenising effects of mass culture: 'since working people rarely find their work experiences reflected in the mass media, this also devalues those experiences and the self-esteem achieved through working' (*Caper 18*, 1983: 13). In these examples working class culture was not defined through the identification of specific forms. Rather, the cultural interests of the working class were articulated as *opposed* to both bourgeois class privilege and the hegemony of mass culture.

The historical and the contemporary articulations of 'working class culture' in *Caper 18* were based on different assumptions and had different effects. In the first, the use of tradition implied an intrinsic relation between certain cultural forms and the working class that bordered on class essentialism. Explanations of the contemporary relationship between class and culture in *Caper 18* were more progressive because they represented class as a relation rather than an enclave. The working class were not defined in terms of distinctive artefacts and rituals but in terms of shifting political and cultural interests that emerged always in relations of domination and subordination. In this framework two important processes in the alignment between class and culture can be identified: first, how cultural forms are used to articulate and claim class interests; and second, how cultural distinctions are mobilised to express differences in power and status (Frow, 1986: 124). In representing the working class as a constituency, AWL policy had to situate 'them' within the broader field of cultural policy. Endowing the working class with culture was essential but this did not automatically guarantee a progressive challenge to existing policy structures. How this alignment between class and culture was established had important implications for the oppositional impact of AWL within the Australia Council. Essentialist notions of working class culture did not contest the organising assumptions of cultural policy. They signalled difference and diversity but they did not explain the nature of the relationships between plural cultures and how funding should negotiate these. While the discourse on the working class in *Cuper 18* recognised the cultural power of mass forms and the privileging of bourgeois class interests and pleasures in public support for the arts, it did not offer any substantial account of how cultural domination worked. All that was offered was a rather feeble attempt to articulate working class cultural interests as formed in the struggle to resist the soporific effects of television and the grand authority of opera.

Despite these limitations AWL policy did write the working class into cultural policy. While representations of this constituency were variable and contradictory they did have the important effect of creating a space in policy for a group previously rendered invisible because of its supposed inability to produce an independent and worthy culture. AWL demolished the idea of a single public and it also raised the important question of equity in subsidy: 'This is not simply an argument for the recognition of diverse cultural traditions. It also implies a demand for cultural democracy—i.e. some equality between cultural traditions.' (*Caper 18*, 1983: 13)

Correct artistic practice

While the address to trade unions articulated in many of the policy and promotional texts of AWL was emphatic in its defence of their past and present role, it was less enthusiastic about contemporary art practice. The third theme developed in *Caper 18* focused on a prescription for correct cultural work in the production of AWL projects. A critique of art and artists occupied substantial space in *Caper 18*. This can be read as an attempt to articulate trade unionists' typical suspicions about art:

> . . . trade unionists may also encounter artists who become involved in 'trade union' or 'community' work as a way of enhancing their art world reputations and so fail to produce work which is of genuine use or interest to unions and their members. (*Caper 18*, 1983: 10)

The attack on artists continued with a sweeping dismissal of those who opted for the 'easier option' of working with the new social movements and refused to adapt their undisciplined and individualistic methods to the admittedly often bureaucratic demands of the trade unions. Trade union cultural work was valorised as more properly political than work for environmental, feminist or Aboriginal groups. In this way AWL was distanced from a significant tradition of progressive art practice.

This echoed attacks on community artists at the ACTU Arts conference in 1981. Reporting on this conference, Burn (1982) accused community artists of diluting the political intent of the conference because they refused to see their work in terms of struggle or opposition: 'it has been rare for community arts programmes to provide means of expression for the outrage, anger and opposition that people should and do feel' (Burn, 1982: 37). The implication here was that community arts could not be considered progressive. Its emphasis on harmony and integration limited the possibilities for a genuinely radical cultural practice. In both these cases AWL was constituted in opposition to existing 'alternative' art practices. The rejection of community arts and the work of artists in various social movements as not properly 'political' confirmed the trade union and its cultural traditions as the almost exclusive source of true radical practice.

Related to the critique of artists was an argument about the social distribution of creativity. Creativity was not the exclusive preserve of artists. Unions were identified as a creative force in society, 'perhaps the most creative', because of their capacity to produce 'conditions guaranteeing the social well-being of future generations' (*Caper 18*, 1983: 14). However, these claims about the central place of unions in the struggle for social justice ring a little hollow when issues such as land rights, disarmament and feminism feature so little on the official platforms of most unions. As Charles Merewether points out these are 'precisely those issues that some artists condemned as romantic leftists have sought to address for many years' (1987a: 33).

Artists were also accused of having a poorly developed industrial consciousness. The failure to see themselves as workers was evident in their very low levels of unionisation and the difficulties they experienced in working collaboratively, in throwing off the claim to individual authorship. Collaborative authorship was posed as automatically progressive and artists were urged to contribute their skills to the trade union movement. While mutual benefits for artists and unions were the outcome, the emphasis in *Caper 18* was firmly on the union determining the role of the artist, on the artist as service worker and the art as functional to union interests (1983: 14).

The discourse on artists was established through a mixture of critique and prescription. The attack on artists was unrelenting, condemning all but a minority who had abandoned their creative egos and learnt to work under direction from the union. This argument explicitly privileged a notion of the artist as craftsworker or technician able to translate union requirements into acceptable designs. The conceptual and critical abilities of artists were denied, reducing the idea of collaboration with unions almost to a master–servant relationship. This prescription for correct art practice also had implications for the types of forms favoured in AWL projects. The emphasis on reviving and celebrating past cultural traditions placed the artist in the role of artisan, carefully maintaining already established formal conventions. The possibilities for innovation and experimentation were slight as the artist was positioned in a deferential relationship to both union management and past cultural forms.

In the formation of AWL policy the three themes outlined here were used to justify the program to the Australia Council and the trade unions. AWL was represented as a program supporting the resurgence of a great past tradition, offering new contexts and roles for art and artists and facilitating the identification of new audiences of workers. The effects of these policy discourses on the sorts of projects funded, on the texts produced in the name of AWL, cannot be ignored. The expressions of working life which projects generated have to be considered in relationship to the meanings and conventions privileged in policy. This is the focus of the next section.

Retrenchment—Denying Skills: a photo project

In selecting an AWL project for analysis the intention is to explore how one exhibition of photographs produced meanings for art and work within the broader field of policy discourses. The preceding section read policy as texts which constituted a set of knowledges about AWL, and this is also the purpose of this section. The difference here is that the focus is on a series of photographs, on visual rather than literary texts.

There are other differences between policy and project texts. Apart from their forms, each is the result of distinctive conditions of production and circulation. However, they also emerge in relationship to each other. This relationship is not deterministic. It would be dangerously crude to reduce projects to the demands, guidelines and economic power of the funding institution. Projects are conceived with these guidelines in mind and successful submissions depend on addressing the funding source in its own terms. Nevertheless, they are also conceived with a constituency in mind, an intended group of participants and potential audience. Projects have to negotiate both these fields.

Retrenchment—Denying Skills (RDS) was initiated by the Workers'

Cultural Action Committee of Newcastle Trades Hall in 1983. This committee was established in 1974, with the aim of counteracting:

> the lack of alternative cultural events and activities for working people in Newcastle. Emphasis was given to taking the arts to where workers spend a good deal of their time—the workplace. Conventional wisdom dictated that it was unrealistic to expect workers to seek out cultural institutions, art galleries, theatres and so on, in their leisure hours. We felt that lunchtime performances in the workplace would not only stimulate an interest in arts activities not normally accessible to workers, but would eventually lead to workers' participation in cultural events and production. (*Caper 19*, 1983: 4)

The parallel between this argument for cultural activity and those promoted by the Community Arts Program in its early days is striking. Both represent cultural programs in workplaces in terms which invoke an almost missionary zeal. The industrial worker trapped in wage slavery is to have culture brought to 'him', so that in the long term its uplifting effects may be discovered and the worker shall seek it out himself. Access leads to participation. Implicit in the Workers' Cultural Action Committee's discourse, however, is a tension between workers needing Art and workers needing an alternative culture, one that would help foster class consciousness.

This tension is evident in the pattern of grants made to the committee since its inception. In the 1974–75 budget of the Community Arts Program $2000 was granted to this organisation to carry out programs of concerts and art workshops for workers and their families (AC, AR 1974–75: 27). This level of grant continued throughout the 1970s but the focus of the projects shifted away from arts access and towards the support of working class cultural traditions and the provision of an alternative to commercial culture and its dangerous effects:

> We made moves to broaden the program to include taking activities to workers' recreation centres, clubs and pubs. We aimed to make a covert attack on club culture, to woo people away from the pokies and 'tits-and-bums' shows, if only for half an hour of good, solid, thought-provoking, right-line performances. (*Caper 19*, 1983: 5)

Retrenchment—Denying Skills was originally conceived by the Workers' Cultural Action Committee as a project employing a photographer-in-residence at Trades Hall for six months to 'record the skills which were becoming redundant due to rapid changes in technology' (RDS Exhibition Catalogue: 3). The title of the project on the submission to the CAB was 'It's a Dying Art' which stressed disappearing art and craft skills in the workplace. In May 1983 Warwick Pearse began work as the photographer. He was appointed for two main reasons. First, he was *not* an artist: the committee was adamant that an 'artist' would be ignorant of union issues and unable to work collaboratively. Second, he had extensive experience working with workers and trade unions having been previously employed at the Workers' Health Centre,

Lidcombe (Pearse, *Interview* 26-3-88). It was fortuitous that he was also a skilled amateur photographer.

The appointment of the photographer triggered a reformulation of the aims of the project. The abstract idea was remodelled with the input of Pearse's experience over the first couple of weeks and his different analysis of skill loss. Pearse argued for a shift in the focus of the project away from loss of skills and 'dying arts' towards the more general issue of economic restructuring and retrenchment. This change was significant. The earliest ideas about this project articulated similar discourses to those set down in *Caper 18*. The great craft traditions of the past were under threat; the worker was 'his' craft; traditions had to be recorded. Pearse's changes challenged this nostalgia. He redirected the project towards a more immediate and functional orientation with the argument that the project should have useful outcomes, specifically the production of photos of and for struggle (Pearse, *Interview*, 26-3-88).

A second important element in the development of this project concerns the choice of media. Within the visual arts, AWL projects have privileged certain forms: murals, banners, posters, photography and, more recently, postcards. The consequences of these choices are significant. For a start they immediately signal a distance from dominant fine art forms and their particular cultural authority. Instead 'other' forms are legitimated. Embedded in these choices are assumptions about the audience. The selection of alternative, low-tech, popular forms implies that images will be easily accessible and appropriated. The choice of photography as the medium for *Retrenchment—Denying Skills* reflects these assumptions. Not only was the camera privileged as the most effective tool for documenting economic and social change but photos were also assumed to be the most effective form for communicating those changes to the potential audience.

The choice of the camera had other implications. In this project the absence of a darkroom at Trades Hall meant that Pearse was forced to work out of the Photography Department of the Newcastle College of Advanced Education. In order to establish this deal students and staff from this department were encouraged to produce images for the exhibition. This arrangement, essential to the implementation of the project, meant that any tendency towards the presentation of the photos as the work of a single talented 'artist' was undercut. The final exhibition contained the work of many photographers, and while Pearse's images were in the majority the emphasis on social concern and documentation countered the idea of the exhibition as art. Claims to authorship were relinquished in other ways. The ownership of the images belonged to the WCAC, who retained control over the photos and their circulation after the completion of the project.

The question of authorship remains a problem in photography. Part of the struggle to assert photography's aesthetic credentials, to claim a legitimate place for it in the fine arts, involves the promotion of a controlling authorial voice. The representation of the photographer as an artist has depended on challenging the idea that photography is a form dependent only on technical mastery (Sekula, 1983: 200). The refusal of authorship takes place in relation to this, and is central to the practices privileged in community arts and AWL projects. The denial of a single authorial voice is one of the major ways in which these projects declare an oppositional content. The emphasis on collaborative work, on the participation of the subjects in the construction of the image, on non-exploitative devices which represent subjects in terms which they control, are all claimed by community arts and AWL practitioners to be evidence of their progressive intentions and effects.

However, the claims that these practices are unique to community cultural practice and that they are intrinsically radical must be scrutinised. As Alan Sekula (1983: 200) points out, these practices are also central to a lot of commercial photography where, in the interests of economic survival, the work involves the negotiation of the author's craft with the demands and expectations of the clients.

In order to establish a reading of this project it is necessary to trace the patterns of aesthetic decisions not as separate from these contextual conditions but as deeply interconnected with them. The emphasis on the institutional and discursive origins of *Retrenchment—Denying Skills* counters the tendency to fetishise the visual texts; to fix meanings only within formal criteria. Instead, the social relationships inscribed within the photographs, their conditions of production and use are recognised along with formal properties (Braden, 1983: 89).

At first glance the images of *Retrenchment—Denying Skills* are easily categorised as social realist. Devices like the straightforward frontal camera angles, the sense of purposeful documentation, the use of captions to provide related statistical information, the unsmiling gaze of the subjects, all accumulate to produce an effect of 'reality' recorded. These are images that evoke 'concern' and 'commitment' rather than 'art'. Their aura of literality emphasises the photo as truth and evidence, as direct transcription of the real. However, as John Tagg (1980) argues, realist texts are constituted. They deploy particular codes and devices as do all forms, but these processes of production are elided in the apparent innocence and naturalness of the image.

Retrenchment—Denying Skills deploys a variety of photo-realisms. Some images refer to photo-journalism, while others use the discourses of family photography and the snapshot. There are also images evocative of the use of the camera in campaigns for social reform, specifically the sorts of photos which 'discover' the working class as fascinating subjects of bourgeois concern. In others realism is given a socialist inflection with the worker posed as the heroic subject of class struggle. Photos were arranged on panels usually representing a single workplace or worker organisation. Panels often combined several different styles of photo, text and, occasionally, montage. These different but related realist devices and design techniques point to the complexity of this project; there is no unified mode of address, but several. Some photos place the viewer outside, as a witness to otherness. This involves what Dermody and Jacka (1988a: 41) have described as a 'social work' position toward the 'client' subject where representations of social problems establish the viewer as 'concerned'. In other photos the mode of address is celebratory with the viewer addressed as inside the subjects' class culture.

These various registers in the panels of *Retrenchment—Denying Skills* highlight a fundamental tension in the project. Just as AWL policy shifted between celebration and nostalgia so too do these images. Celebration depends on the recognition and affirmation of submerged and marginalised cultures, its critical potential is in the defiant assertion and pleasure of difference. In contrast, nostalgia's backward-looking sense of loss only fuels the idea of the working class as objects of both pity and imminent extinction. The surfaces of this project present a vast collection of imagery and data about the organisation of work, ranging from technological change to workplace hierarchies. At this level it functions as an important political record and resource. But beyond this are contradictory representations of the worker, who is both the essential human subject of all workplaces and a mere object of machine and management discipline.

Concern for the disappearing worker is established through documentations of technological change. Here the organisation of the panels is conceptually and aesthetically complex with the worker placed in various relations with machines. In the panel documenting the Comsteel factory the impact of computerised lathes on the organisation of heavy metal manufacturing is explored. In this panel machines dominate. While workers are represented, they are not foregrounded. Instead they appear as appendages, as props to machines. A disembodied hand turns a wheel, a man glances at the camera distracted from his supervision of a machine-based production process, a worker's back almost fills one image but the machine is still privileged, both the worker and the camera face it. The text cutting across two of the photos details the changes in levels of production that have occurred since the introduction of computerised technology. This reinforces the discourse of realism as neutral information, the abstract statistical data of economic restructuring. In the Comsteel panel machines are privileged, the worker services them but work is the product of mechanical not human labour.

In the coal loader panel (plate 7.1) machines are also central. The awesome spectacle of immense mountains of coal is juxtaposed with images of the machinery which move it. But in this instance the workers' presence is quite different from the Comsteel photos; they appear as portraits at the bottom of the panel, underneath the

Plate 7.1 Port Waratah Coal Loader, Carrington. Photographer: Warwick Pearse, *Retrenchment—Denying Skills*, 1983

'empirical' record. In one of these images the background is a brick wall. Context becomes anonymous and connotations of the mug-shot creep in. The text below asserts identity and experience, the oral is used to authenticate. Doug Oliver, the subject, is quoted:

> The reason I look so tired is this boring fucking job. Before automation we worked our arses off but at least we were active for forty hours a week and we were masters of our own destiny, we controlled the pace and the order of the work. In fact it was our hard work that created the wealth that enabled them to automate the place. (Text on the coal loader panel, RDS, plate 7.1)

In both these panels an iconography of technology is established that aestheticises machines. But whereas the Comsteel panel confirms the disappearance of the worker, the coal loader panel acknowledges resistance and the impact of technology on work organisation and worker identity. The portraits in the coal loader panel evoke the archetypal image of the worker who is at the heart of all workplaces. The worker who is working class; the overalls and the hardhat signifying the culture of class difference/class dignity. These panels explore different relations between people and machines. Comsteel is represented as a victory for machines, while the coal loader panel signals the political context of technological change.

Representations of the content of work are the subject of many of the panels. Here the choice of the camera presents particular limitations, for working class work is by and large routine, repetitious and marked by power relations. While these power relations may be explained in general terms as exploitative, each workplace constitutes these relations and is constituted by them according to its particular history.

In *Retrenchment—Denying Skills* representations of working class work processes are the focus in the panels of Stockton hospital for the severely disabled, Rundles clothes manufacturer (plate 7.2) and a retailing outlet. All these panels use sequential images in order to document the stages of a specific work function. Time-and-motion photographic segments are employed to capture, for example, the process of two nurses lifting a patient from the floor into a wheelchair and the sequence of hand movements used in the sewing of a shirt. A photographic technique associated with scientific management is appropriated in order to render visible work as predetermined rules and repeated procedures (Moore, 1988: 165). This use of sequential images is a partial solution to the specific problems of representing work with a camera: it sets up a narrative in response to the photo image which freezes time (Alvarado, 1979–80).

The use of the hand sequence to signify the essential processes of this work is also important. Significantly these are all female hands reiterating the ideology of female manual dexterity. These are not

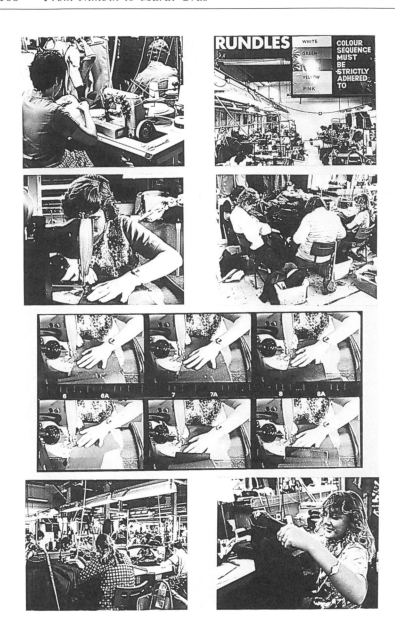

Plate 7.2 Rundles Clothing Factory, Newcastle. Photographer: Warwick Pearse, *Retrenchment—Denying Skills*, 1993

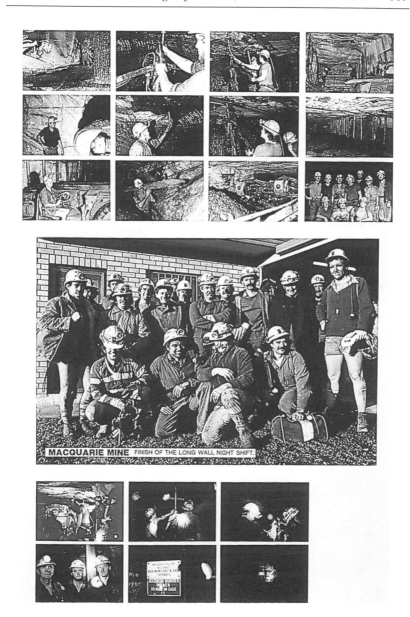

Plate 7.3 Macquarie Mine, Teralba. Photographer: Warwick Pearse, *Retrenchment—Denying Skills*, 1983

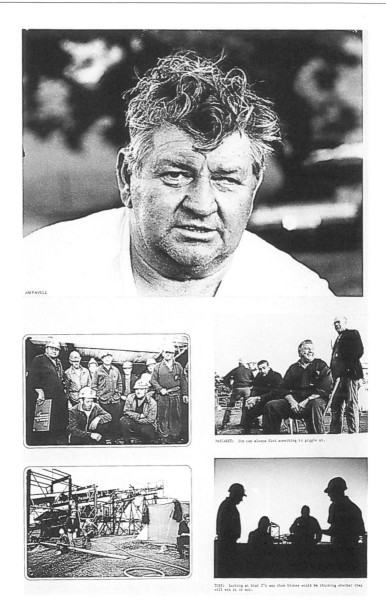

Plate 7.4 Preston Miners Sit-in, Gunnedah. Photographer: Warwick Pearse, *Retrenchment—Denying Skills*, 1983

artisanal hands expressing the freedom of creativity but hands which are dictated to by machines. The hand becomes the symbol of repetitive manual work.

Representations of power relations in workplaces are established via the use of several related conventions. A recurring technique places group shots of workers as the central image on a panel. The Macquarie Mine panel (plate 7.3) is the best example of this. Here worker power is signified as collectivity. The group shot celebrates the social relations of work, the associations which management cannot completely control or obliterate. These images of the social character of work invoke both teamwork and resistance. Unlike the school photo, where the authority of the teacher standing guard in the back row maintains power relations, here workers are grouped in a relaxed and confident pose asserting their power in the workplace. And unlike panels which represent work as hands, machines and repetition here work is workers: organised, united, powerful and *male*. The polemical and celebratory rhetoric of these images establishes an affectionate and 'inside' sense of coalminers' subculture.

In the panels recording a sit-in protesting the closure of the Preston Mine (plate 7.4) power relations are placed within the context of struggle. Group shots predominate but they are fixed within a discourse of campaigning. Here images of individuals take on connotations of the heroic worker. Struggles against redundancy rarely produce positive results and in the Preston Mine panels the atmosphere of defeat is countered with an aesthetic language reminiscent of socialist realism. The campaign context places the worker in history, as the subject of class struggle. One image is of a banner proclaiming 'Preston Stockade 1856–1983'. This relation between character and history is central to socialist realist narratives where individuals function as social types, as embodiments of social and historical characteristics (Kuhn, 1982: 141). Many of the devices of socialist realism are evident here: the low angle shots; the heroic, unsmiling portraits of workers; the group shot in silhouette. While these are images of contested power, of the demand to protect jobs, the aesthetic language undercuts this with a privileging of the worker as the archetypal expression of class. This implies that the individual's fate is transcended by the inevitabilities of history, which marches on regardless (Kuhn, 1982: 144). There is a tension between the worker as the heroic subject of history and the worker as the victim of history.

Apart from these images there are also several which show workers with their families: the son trying on his father's hardhat; women laughing together; a woman with her hand on her husband's knee. A sentimental mode of address creeps in, with images of everyday life and the casual intimacy of the mining community, of the social relations which surround and support work. These tend to counter some of the effects of the more heroic shots by placing the worker in the family, by giving him an identity outside of struggle; the hero is personalised. The majority of panels in *Retrenchment—Denying Skills* represent working class manual work. While there are also panels depicting unemployed youth taking over the council chambers, the Women and Work campaign and the local Aboriginal co-operative the overall effect is of a series of photos which constitute work as manual and workers as male. In this context the attempt to recognise workers outside the official organisation of trade unionism is only partially successful. The marginalisation of women, the unemployed and Aborigines is reproduced in the structure of the exhibition. This echoes the discursive themes and organisation of AWL policy where the invocation of class and tradition restricted the ability to document the diversity of workers and work organisations.

The panels on women's work highlight this problem of how to represent 'other' manifestations of work. Recognition of gender divisions in the labour market have to entail more than just a commitment to 'balance' and equal time. The difference of women's work has to be established and explored and this takes place always in relation to dominant representations of masculinity and male manual labour. Women workers are present in this project. Several panels document female-dominated workplaces: the telephone exchange, Stockton hospital, Rundles and retailing. In several of these panels the managerial hierarchy of workplaces is captured in ways that record how work discipline is gendered.

The Hamilton Telephone Exchange panel (plate 7.5) is dominated by images of workbenches where regimented lines of women work without apparent contact with each other. The photos reflect a managerial visual field, the camera surveys the workers. The photo of the male supervisor gazing at a passive and compliant row of telephonists documents the operations of gender and power at work in techniques of management control. This rare image of the hierarchy of workplaces is in stark contrast to the camaraderie of many of the mining shots where male workers are represented in solidarity and imaginary control. The celebratory rhetoric of male workers and workplaces depends on dismissing management as absent and irrelevant. It also depends on dismissing women. The romanticism of the heroic worker implies a double exclusion: together men stand, apart from bosses and women. In the telephone exchange, celebration is impossible not simply because supervision and regulation are omnipresent but also because the visual language of worker solidarity obscures women. Women workers are obedient and isolated. In a second panel on the telephone exchange (not reproduced) a series of newspaper clippings record the successful campaign to save jobs. Despite this victory, there are no images of unity and struggle here.

Tracing patterns of aesthetic organisation in *Retrenchment—Denying*

Plate 7.5 Telephone Exchange, Hamilton. Photographer: Warwick Pearse,
Retrenchment—Denying Skills, 1983

Skills and the project's production processes and institutional origins does not offer a complete picture. It is also essential to consider patterns of distribution and reception. But this is the hardest part of the picture to fill in. There was no attempt to record audience size or responses to this project and only fragments of information are available about exhibition strategies. *Retrenchment—Denying Skills* was 'premiered' in a room at the Newcastle Workers Club, a large recreational club providing several levels of food, discos and live entertainment. Workers were the captive audience, forced to encounter the photos as they walked from one section of the club to another. A photographic exhibition of workers at work, displayed to workers in their leisure was one of the many ironies produced by this method of display. Despite the concern to make the images accessible, their exhibition in a place of mass entertainment amplified the idea of photos as 'art' in opposition to discos, poker machines and bands as 'fun'. One club member was even hostile to the exhibition, commenting to Pearse that he went to the club to get away from work (Pearse, *Interview,* 26-3-88).

Conclusion

The discourses of art and work constituted in *Retrenchment—Denying Skills* reiterate many of the themes established in AWL policy. The suspicion of artists expressed in *Caper 18* is also evident in the Worker's Cultural Action Committee's decision to employ Pearse. So too is the deliberate distancing in the policy and the project from any connotations of art as 'high' or imposed. 'Access' means alternative forms, social realism, collaborative production processes, union involvement, cultural forms designed for campaigns and exhibitions in popular sites. But beyond these fairly straightforward reflections is the more complex question of how questions about class, culture and tradition are resolved in these two manifestations of AWL.

Caper 18 and *Retrenchment—Denying Skills* both have a polemical intent. Their rhetoric asserts the significance of working class collectivity and organisation. But in both these texts class is an unstable concept. In *Caper 18* the problem of other structures of difference is sidestepped with the wholesale endorsement of trade unions as the official and only acceptable voice of 'the people'. In the project there is a much more conscientious commitment to including those outside the mainstream of union organisation. The unemployed and Aborigines are accorded a place, as are women. While these inclusions are overshadowed by the masculinist discourse on work they still signal the complex relation of class with other structures of difference from gender to ethnicity; 'unity' is made problematic.

The invocation of tradition is also a point of difference. While *Caper*

18 uses tradition to write AWL into the history of trade union culture, *Retrenchment—Denying Skills* only occasionally points to the past. Instead the emphasis is on the contemporary, on immediate threats to workers and jobs. The use of newspaper clippings amplifies the photo-journalist style of many of the panels and invokes the urgency of the political campaign.

Finally, what both these texts reveal is the tension between notions of difference and disadvantage. While the AWL program may have been presented as the most complete resolution of this tension, as a program legitimating workers as differently cultured rather than without culture, this resolution is never complete. In the project and policy assessed in this chapter it is possible to find celebration, polemic, cultural revival and defiance, but it is also possible to find nostalgia, pity and patronising expressions of social concern. While AWL high-lights how certain cultural traditions have been selectively disadvan-taged by entrenched and elitist patterns of public subsidy it also highlights the difficulties in creating a space for the working class in cultural policy. The official culture enshrined in arts policy is bour-geois. This bourgeois 'ownership' is naturalised and while recognition of 'other' cultures may be allowed through special programs and subsidy these other cultures still remain both different and disadvan-taged.

8
Amateurs and artists

Community arts are arts events in which members of the community participate as doers and learners; in which they are actively involved at the grass-roots level of the artistic experience—learning to make pots, painting, weaving, acting, music-making, folk dancing, using film and video-tape, writing and illustrating and collating local history, poetry or stories. (Bower, 1981b: 7)

The idea of community arts as a distinctive cultural practice was central to the ongoing discursive formation of the program. It is for this reason that the shifting prescriptions for community arts practice demand close and separate attention. This is the focus of this chapter. However, in order to understand the significance of this theme it is important to recognise that it was formed in relation to the discourses on art and artists dominant within the rest of the Australia Council. In many of the arguments for the need for community arts, 'mainstream' art practices and artists were dismissed as alienated and alienating; as irrelevant to the majority of the population and obsessed with self-reflection. Community arts emerged as an antidote, as a method for establishing more authentic relations between artists and their audiences (Braden, 1978: 130). The justification for new techniques for practising the arts was based on the contradictory desire both to rescue and reject mainstream art. While art needed to be transformed in order to make it relevant to the majority it was also, at the same time, peripheral to most people's pleasure and leisure.

The discourse on cultural participation was structured around a fundamental question: what should be the relation between communities and artists? At different periods in the development of the Community Arts Program different answers were proposed. During the 1970s the focus was most definitely on the community. Community arts practice was something that generally excluded artists and any semblance of professionalism or 'standards'. 'Informal creativity' loosely describes a range of cultural activity identified in policy as problematic. While community arts began with the assertion of cultural lack the rush of funding requests for anything from a street festival to a children's pottery class forced a reluctant acknowledgement of an immense variety of local cultural practice. These practices produced a policy dilemma: should informal creativity be ignored, celebrated or improved?

Throughout the 1970s the idea that artists were not only irrelevant but often counter-productive to the struggle for increased access to the arts dominated definitions of community arts practice. However, from 1980 the focus began to shift from amateurs to artists. Around this time projects for artists-in-community began to be funded. This development signalled a relatively late admission that artists had a role to play in facilitating community arts practice. Initially the arguments about artists focused on community-based practice as a new source of inspiration for artists; as a way of 're-entering social relations' (Braden, 1978: 133). However, this emphasis quickly gave way to a concern to establish how artists should work *with* a community rather than simply in it; to the idea of collaborative work as a radical cultural practice.

So it was not until the early 1980s that the discourse on community arts practice established an oppositional framework. In focusing on the relationship between artists and communities the meaning of 'participation' was changed. Participation was no longer something communities did as a form of therapy or something that artists did in order to revive jaded creativity. It was artists and communities working together in cultural production. Cultural participation became a resource for the affirmation of different social groups and the expression of various issues. Community arts practice was now a method for aligning the skills of artists with unrepresented groups in the struggle for cultural self-determination.

Tracing the discourse on practice involves an initial consideration of the meaning of participation for communities and artists. Only then can the nature of the proposed relationship between these two groups be assessed. Extending involvement in cultural activities was one of the central objectives of community arts policy and, in order to comprehend the significance of this rationale for arts support, it is again necessary to look beyond policy to projects. In the final section of this chapter the Sydney Gay and Lesbian Mardi Gras will be discussed, for in this example the significance of community arts as a distinctive cultural practice is revealed.

'Amateurs': the problem of informal creativity

Definitions of cultural disadvantage dominated the earliest policies of community arts. Participation in the arts was uneven because some groups suffered from cultural lack or ignorance. The 'solution' to this was the redistribution of arts money in order to facilitate wider awareness of and access to the arts. Despite its democratic appeal, this argument was difficult to sustain because it depended on defining cultural lack in terms of indifference to or ignorance of high culture. As soon as the money started to flow the flaws in this rationale surfaced:

> It became abundantly clear that the 'silent majority', often thought to be hostile to the arts, was in fact humming with interest in its own multifarious artistic pursuits, and (if met on its own grounds) is *eager to move towards higher standards and new ventures.* (AC, AR, 1975–76: 16) [emphasis added]

The discovery of the 'silent majority' busy with its own 'multifarious artistic pursuits' was a paradoxical effect of patronage. The offer of subsidy produced a steadily increasing flow of grant requests from mainly non-arts organisations for activities able to be represented as community arts. Granting money to these activities meant legitimation but it was a legitimation marked by profound ambivalence. While their existence could not be denied, how to assess them remained a problem. In the first years of the Community Arts Program debates about practice focused on what to do about local cultural expression. Different cultural forms and activities were generally not celebrated as signs of healthy cultural diversity. They were evidence, instead, of creativity unaware of professional definitions of quality. These cultural activities may have been popular but they were definitely inferior and unsophisticated.

These 'other' cultures were given a variety of labels: amateur, folk, leisure, self-expression, traditional, craft. Common to all these terms was the implication that these were residual activities negatively defined in relation to high culture (Bennett, 1980: 22). They were not art; nor were they represented as in any way oppositional. Their status was unequivocally lesser in two significant ways. First, their conditions of production usually did not depend on the skills of artists, and second, they originated from social groups excluded from the elite valuing community constituted by the ideology of excellence.

The earliest discourses of community arts were marked by contradiction. On the one hand communities in need of access were constructed as cultureless. On the other, they were represented as excessively creative, busy with festivals, folk dancing and brass bands. A partial solution was to place these cultural activities within the realm of self-expression, not Culture. They had value for the practitioners but not aesthetic value. While everyday creativity was accepted it did not necessarily have anything to do with art. In fact, it was most often represented as leisure activity or hobbies. Informal cultural practices were equated with well-being; like exercise they were good for people. When artists were occasionally mentioned in these instances, they were valorised as the possessors of 'true' genius and inspiration. They were creative, while others were merely 'expressing themselves'.

While the Community Arts Program granted recognition to these quaint 'unofficial' cultures on the basis of their therapeutic benefits, there was, at the same time, a drive to improve them. Arguments about cultural disadvantage persisted. In the 1970s community arts practice often meant projects seeking to introduce communities to more sophisticated forms. In the 1975–76 Annual Report of the Australia Council the funding of amateur activities was accepted only if the purpose of the project was to 'raise standards' (AC, AR, 1975–76: 16). Festival organisers were urged to incorporate more 'arts content' in order to counter the overwhelming influence of 'marching girls, queen competitions, commercial floats and piped music' (AC, AR, 1975–76: 17). Raising standards usually meant employing professional artists or companies. Their role was not so much to collaborate in local creative projects as to educate in correct methods.

The improvement of informal creativity was justified on the grounds that participation did not mean appreciation. The original argument about cultural lack was modified: it was not that certain groups were without culture but rather that they participated in inferior cultures. Speaking in 1980 as Director of the CAB to a national community arts conference, Ros Bower summarised the limitations of mere participation:

> We must not confuse opportunities to participate in the arts with opportunities to enjoy the work of artists. In terms of day to day developments in the arts, or the range of arts activities accessible to the community, however, nobody can *dictate* about standards. We have to accept that they will vary, that a thousand pottery ashtrays will bloom and languish on craft stalls; that a thousand gum trees will offer themselves to the axe of indifference which is the Herald Outdoor Art Show; that a thousand 'Charley's Aunts' and 'Salad Days' will be re-enacted. . . But it is only David Humphries, or the artist potter, or Gordon Chater, or the sculptor or dancer who can ultimately demonstrate the difference. Their aim—the aim of artists—will not be to pour contempt on prevailing taste, the amateur or the local people's preferences. Their aim will be to offer works of art; to open up enjoyment of the arts; to widen horizons, to evoke the 'Aha! I see! That's great isn't it?' (Bower, 1981a: 1–2) [emphasis in the original]

In this argument for the initiation of subordinate groups into the illuminating benefits of high culture, participation was deemed a *lesser* cultural practice than appreciation. Strategies for extending access to the arts depended on diverting various communities away from their existing cultural pleasures and practices into 'better' forms and 'better' techniques for consuming them. Participation had to be converted into disinterested appreciation.

Despite Bower's warning against 'pouring contempt on prevailing taste' this is precisely what she did in this speech. Beyond the references to gum trees and pottery ashtrays was a wholesale endorsement of the superior and mystical benefits to be gained from the contemplation of art. Central to this prescription for community arts practice was a distinction between amateur and professional cultural activities. While the pleasure of amateur cultural practices was acknowledged it was a pleasure with little lasting value. Imperfect techniques, inferior knowledge and informal organisation all meant fun without real cultural significance. Cultural production for the sake of it, for the pleasure of doing it yourself, could not stand alone. If these activities were to be publicly funded then subsidy had to be used to transform, educate and improve.

The desire to convert participation into appreciation was also used to justify the funding of arts programs in schools. Here cultural socialisation was recognised as a long and arduous process. Only children had the time and appropriate institutional context to be rescued from the damaging effects of mass culture and poor parental conditioning (AC, AR, 1973: 16). The school was the best place to teach a love of the arts. In 1978 the CAB initiated an Arts in Schools program 'to stimulate interest in and understanding of the arts' (AC, AR, 1980–81: 27). The incorporation of arts education in the curriculum was justified on the grounds that the intention was merely to inform all children of the cultural choices available to them. Rowse (1985a: 45), drawing on Bourdieu, identifies the naivety of these assumptions. Not only did they avoid identifying which 'arts' would be included and how, they also ignored the processes of differentiation embedded in school structures which privilege middle class knowledge, skills and taste.

While many forms of creativity were deemed amateur, inferior and not conducive to true appreciation, some were acceptable. The story of ethnic arts reveals a different response to 'other' cultural practices. Ethnic arts were represented as traditional and folk-based. 'Ethnics' were naturally cultured. Their cultural pleasures did not need to be improved because they fulfilled the important function of maintaining self-esteem and identity. In the funding of ethnic festivals, folk dancing classes or music performances, for example, the concern was not so much for quality as for the continued practice of an essential creativity. Ethnic arts were an important sign of migrants' difference and they were acceptable because a connection between culture and consciousness could be established: to be ethnic meant to have culture. These articulations of migrant creativity implicitly acknowledged the relationship between cultural practice and cultural survival, but this relationship was not granted any political import. Migrant creativity was legitimated on the grounds that it was 'natural', because without it identity suffered. Ethnic arts policy remained trapped within the rhetoric of welfare.

In early community arts policy the recognition of migrant cultural activities was unequivocal. In sharp contrast to this was the deep ambivalence about other social groups and their cultural pleasures. While the cultural expressions of old people, rural dwellers, people living in the western suburbs or children were acknowledged these constituencies were also targeted for cultural development. Their cultural practices had to be improved rather than merely maintained. To read the lists of grants from the Community Arts Program between 1973 and 1980 is to sense a vast world of local cultural activity. From the lounge room to the youth centre, to the Italian Club, people were busy producing cultures, enjoying themselves and expressing individual and collective pleasures and identities. Community arts funding triggered responses from these multiple sites of informal creativity. Subsidy recognised the reality of extensive cultural participation outside the ambit of art and artists. However, the problem was how to assess these various practices. How to justify subsidy especially in the context of a national funding body dominated by the support of high culture and the pursuit of excellence. The language of community arts policy was equivocal. The continual references to informal creativities as 'self-expression', 'recreation' or 'amateur' reinforced the residual status of these activities. The insistence that participation was a lesser cultural activity in comparison to appreciation established a sharp distinction between more and less sophisticated cultural practices.

These early references to community arts as a distinctive cultural practice indicate a fundamental tension between social and aesthetic measures of value. The emphasis on participation and activity highlighted the crucial relationship between cultural practice and social identity. 'Domestic', 'folk', 'amateur', whatever such expressions were called, they all stressed the pleasure of self-validation through making and creating. But these tentative arguments for the social value of cultural participation were continually undermined by the almost evangelical drive to convert participation into appreciation. In this counter representation of community-based cultural practice as 'unsophisticated' the hegemony of aesthetics was revealed. Community arts practice was not posed in opposition to 'high' cultural production and consumption. It was, instead, an alternative for all those constituencies unable to achieve the superior position of appreciation.

While there was a persistent emphasis on educating and improving popular tastes a certain fatalism surrounded this objective. Subordinate groups would never really acquire the necessary cultural capital to genuinely enjoy and understand art. What the conversion of participation into appreciation meant was that these other groups would at least realise the greater value of certain cultural activities. 'High' culture would be recognised as worthy but unintelligible.

Artists: ethnographers or activists?

The silence on artists in the first seven years of the Community Arts Program was significant. While they were occasionally mentioned they were not the subject of community arts discourse. They may have been necessary to the successful operation of art workshops or tours to isolated regions but they were not practitioners of community arts. This was something various constituencies did largely independently of artists.

This distance from artists was an important element in the Community Arts Program's initial identification of a field of responsibility. It was equally characteristic of the Aboriginal Arts Board and the Crafts Board. One of the reasons why these three funding areas clustered on the margins of the Australia Council was their support of cultural forms and activities that were not dependent on artists. In these Boards 'the artist' was not valorised as the essential element in creative practice. The emphasis on local production and participation democratised the creative process and generally rendered the artist a peripheral figure.

However, in the rest of the Australia Council artists were valorised almost as an endangered species. One of the legacies of the Whitlam years was a concern to redress the neglect and low status of artists. This was often presented in terms of artists' unique contribution to the nation:

> Too many of our finest talents have been lost to overseas. We want to ensure that our greatest artists remain in Australia and prosper in Australia, and that the whole Australian community is the richer for their presence. (Whitlam quoted in ACFTA, AR, 1974: 8)

In the conversion of the ACFTA into the Australia Council artists were recognised in a number of different ways. They were nominated to membership of Council and the Boards in order to fulfill Whitlam's demand for peer group assessment of both policy and grants. Apart from this commitment to participatory democracy the structure of subsidy also privileged artists. Grants to support professional cultural production and producers dominated in most of the Boards. Subsidy was represented as a form of urgent first aid for artists and became incorporated into discourses on fame and talent. Getting a grant as a writer, painter or whatever became an important part of an artistic career.

So, while the rhetoric of excellence and national identity justified subsidy to artists the rhetoric of access and participation justified subsidy to 'non-artists'. This distinction, established in the first years of the Australia Council, was firmly entrenched in the Community Arts Program. It was not until the first years of the CAB that 'the artist' began to feature in community arts policy—and then as a subject of concern. Initially this concern was expressed in terms of their isolation from the community: 'Australia lacks a coherent cultural background. In terms of our national cultural objectives the re-integration of the artist into the community is of crucial importance' (Bower quoted in AC, AR, 1980–81: 23).

The idea of isolation was central to the discovery of the artist by the CAB. It was invoked in order to explain anything from widespread lack of interest in the arts to the absence of a national culture. In this process explanations for the causes of cultural disadvantage shifted from the failings of special populations to the problems of contemporary artistic practice. Community arts became the saviour of artists, the method for placing them back in the social. However, what was so problematic about this representation of the artist was the uncritical reiteration of the ideology of isolation. Initially community arts policy did not challenge this ideology but perpetuated it. The myth of the outcast artist was posed in opposition to the fully integrated 'community artist'.

The origins and effects of the ideology of the isolated artist have been explored by Janet Wolff (1981). She identifies it as a product of the rise of individualism concomitant with the development of industrial capitalism. Not only did industrialisation push artistic production to the margins, making it appear as play rather than work, but it also represented creativity as the exclusive gift of select, talented individuals. New market-based systems of patronage also had the effect of connecting the value of artforms to the cult of the artist. Ultimately, the ideology of the isolated artist denies the collaborative nature of much creative work and the reality of many artists who are 'integrated, *as* artists, into various branches of capitalist production and social organisation' (Wolff, 1981: 12) [emphasis in the original].

The CAB's first official deliberations about artists did not challenge these tendencies. In setting up 'the community' as a site where artists could be repatriated romantic myths remained intact. The community was represented as an exotic other world where inspiration for jaded, *male* creativity could be found:

> The artist needs to become the spokesman, the interpreter, the image maker and the prophet. He cannot do it in isolation. He must do it by working with the people. He must help them to piece together their local history, their local traditions, their folklore, the drama and the visual imagery of their lives. And in doing this, he will enrich and give identity to his work as an artist. (AC, AR, 1980–81: 23)

In this example the artist's venture into the community was presented in a language evocative of ethnography. Like ethnographic authority, the artist's authority was established from an observational standpoint, from the position of outsider who represented others. But while traditional ethnographic texts addressed other anthropologists, the artist-in-community was placed in the role of representing others to themselves. The effects were the same, as James Clifford so neatly summarises: 'You are there, because I was there' (1983: 118).

From 1980 the placement of artists in the community began to feature in policy statements as a new focus for the Community Arts Program.

In the 1981–82 Annual Report of the Australia Council the CAB stated that one of its five priority areas was the placement of 'professional artists working in community contexts as creative artists and/or teachers and catalysts' (AC, AR, 1981–82: 31). The idea of artists serving the community was not yet the main emphasis. Teaching or acting as a catalyst was an adjunct to their primary role as individual creators. The artist-in-community was initially conceived in terms similar to residencies, with the community replacing traditional sites like the university. This strategy was regarded as experimental and most of the artist-in-community projects were funded under the Pilot Projects category. However, by 1982 this approach had become institutionalised enough to warrant a separate funding category and the establishment of a training program for artists seeking to work in this 'new' site (AC, AR, 1981–82: 31).

The provision of training for artists keen to venture out of their garrets was the result of demands from those who found traditional skills inadequate when confronted with a community context for their work (see AC, AR, 1981–82: 31). While the idea of a residency implied a neutral site where the artist continued work as usual, the reality of community-based practice for artists was quite different. Responses to the presence of an artist were unpredictable ranging from excessive demands for assistance to polite apathy (Braden, 1978: 169). Accounts of the shocks experienced by artists during these projects were once again reminiscent of the ethnographer. Self-discovery is an inevitable effect of ethnographic practice, the rites of passage of the ethnographer being a familiar sub-text in anthropological writing (Clifford, 1986: 109). The same effect can be detected in this description of an artist's concern about working in the community:

> Ann's initial doubts were to do with how to approach people in the community situation after having spent so long in a tertiary institution and how she would be accepted, particularly her appearance. . . Ann still finds communication the most difficult aspect of the position. She is confident in addressing groups . . . but finds it difficult to engage in one to one discussions with people who state different, more conservative or sexist attitudes, particularly if they seek or assume agreement. (Muir, no date: 12)

What is so remarkable here is the sense in which it is the artist who is 'other', not the community; the subject of otherness is never fixed.

The discovery of the artist reoriented the discourse on community arts practice. Prior to 1980 practice had been defined as spontaneous and therapeutic, emerging from the creative wellsprings of 'the people'. While these activities were problematic it was generally up to arts organisers, Community Arts Officers or Field Officers, not artists, to culturally improve the community. The growing emphasis on the artist-in-community shifted attention away from questions of informal creativity and onto questions about how professional artistic practice could be adapted to suit new contexts. Community arts practice became the practice of artists, whose creativity was now placed in new social relations and new sites.

Once artists had been inserted into the discourse on community arts practice definitions of their role began to proliferate. Initially, the artist's practice was not to work with the community but in it. The community was the place where the arts could become involved with everyday life (see Pascoe, 1983: 8). By 1983 the artist-in-community began to acquire different functions. The illusion of the community as a passive source of stimulation collapsed and discussions about practice began to focus on the nature of the relationship between artists and communities. Community arts practice was now described as a collaboration with the artist deferring to the community context, and 'what would emerge would be a . . . product informed directly by the concerns of the communities and executed with a high degree of technical skill' (Hawkes, 1986: 2).

In this new emphasis the term 'community artist'· gained fresh meaning and replaced 'artist-in-community'. This implied that artists' creativity was to be put to work *for* the community rather than *in* the community. This seemingly innocuous name change signalled a shift away from the artist as ethnographer towards the artist as activist. Community artists collaborated with the community in cultural production; there was creative equality between the artist and the community. In 1984 Jon Hawkes (Director of the CAB) announced the arrival of the community artist who was now an activist and *female*:

> Being creative with others would be the most important part of the job. The 'with others' bit is what requires skills in social communication, group dynamics, diplomacy etc. . . One would expect the arts worker to be an active contributor to the collective experience and the effort involved in realising the art. Their obvious contribution to the end result (if there is one) may be invisible or huge but whatever the appearance, the arts worker must have joined in. It is not the primary role of a community artist to organise the arts activities of others or just to teach arts skills—the community artist gets her hands dirty in the creative act along with everyone else. (Hawkes, 1984: 8–9)

This definition put to rest any semblance of the romantic artist. The artist had become 'arts worker', individual authorship was irrelevant, cultural production a collective process, specialist creative skills of only peripheral importance and end results a nice, but not essential, by-product. The idea of isolation as fundamental to an artist's capacity to create and, more importantly, to critically reflect or oppose was refused. Art and artists had to be socially engaged.

In each of these assertions community arts practice reflected broader debates about the role of the artist and the place of culture in struggles for social change. The emphasis on the organising function of culture echoed Walter Benjamin's argument in his essay 'The Author as Producer'. For Benjamin the author:

will never be concerned with products alone, but always, at the same time, with the means of production. In other words, his products must possess an organizing function besides and before their character as finished works. And their organizational usefulness must on no account be confined to propagandistic use. Commitment alone will not do it. (Benjamin, 1973a: 98)

Benjamin's interest in the means of cultural production and the historical and social conditions which situated 'the author as producer' prefigured community arts' emphasis on process over products and the artist as activist. Benjamin's insistence on the need to demystify the production processes of culture and turn 'readers and spectators into collaborators' was picked up by community arts commentators as a model for correct cultural practice (see Braden, 1978: ch. 6; Marsh, 1984).

However, Benjamin also insisted on a balance between a concern for production processes and products. He rejected the idea of liberating the means of cultural production so that the people could simply 'express themselves'. *What* was produced was equally important. Works manifesting the correct tendency were dismissed. For Benjamin, progressive cultural practice did not mean an end to formal innovation, and herein lay his endorsement of montage and epic theatre as exemplary forms. Evidence of commitment was no substitute for aesthetic quality.

These counter arguments in Benjamin's thesis were generally ignored by community arts ideologues. In constituting the parameters for radical community arts practice questions about forms were persistently avoided. Opposition emerged from new relationships between artists and communities, not through aesthetic innovation. The role of the community artist was to establish alliances with disenfranchised groups, to work with them in struggle. This rhetoric echoed familiar left ideology about community-based activism. It was also in stark contrast to earlier discourses on practice. The 1970s emphasis on cultural participation as therapy was replaced with an insistence on culture as commitment.

More significant, however, was the way in which the emergence of the community artist challenged traditional notions of authorship. Collaboration, participation, creative equality—whatever it was called—placed the artist in a different relationship to both audience and artefact. Taken to extremes community arts practice meant the end of any status for the artist, the denial of any specialist skills: 'the artist is not a special kind of person, rather each person is a special kind of artist' (CAB, *Minutes*, 15-7-82: 2). But the problems of defining an artist were not solved by this counter cultural essentialism. Gradually the term 'artworker' gained popularity in the discourses of community arts signifying a more sophisticated critique of the dominant language of creativity.

By 1983 the 'community artist' or 'artworker' was identified as the central player in community arts practice. This was symptomatic of the wider shift in policy from cultural disadvantage to cultural difference. Artworkers were now crucial resources for the expression and affirmation of different constituencies and cultures. In this way cultural practice was represented as political practice; the production of culture was a mechanism for both organising and contesting.

Because 'practice' was no longer a matter of getting communities to participate in 'good' culture but, rather, getting artists to participate in communities, community arts became a measure of an artist's commitment. A willingness to work with communities was a sign that an artist had abandoned reactionary notions about individual talent and aesthetic excellence. For what the rhetoric of collaboration always implied was that 'quality' must be forsaken for participation. This was reflected in the dominant form of documentation of community arts projects, which was a narrative history of the production process obsessively describing the shifting relations between artworkers and constituencies (see *Caper 17* and *Caper 20*).

The value of this attention to the complexities of collaboration is that it reveals community-based cultural production as a continual process of negotiation over what and how to produce. This negotiation is structured by the power relations between artists and communities which are never fixed. While some projects may establish deference to the artist's authority and special skills, this was generally disapproved of as a form of cultural imperialism. In other projects the reverse was the case. Karen Merkel describes the problems inherent in artists' deference to the community in this way:

> . . . the usual producer/consumer relationship cannot be simply cited since most of this work is produced collectively. Therefore, in order not to fall out over probable irreconcilable issues of taste, people settle for humourless issue-based hybrids. (Merkel, 1987: 3)

For Merkel one source of the problem of how to establish creative equality is the class differences between artists and most community groups. These are nowhere more manifest than in the dilemma over what to do with the artist's specialist knowledge. The place of the artist in collaborative work cannot be as a mere functionary, providing access to the means of cultural production and knowledge of technical skills. The artist has a legitimate role in expressing judgements and opinions and discussing the basis of these (Kelly, 1984: 111). The application of skills has to be contextualised. It is not a matter of avoiding standards in deference to 'the community' or imposing foreign standards but of collectively establishing others.

While collaborative production disrupts usual notions of authorship it does not get rid of them altogether. Although some descriptions of the practice of community artists completely deskill them, making them 'one of the team', others describe a process of co-authorship in which the artist's skills are acknowledged as one part of the creation, but not the only or most important. Different contributions are recognised but not ranked.

For many community arts projects the form expresses, even celebrates, plural authorship. Participation in the mural, the festival, the theatre production is inscribed in the evidence of many voices, in the idea of the community speaking. While this polyphony may dislodge the authority of artists, their role as instigator, coordinator and editor of community arts projects generally remains. In this sense the community artist's role is enabling, the coordination of multiple inputs into a coherent whole becomes the unique and crucial role of the artist. As Clifford points out, 'the authoritative stance of "giving voice" to the other is not fully transcended' (1983: 140).

Discussions about the nature of collaboration reveal the difficulties in establishing creative equality between artists and communities. They also reveal the centrality of the discourse on practice in the construction of community arts. The main effect of this discourse was the insistence that processes of cultural production were far more important than products. The shifting meanings for community arts practice were a major force in the establishment of non-aesthetic measures of value. They identified a variety of objectives for community arts from therapy to the affirmation of identity to opposition. Each of these social or political objectives was placed above the pursuit of art or an 'excellent' finished product.

The shift from access to art to participation in culture was crucial. It signified a new interpretation of the idea that art had transformative qualities. Community arts practice was no longer a matter of trying to improve popular tastes but a valorisation of other constituencies and other cultural practices. Participation was no longer the poor relation to appreciation, but rather the fundamental objective of good community arts practice. It was the essence of oppositional measures of value. In declaring participation as the most important cultural practice community arts rejected the cerebral basis of appreciation. Culture was not something internal (in your head) which some recognised and others did not, it was external, a form of praxis or activity which different people used in different ways.

Assessing community arts practice: the example of the Gay and Lesbian Mardi Gras

While policy has produced changing prescriptions for community arts practice it is in the documentation of projects that the complexities and contradictions are revealed. In this section the Sydney Gay and Lesbian Mardi Gras will be analysed as an example of community arts practice. In selecting Mardi Gras the idea of the festival as an archetypal community arts activity is reinforced. For nothing symbolises the idea of collective creativity more powerfully than 'the people' taking over the streets.

The Gay and Lesbian Mardi Gras is an annual parade down Oxford Street in Sydney that began as a political march in 1978. By 1990 the march had become a month-long festival featuring gay film, performing arts, television and visual arts events, community activities, sports programs and forums. The highlight of the festival remains the street parade which has shed connotations of the demonstration in favour of a celebratory carnival. For Eric Michaels the parade 'has become a theatrical event that gay people perform as an offering to the city at large' (1988b: 4).

In the 1990 program Mardi Gras was described as the 'largest community arts association in Australia' (Phillips, 1990: 8). In terms of budget this is probably correct. The Mardi Gras Association has an annual turnover of approximately $1 000 000 generated through an ongoing series of cultural events ranging from parties to a parade award night. This financial independence definitely sets Mardi Gras apart from the majority of community arts organisations which are almost completely dependent on federal, state or local government subsidy. Mardi Gras has, however, had brief contact with the subsidy circuit. In 1983 it received a $6000 grant from the CAB but the resulting controversy over public support for homosexuality made this option more trouble than it was worth (Galbraith, 1990: 10).

Survival in a commercial rather than a subsidy economy does not disqualify Mardi Gras from community arts status. The parade, especially, manifests all the elements of informal creativity. Apart from the obvious celebration of gay community identifications and attachments, it is participatory, setting few limits on the nature of gay individuals' or organisations' involvement. The parade is also not a unified or coherent cultural product; chaos, diversity and different standards of production and performance are all in evidence.

What is so interesting about the example of Mardi Gras is the way in which it reconfigures the 1970s discourse on community arts practice. In this period, before the discovery of the community artist, community arts practice was dominated by references to self-expression, recreation, amateurs and local cultural activity. Mardi Gras reflects all of this but its organisation and effects place this popular creativity not in the realm of therapy or alternative 'activities' but, rather, in the realm of celebration, affirmation and opposition.

Michaels' wonderfully evocative insider's account of the 1988 parade situates the event within the tradition of carnival. Not only does it allow a series of ritualised transgressions about gender but, as a form, it eliminates distinctions between producers and consumers, artists and audience:

Authentic Carnivale, like other ritual theatre, does not separate spectator from event—audience from actor—across the boundary of the proscenium arch. This is one of the sources of the power of ritual theatre: everyone is drawn in; safe defensible lines are breached. This defines a site of danger, excitement and political potential like no stage show can. This is what 'Act 1' of the Gay Mardi Gras parade lacked. There the boundaries were drawn: street/walkway; revellers/audience; us/them. Probably these boundaries are necessary to permit Mr and Mrs Suburbia to be spectators at a gay event comfortably. But with the last float, the line collapsed, and for a remarkably protracted moment, all boundaries, social as well as spatial, were up for grabs. (Michaels, 1988b: 7)

What this account establishes, in opposition to the early policy on community arts practice, is the political importance and pleasure of self-representation, the authority of people speaking for themselves. But it is not just people claiming their 'cultural rights' that is important. *How* they do this warrants equal attention. The fact that Mardi Gras is a piece of street theatre, is carnivale, has implications for what is said. The parody of the three and a half metre high papier-mache 'macho man' is reminiscent of Bakhtin's discussion of folk humour with its capacity to ridicule both officialdom and 'the people'. This is not the laughter of satire but the pleasure of self-mockery (Bakhtin, 1984: 12). It is also evidence of the form *allowing* certain expressions. What carnivale provides is the possibility for gays to 'perform homosexuality' (Michaels, 1988b: 5) to themselves and others in ways that are both celebratory and diverse.

The description 'amateur' is meaningless in this example. This is not a cultural practice established to mimic high culture forms; it is oblivious to dominant ideas about standards. Mardi Gras allows participants ritualised expression. It does not establish a hierarchy amongst performers, nor does it valorise the work of artists as more creative. While artists are employed by the Mardi Gras organisation their task is to run a workshop where assistance with design and preparation of floats and costumes is provided. Artists also prepare some of the major floats around changing themes. In 1990 a Parade Designer was employed for the first time to coordinate the multiple participants but this did not alter the overwhelmingly popular and inclusive feel of the event (Westmore, 1990: 17). The parade celebrates spectacle, design, preparation and, most importantly, collective creativity; this is what is inscribed in the sprawling assortment of performers and floats.

Recognising creativity outside of the practices of art and artists is a central element in the discourse on community arts practice. However, the nature of this recognition varies. When popular cultural practices are constituted as residual in relation to high culture, their status as non-art remains problematic and produces strategies for improvement. When these practices are placed within the context of cultural rights, of people representing themselves, then their progressive potential is revealed. What the example of Mardi Gras so convincingly displays is the power of direct participation in culture. This participation evokes the pleasure of expression and creativities that are not only collaborative but also profoundly affirming.

Apart from the predictable expressions of horror from the extreme right about Mardi Gras' 'promotion of homosexuality' it has also been attacked from the left. The accusations from this side focus on the transformation from demonstration to parade. In this process, the critics claim, political content has been replaced with a celebration of lifestyle. What this mean-spirited attack manifests is a narrow and puritanical notion of 'politics' that excludes pleasurable cultural expressions. The annual ritual of Mardi Gras is central to the political survival of the gay community because it is in the capacity to produce and practise culture that gay identity and organisation are both celebrated and maintained.

Conclusion

While the discourse on practice explored the relationship between artists and amateurs one is still left wondering what was produced and who was watching? In so many documentations of community arts projects the emphasis on the context of cultural production is overwhelming. In the rush to define success in terms of the number of people involved or the worthiness of the issue selected, the silence on the formal organisation and outcomes of 'community arts practice' is resounding. This relentless emphasis on the social conditions of cultural production fuels a rigid distinction between texts and contexts. In the CAB's refusal to prescribe official forms the fundamental relationship between processes and products has been ignored. But while questions about forms are displaced they cannot be avoided altogether. The problem still remains of how to assess the impact of production processes on forms; how is community arts practice evident? The privileging of context in opposition to the fetishism of the text does not solve the problem of evaluation but perpetuates it. Questions about the meaning and value of community arts projects remain problematic in the discourse on practice precisely because of the maintenance of the text/context separation.

The challenge is not to find the correct balance between textual and contextual measures of value but to abandon this dualism altogether. Tom Burvill's (1984) idea of the 'social aesthetic' offers a valuable way forward. In his discussion of the work of the community theatre company Sidetrack he shifts between an analysis of the methods of production and the formal organisation of the plays. This approach makes it possible to see *how* this theatre has meaning to the community in which it was produced; how measures of value and success are determined by the close interaction of performers and audience. It recognises that different cultural practices create different aesthetics that have to be judged against their own criteria.

Another absence in this discourse was the audience. What the focus on participation produced was a cultural scenario in which everyone was involved, everyone was a cultural producer. In this sense the audience, with its connotations of passive consumption, was rendered both abhorrent and irrelevant. In the rare moments when an audience was acknowledged it was often represented as 'the community', perpetuating the idea of community arts as marginal and parochial; as cultural forms which spoke only to themselves. In the drive to collapse the social distance between artists and audiences community arts became something that everybody did and nobody watched.

While these effects of the discourse on practice are problematic they do not undercut the political importance of the idea of cultural participation. Community arts practice valorised modes of cultural production and reception that were outside the ambit of official culture. The insistence on *doing* rather than *contemplating* shattered the usual distinctions between cultivated and uncultivated, artist and amateur, audience and performer. The discourse on practice also emphasised the specificity of most arts whose origins and impacts are firmly rooted within particular times and within particular cultures. In making culture a resource for various unrepresented constituencies community arts practice reinforced the fundamental relationship between cultural production and social identity, and this was its radical challenge.

9
The aesthetics of affirmation

'With assistance from the Community Arts Board'. This acknowledgement appears on the bottom of posters, at the end of theatre programs, on the opening pages of local histories, on all the various cultural activities funded by the Community Arts Program. It is the public recognition of patronage. Behind this obligatory display of gratitude exists the complex relationship between projects and funding body. Before considering three visual arts projects in detail, this relationship needs to be examined.

The cultural activities supported by the Community Arts Program reflect the process whereby money is translated into cultural artefacts. Projects emerge in relation to the Community Arts Program via the work of preparing a submission, representing the project in terms laid down by the funding guidelines and awaiting assessment. However, after funds are granted, projects acquire a relative autonomy and produce their own meanings for community arts within the specific conditions of their production and circulation.

One model for explaining the relationship between the funding institution and projects treats projects as a simple realisation of policy objectives. This implies that patronage is a one-way relationship, with all control in the hands of the funding body:

> Funding addiction has its own hazards; the style, scope and subject matter . . . become limited by the guidelines laid down by funding bodies. While the official artist-in-community projects have their value, it is important to recognise that they are state and corporate owned and will necessarily reflect the opinions and tastes of the sponsors. (Church, 1986: 5)

Such economic determinism is not uncommon in analyses of community arts which depend on representations of the state as monolithic and power as a zero sum. Here projects are understood in terms of the intentions of patronage and the attribution of various motives to the funding institution.

Several recent studies of the relations between funding bodies and

133

the cultural forms which they support have begun to challenge this determinism. These accounts represent funding as a *practice* marked by a continual process of negotiation and always inscribed in the play of power (Kuhn, 1988: 6). Annette Kuhn's (1988) history of film censorship is an excellent example of this approach. This study breaks with the tendency to think of institutions and texts as separate with the latter subordinate to the former. Instead Kuhn focuses on the interactions between the various parts of the 'film censorship apparatus'.

Jeni Thornley's (1987) history of the Women's Film Fund documents the influence of the Sydney Women's Film Group on its policies and practices and traces how this relationship between a funding institution and a lobby group was reflected in the shifting content and forms of the films produced with these funds. Susan Dermody and Elizabeth Jacka's (1987 and 1988a) analyses of the 'Australian Film Commission genre' show how policy discourse was inscribed in forms through the repetition of certain aesthetic decisions. Through this repetition identifiable styles emerged (1988a: 28). For Dermody and Jacka the representation of Australianness in films produced between 1975 and 1980–81 was a product of this interaction between official and aesthetic discourse (1988a: 31).

In these examples funding is practised within an organised field of relationships and the effects on texts are complex and shifting. Funding guidelines and preferences are not simply written in policy, they are also made in the practice of assessing submissions. Funding decisions are always an interpretation of policy. What to fund is as much a product of what types of submissions are received as it is an enactment of fixed policy. Deterministic accounts of patronage assume that once guidelines are written that is the end of the story. The approach taken here sees guidelines as one part of the practice of patronage. While guidelines shape the ways in which community arts projects are proposed, the request for funds is often marked by processes of informal negotiation between applicants and CAB staff. It is here that projects are adapted to meet various criteria and also that guidelines are stretched to accommodate interesting projects. Guidelines are what their name implies, a set of loose boundaries within which patronage is practised.

In this discussion of projects the intention is to investigate how they articulate certain notions about community arts and how these notions both repeat and remake various institutional discourses. Patronage is a relationship where money and meaning circulate and projects have to be considered as one part of the community arts complex: an assemblage of institutions, practices, discourses and strategies which involves the formation of policy, the disbursement of funds, production of various cultural forms, promotion and distribution. The first point to acknowledge about projects is that while they may be constituted in relationship to the funding body, their history after this is a product of very different conditions and concerns, according to how and where they are carried out.

Some models for reading projects

Having located projects' place in the community arts complex, the next step is to establish how to read them. The very category 'project' presents immediate problems because it implies not just an artefact but its context, its conditions of production and circulation. This ambiguity signals other standards and languages of appreciation. These are 'projects' rather than art, in much the same way as migrant writing is 'writing' not literature (Gunew, 1983). The popularity of this term is an indicator of how much actual works or objects are peripheral to the discourses of value that circulate in the community arts field. It is also an indicator of how much community arts is defined as a cultural practice rather than as a distinctive form.

Two examples provide interesting models of how to read projects without reducing them to context (as do so many of the *Caper* papers) or, conversely, fetishising the texts. Eric Michaels' (1987a) discussion of the work of the Walpiri Media Association is both a documentation of a significant cultural activity and an analysis of how the videos produced successfully negotiated and expressed the social relationships and laws of the Yuendumu community. While Michaels offers a reading of several videos he places his interpretations within a wider description of the origins and work of the media association and its relationship to the cultural practices of the Walpiri. The effect of this method is to establish not only what these video tapes mean to the Walpiri but *how* they mean. To explore, from the inside, the relationship between video production and the cultural reproduction and survival of an Aboriginal community.

In her review of a community photography project, Anne-Marie Willis (1984) uses a similar approach. She traces the history of this project and reads the images as both a reflection and a construction of Caulfield, Melbourne, where they were produced. The aesthetic devices employed are read as a product of the interaction between the cultural practices privileged, amateur photography, and the discourses of community work which encourage positive, accessible representations.

Where these two examples differ is in the question of attributing value to these projects. While they use similar methods of documentation, they diverge when it comes to deciding how to assess this work as good or bad. While Willis is cautiously uneasy about what she identifies as an 'aesthetic conservatism' (1984: 6) ultimately she abandons a position of judgement with recourse to what is seen as the inherent worthiness of community arts projects. Her final sentence reflects this: 'such photographs work in direct and simple ways to establish senses of continuity and belonging to a community' (1984: 7). In this review 'worthiness' and 'community' provide an escape from judgement. They are invoked to place the project beyond criticism. Willis perpetuates an avoidance of critical discussion of community arts projects.

What Michaels proposes is assessment which neither uncritically overvalues nor dismisses out of hand projects which are produced outside of traditional art institutions and which explicitly challenge hegemonic discourses of value. The recourse in mainstream art criticism to judgements based either on the talent of the artist or on the placement of the text in a particular formal tradition become meaningless when assessing texts with other origins, audiences and distribution. Instead, it is crucial to establish value in terms that recognise who community arts projects are for and how they are carried out. This does not mean patronising acceptance or refusal to judge. When Michaels refers to 'alien readings of the text' he means readings which either appropriate these forms or impose standards that are foreign and irrelevant to the cultures producing them. While there is no such thing as a correct reading, assessments about whether a project is good or bad must begin from a recognition of how these values are first of all established within the original constituency. Questions of value cannot be abandoned with an uncritical reliance on notions about the implicit wholesomeness of arts in the community, but nor can they be be posed in terms which refuse to recognise what is distinctive about community arts. Michaels (1987b) argues that critical analysis should be expanded in order to consider:

> evidence of the conditions of making, transmitting and viewing, and to acknowledge that texts come into existence, and must be described, in terms of the social relations between institutionally situated audiences and producers, and that meanings arise in these relationships between text and context in ways that require a precise description in each case. (Michaels, 1987b: 60)

Three community visual arts projects funded by the CAB (though other sources were also involved) have been selected for discussion: *House About Wollongong* (1984–85), a history of Wollongong through its houses; *Mothers' Memories Others' Memories* (1979–81), a project exploring the lives of women through their domestic creativity; and *Land of Promises* (1983), a series of posters about the experience of migration.

All these projects were produced after 1979 and were funded by the CAB rather than the CAC. This historical context means that they have to be considered as part of the shift in policy from disadvantage to difference that began in the early 1980s. There is no intention to argue that they are representative. They have been selected as case studies rather than as definitive examples of community arts. Their selection, however, was not random. Each of these projects has a reputation, mostly as a result of the CAB's decision to promote it as exemplary. These projects have been taken up by the funding body in different ways and have been used to define and defend community arts; they have been given the official nod of approval.

Rather than consider each of the projects in turn it is more useful to review them thematically. Thematic analysis facilitates an investigation of community arts projects in terms of their common aesthetics. While each of the projects selected employs a different visual form and there are variations in the cultural practices used to produce them, their discourses are remarkably similar. One of the main arguments underpinning this discussion of projects is that their similarities reflect what has been described as an aesthetics of affirmation (Kirby, 1982).

Descriptions of community arts as affirming the cultures of various disenfranchised groups are common (see Kelly, 1984; Connell, 1983; Hull, 1983; Greenwood, 1983). Affirmation was justified on the grounds that exclusion and domination denied positive identities to the marginal. In community arts a politics of representation meant the production of positive images of others, it meant giving the power to represent to those who were underrepresented or negatively represented in public culture. While the possibilities and limitations of this approach will be explored throughout the rest of this chapter, its political implications cannot be denied. In seeking to recognise diversity rather than fill in a cultural lack community arts policy in the 1980s began from a position of respect for divergent values. It encouraged the development of cultural practices that acknowledged difference and that allowed the silenced and marginalised a space in which to express their experience and culture.

The diversity of these projects cannot be denied but they all, in different ways, affirm the contexts in which they were carried out. *Mothers' Memories* and *Land of Promises* were participatory projects aimed at giving marginal groups the opportunity to speak. Their aesthetics of affirmation privileged notions of the self-esteem of participants. Rescuing damaged identity was an often-mentioned project intention. In this process affirmation and opposition were interconnected discursive themes. Voices from the margins are always produced in relation to hegemonic voices. In *Mothers' Memories* and *Land of Promises* many of the images bear witness to women's and migrants' experience of loss, suffering and exclusion and to their endurance, resistance and community. This art becomes both a recognition of oppression and a celebration of collective identity. In this way the commitment to affirm was also, at the same time, a confrontation of marginality.

In contrast, *House About Wollongong* involved no community participation beyond consent to having one's house photographed. The final exhibition included only the occasional image of a person. For a community arts project this absence of smiling faces, of an ever-present populism, is a significant part of its fascination. Yet affirmation is still the dominant effect. In tracing the immense variety of owner-built housing styles and decoration in Wollongong this project celebrates domestic architecture in a working class region. It recognises and records different cultural practices and pleasures around that central icon of the Australian dream, the house.

Sandy Kirby defines the art of affirmation as 'an art that returns to its source, that draws on the knowledge, skill and experience of the community as a whole' (1982: 39). This representation of community as the source of authenticity is another central and problematic element in the aesthetics of community arts. Each of these projects, in different ways, constructs community; it is not something there waiting to be uncovered. The process of establishing a group willing to participate means that community arts projects often depend on establishing constituencies, on generating a sense of common interest through the evolution of the project. Assumptions about audience also involve the recognition of other discourses of value and the production of texts that explicitly address specific social groups, that constitute different valuing communities.

Three themes have been identified in the aesthetics of affirmation: the voice of experience, the recognition of informal creativity, and the production of a discourse on art and community. Each shall be considered in turn. Embedded in these themes are the oppositions that have been crucial in policy formation. In the history of these projects there was a continual tension between the idea of 'standards' and the commitment to participation and access, between notions of cultural difference versus cultural disadvantage and between the boundaries which separate art from non-art.

The voice of experience

Mothers' Memories Others' Memories (MM) and *Land of Promises* (LOP) take as their respective subjects women and migrants—two groups who have increasingly come to signify the representative oppressed (Gunew, 1985a: 148). In this section these projects will be the focus because they both rely on personal testimony as the dominant mode of address. As Sneja Gunew (1985a) argues, the marginal voices of women and migrants are most often provided with the authority to speak using the first person. Lived experience becomes their discursive 'truth'.

Mothers' Memories was a project spanning two and a half years. In 1979 artist Vivienne Binns received a small grant from the Visual Arts Board to work as an artist-in-residence in the General Studies Department of the University of New South Wales. The success of this initial stage led to a grant of $9300 from the CAB in 1979–80 and to further grants in 1980–81 from the CAB and the Crafts Board to transfer the project to Blacktown where Binns worked as an artist-in-community (Hull, 1981a). Through a process of group discussion and sharing of photos, stories and experiences Binns encouraged participants to express their ideas about mothers and mothering through some sort of creative display. The results are difficult to categorise. Formal diversity is perhaps the most striking element of *Mothers' Memories*. However, there are recurring devices. Most of the displays rely heavily on the use of family snapshots. Some are organised into albums, while others are displayed on panels with thematic organisation and accompanying text. Whatever their arrangement, photos feature as the archetypal document of memory.

According to Hull (*Interview*, 11-9-87) *Mothers' Memories* was pro moted by the CAB as an example of the exciting possibilities for community arts practice to establish new methods and sites for artists' work. This valorisation of the project was symptomatic of the shift in the discourse on practice away from the reform of informal creativity towards new relationships between artists and communities.

Land of Promises was also an artist-in-community project. In 1982–83 Andrew and Eugenia Hill were successful in getting grants from the CAB and the Visual Arts Board to work with migrants documenting their experiences of post–World War Two migration and resettlement. Based at the Community Media Association in Adelaide, this project also involved participation: migrants were to be both the subjects and objects of *Land of Promises*. Like *Mothers' Memories* the idea for the project did not spring spontaneously from the community but came from artists who had to construct constituencies. The first stage of *Land of Promises* involved finding migrants who were interested in participating.

The parallels with *Mothers' Memories* continue. In *Land of Promises*, photos, letters, passports and naturalisation documents were used as source material and the process of group discussion, trust and exchange was a central part of the creative practice (LOP, Project Booklet, 1983: 5–6). There is, however, one point of significant difference. *Land of Promises* used one form only, issue-based photo silkscreen prints. In contrast to *Mothers' Memories* with its formal diversity and open-endedness, *Land of Promises* was formally unified, with similar aesthetic devices repeated in each poster. Where *Mothers' Memories* refused to impose standards or demand artistic competence in participants, *Land of Promises* insisted that amateurs measure up with the production of acceptably aesthetic posters. These variations imply very different strategies on the part of the artists-in-community. The tension between access and excellence was resolved in different ways.

Land of Promises was also considered a model project by the CAB which held it up as exemplary in the 1982–83 Annual Report (AC, AR,

1982–83: 43). It toured extensively after its completion and was used as evidence of the CAB's partial break with the ethnic arts straight-jacket. Projects which documented migrant experience were identified as more progressive than those which supported folkloric fun and diversity because they addressed Anglo–Saxon cultural hegemony rather than closed ethnic communities. This shift from ethnic diversity to migrant experience was significant. In constructing the project in this way, ethnic culture as something different and quaint was replaced with the migrant as excluded, suffering and angry. Marginality is a shifting discourse, with the margins framed in different ways.

The stated intention of both these projects was to use cultural practice as a mechanism for conferring identity. The granting of money gave these others a voice. However, women and migrants had already been produced by the CAB: official policy, research into their needs, and special programs had all represented them. What a reading of projects has to consider is how women and migrants produce themselves.

Both these projects were valorised for their authenticity but, like all representations, images of 'experience' depend on the mobilisation of conventions. The conventions through which women and migrants speak themselves are similar, they are autobiographical. Their visual imagery is about the revelation of self through stories, oral history, personal documents, memorabilia. The appeals to authenticity and truth come from this confessional mode, this exposure of the private experience made public. Nowhere is this more evident than in the repeated use of the snapshot. The family album was raided to both reclaim and reconstruct migrant and female social history.

Most of the displays in *Mothers' Memories* present a positive celebration of women's domestic lives, knowledges and identities. Women's different culture is affirmed through their participation and dominance in the domestic sphere. By re-framing the family album these displays become acts of recovery that place women in the centre. Men—fathers, husbands and brothers—are pushed to the sidelines, their authority weakened. In many of the panels the arrangement is chronological. Fragments of lives are neatly organised into biographical narratives. The images are ordered to reinforce the biological inevitability of growing up: the baby, the child, the young woman. The text under the photos is explanatory, identifying primary relationships. Despite the mystery surrounding the subjects the celebratory display of images is comfortably familiar. The conventions of the snapshot reassure, family relations are represented in a continuum of warmth, identification and support (Moore, 1988: 142).

Despite the overwhelming emphasis on women's domestic subculture and sisterhood a few of the diplays in *Mothers' Memories* attempt to deconstruct rather than valorise women's position in the family. In two panels titled 'Memories or Misery' and 'The Holey Family' text and organisation undermine the snapshot's smiling faces. These panels interrogate the overwhelming effect of nostalgia so easily mobilised when the family album is dragged out. Not only do they resist a narrative structure but they also make problematic the family and women's contradictory position in it. Gender relations are reflected on; power, domination and violence are alluded to. These displays facilitate critique rather than celebration. The family here is a profoundly ambivalent attachment, something loathed and rejected but also longed for.

There is a tension in *Mothers' Memories* between analysis and celebration and this is connected to the central use of the snapshot. In many panels the conventions of the snapshot are unexamined. The sense in which photos are always fragments, always images of past time means that the panels in this project represent not so much a life as bits of lives—specifically those bits captured on the family Kodak. Susan Sontag's (1977) observations are confirmed: the family photo is a document of happy moments. But the effect of assemblage is also in the absences, the bits of family life that are unrecorded—the fights, the tensions, the tragedies, the 'domestics'. They are censored but their presence remains. The fascination with the material left out intensifies (Coward, 1984: 51).

In many panels assembling biographies out of snapshots reinforces the ideological effects of these images of family. However liberating the production process may have been in *Mothers' Memories*, these panels tell a different story. Mothers are represented in terms little different from advertising's excesses: gratitude, adoration, celebration. The happy haven is signified through a series of milestones: children, the first home, weddings, the new car, and at the heart of it all the mother. This highlights a fundamental dilemma in the search for 'positive' representations of women, a search which always takes place in relationship to other available discourses on women. In seeking to 'correct' the exclusion of women in public culture celebratory strategies naively revalue women's domestic culture as the source of their special and essential difference.

Beyond the particular limitations and possibilities of appropriating the snapshot its function in female cultural practice remains. Photos have always been used as a means for producing memory; this is a fundamental part of their power and pleasure. What *Mothers' Memories* reflects is how much the collection and preservation of family photos is a female activity. While the taking of photos may be dominated by men (although less so since the introduction of new, easy-to-use cameras pitched at the female market) the organisation and use of photos as icons of memory most often involves women. For Ros Coward women are 'guardians of the unwritten history of the family, women collect and keep photographs' (1984: 50; cf. Bell and Hawkes, 1988). *Mothers' Memories* speaks of women in a number of different ways. It is not simply that the project is about mothers, it is also that the project celebrates the gendered cultural practices that surround the way photos are used to reflect, to reminisce, to look. As an example of community arts practice, the project confirms the potential of cultural participation to legitimate and extend informal creative activities.

In *Land of Promises* the snapshot is also a recurring image, often used as the focal point for poster designs that place it within text and other images. There is a coherence in this project, achieved not only through repeated design techniques but also through the repeated themes of loss, memory, dislocation—this is the 'migrant experience'. Guiliana Otmarich's poster 'In your painful separation from loved ones and homeland we are near in thought and heart' (plate 9.1) is organised around three familiar migrant documents: the archetypal photo of the family gazing over the rails of a boat, the telegram in Italian and the goodbye inscription handwritten in the corner. The photo is ambiguous, are they leaving or arriving? Ultimately it is irrelevant; they are in transit, dislocated, neither here nor there. The migrant self is represented as fragmented, in a constant state of retrospective searching.

In other posters in *Land of Promises* the official rituals of migration are the focus. Eugenia Hill's posters about her parents, 'Despatch to GMH' and 'Bonegilla Training Centre' (plate 9.2), play with the use of the stamp that determines futures. George Lewkowicz's 'Australian Made' appropriates the image of the naturalisation ceremony, the official bestowal of an identity handed down from above. These posters echo Gunew's (1985a) equation of the migrant as child. The migrants' shift in language and culture places them in the position of the child, forced to renegotiate an entry into the social.

In all these posters, the question of what it is to be 'Australian' is repeatedly posed. In most instances migrant is represented as other, as outside, as not Australian. Occasionally there is an attempt to break in, to claim a place inside the nation rather than on its fringes. This involves more than representations of Australia as multicultured, more than appeals to pluralism. In Angelos Aslanidis' poster 'I helped build Australia' (not reproduced) there is a demand for recognition of migrant workers' contribution to national development. This assertion, of the crucial value of migrant labour, confronts the invisibility of the migrant and challenges the ideology of the host country as a benevolent refuge.

The straightforward declaration of Aslanidis' poster is quite different from the text used in many of Andrew Hill's posters. Hill's text is angry and accusatory. For example: 'we have been political slaves' and 'how contemptuously we have been treated'. Despite the attempt at slogans, at a didactic signalling of politics with a capital 'P', these posters speak in the voice of moral outrage, the voice of the migrant as victim, sacrificed for profits and the nation. The invocation of 'we' implies 'you' the spectator. These posters position the spectator as guilty, as complicit in the exploitation of migrants. The effect is to either immobilise the spectator with remorse or spur her on to political

Plate 9.1 'In your painful separation from loved ones and homeland we are near in heart.' Artist: Guiliana Otmarich, colour silkscreen poster, *Land of Promises*, 1983.

Plate 9.2 'Bonegilla Training Centre.' Artist: Eugenia Hill, colour
silkscreen poster, *Land of Promises*, 1983.

action driven by the desire for penance and redemption (Adams, 1989:
42).

Land of Promises generates a discourse on politics not only through
the use of didactic text but also through the deliberate choice of the
screenprint. The connotations of the poster as quick to produce,
designed for the street rather than the gallery and savage in its message
cannot be shaken. The authority for migrants to speak is granted not
through art, not through the display of ethnic traditions, but through
the poster which frames migrant experience as an 'issue'.

The similarities between this project and *Mothers' Memories* are most
evident in their conventionalised expressions of 'experience'. And what
they reveal is the contradictions embedded in the translation of experience into texts. On the one hand the material presented is marked by
the potency of people speaking for themselves—on the other hand it
cannot escape reinforcing the idea of women and migrants as the loci
of experience, as reducible to essences. One of the reasons for this
paradox is the overwhelming reliance on icons of remembering. A
recurring dilemma in *Land of Promises* and *Mothers' Memories* is the
tension between a past–present relation that is nostalgic, that poses
some kind of ideal and lost period, and another that is more politicised,
that places individual testimony and private memory in a broader social
context. Are women and migrants trapped in the past? Does the

insistence on memory, on looking back, on the personal, only work to reinforce notions of fragmented subjectivities and the inability to find a legitimate place in the present? These questions remain. While some displays and posters connect private memories to public events and explore the interaction between public and private, others speak largely to themselves. Here the private is presented in a way that positions the viewer as voyeur and little else, as an uncomfortable witness to grief or confession. These projects both refuse and reiterate marginality.

Gunew's (1983: 18) description of migrant writing as a process of 'writing ourselves into being' is applicable here. *Land of Promises* and *Mothers' Memories* challenge the assumption that migrants and women can only be spoken for or spoken about; the authority of dominant representations is called into question when 'others' portray themselves. These portrayals are not only a series of individual stories. The cumulative effect of these projects is of commonality, of shared experience. While the earliest policies of community arts waxed lyrical about the therapeutic effects of creativity for the 'disadvantaged', what is revealed here is how cultural practice and collaboration can be a process of consciousness-raising rather than personal development. Participation can produce an awareness of experience as a collective phenomenon and this is the significance of these texts. They are projects which reflect the diversity and complexity of migrant and female experience through the detail of individual icons and narratives. But, at the same time, the similarity in stories moves these artefacts from the personal to the political with the representation of others speaking together.

The final point about the discourse on experience is the way in which 'authenticity' is signalled. The use of icons from material culture implies an unmediated presentation of the truth of what it means to be migrant or female. But these icons never stand alone. They are arranged, ordered, used as elements in a design, and in this process of organisation their meanings are transformed. In some of the displays in *Mothers' Memories* arrangement is minimal, the raw materials of biography remaining without a strong structure. The effect is an overwhelming individualism, personal details and documents signifying character, personality and the endless variations of humanity. In *Land of Promises* this tendency is curtailed, to a certain extent, by the poster form which insists on a visual economy. Here the effects of design, the interplay between words and images, produce a more critical edge; lives are reflected on. There is more evidence of analysis and scrutiny; migrant experience is about personal and structural exclusion. A little formalism goes a long way.

Recognising informal creativity: *House About Wollongong*

The shift to *House About Wollongong* is a shift from community arts

Plate 9.3 50 Barina St, Lake Heights. Photographer: Ruth Waller, *House About Wollongong*, 1985.

as an expression of experience to community arts as a mechanism for recording different cultural practices. In this shift images of houses are the focus, rather than images of people. The fascination with this project is not simply a product of its novelty value; like *Land of Promises* and *Mothers' Memories* this project affirms, but it does so using different visual conventions and different production techniques. The organisation of *House About Wollongong* did not involve 'community participation'. The artist, Ruth Waller, worked largely alone photographing Wollongong houses and producing an exhibition. A practice similar to much commissioned photographic work, but with very different results. The evolution of the project did not depend on many of the seemingly essential principles of community arts. It was a not a product of collaborative work. Its promotion and organisation enshrined Waller as an artist-in-residence, rather than a community artist. Indeed the end results were presented to the public at a bastion of regional official culture, Wollongong City Gallery.

The original brief for the project was to develop a residential survey of Wollongong documenting housing styles around three related themes: historical changes, sociological/demographic patterns and pop-

Plate 9.4 44 Kurraba Rd, Woonona. Photographer: Ruth Waller, *House About Wollongong*, 1985.

ular creativity. The final exhibition realised these objectives, a photo-documentary study of Wollongong houses in all their variety. Themat-ically arranged on panels were images of houses, gates and gardens with text ranging from historical information to quotes from occupants. The effect was of two intersecting discourses: Wollongong as place, suburb, community, and the house as a site of creative expression and pleasure. In using the house to construct a social history of Wollongong representations of locality jostled with the celebration of cultural dif-ference. For Wollongong, the meaning of place is inextricably bound up with references to the steel mill and the working class labour that keeps it running and lives on its fringes.

The exclusive use of exterior shots in *House About Wollongong* is crucial in establishing the distinction between houses and homes. In this project the domestic is not constituted using images of interiors which invoke the home as haven and refuge. Instead, the house is presented as viewed from the street. Photos documenting facades, well-weeded gardens, topiary, owner-built fountains and fresh paint all reveal the public face of the domestic (see plate 9.3). The extent of the creativity invested in these facades signifies the ambiguity of 'the front'. While the interior and back may be out of bounds, the facade of the house is both private and public. It may function as the beginning of the boundary around interior domestic life but, in these images, it is also part of a public display, an important site for owners' creative expressions.

Apart from images of exteriors many panels include photos of architectural or garden detail. These record an immense variety of techniques and themes and allow for a focus on minutiae rather than on facades. In the photos of detail two distinct creative 'styles' are recorded: householders' craft skills and popular culture displays. Plate 9.4 records the carpentry skills of an owner–builder. These decorative flourishes are generally features of houses built in the immediate post–World War Two period, documenting a time when shortages of labour and materials led many people to build their own houses. In these images historical and cultural meanings are interwoven. They record an era when 'do it yourself' was encouraged, before the days of mass-produced project homes and standardised designs. They also signify a pleasure and pride in displaying craft skills, in exploring their imaginative design possibilities around the house, outside the restrictions of the workplace.

In this period building your own house was not a sign of reckless eccentricity or counter-cultural deviance, as it often is today. It was often the only way of acquiring a dwelling and it provided immense possibilities for experimentation and expression. The economic necessity of owner-building encouraged creativity and explicitly challenged a dependence on experts or professionals. As the images in *House About Wollongong* show, it was also a period when definitions of 'correct design' were extremely loose, far less controlled than today with housing companies selling three or four variations on a standard layout. Individual touches or flourishes were celebrated as evidence of creative freedom: 'we built it ourselves'.

The skills recorded here are also gendered. Carpentry, welding and bricklaying all imply men at work/leisure. The outside of the house means male territory, the place where their creativity can be legitimately expressed. In contrast *Mothers' Memories* reflects the appropriation of artefacts like embroidery, family albums and fabrics to construct the domestic as female and interior.

What unites all the different elements of *House About Wollongong*—studies of house facades, architectural details, quotations and information—is the enthusiasm they display for the distinctive cultural practices that construct the house in working class suburbs. This project documents one of the central sites of everyday life and it records the richness and imagination that is class culture at work. This is not a project about lack and cultural desolation. Such assumptions are repeatedly challenged by a celebratory design committed to recording diversity, imagination and pleasure in the working class house on display.

The principal objectives behind *House About Wollongong* were documentation and affirmation and this is evident in the straightforward presentation. There is no rhetoric here about 'ordinary people', no attempt to patronise or parody. The basic need for shelter and how this need is met in Wollongong are the key reference points in the exhibition essays and the thematic organisation of the panels.

Intentions do not, however, control meaning. While *House About Wollongong* explicitly refused to apply categories such as taste and kitsch, it still could not escape dominant discourses of value. Exhibition in a prestigious regional gallery led to a series of reviews which evaluated the project from a position of superiority. Mainstream critics could discern 'sophistication and 'taste' and it certainly was not evident in Wollongong:

> This collection of photos shows us the extraordinary measures people have taken to decorate their little suburban boxes. Faces and toadstools are carved out of hedges, rococo environments created in courtyards, and models of famous landmarks, such as the harbour bridge, constructed in front yards. Waller's snapshots, quite apart from their sociological and community art dimensions, are a treasure trove of kitsch. They show householders striving to dress up a depressing environment in the most flamboyant style. (McDonald, 1985: 16)

The categorisation of this work as kitsch meant a refusal to read it in the terms in which the project was conceived and developed. The reviews insisted on evaluating *House About Wollongong* in a negative relation to 'art'. They invoked a discourse of taste which is, as Bourdieu (1986) has shown, always a discourse of power. Cultural difference was reconstituted as cultural deprivation as the critics searched for explanations for such unabashed 'vulgarity'.

While these reviews accept that popular representations of the postwar suburbs as monotonous cultural wastelands are incorrect, especially in the face of such diverse creativity, they still have to place this creativity within a hierarchy. In placing it at the bottom, in the realm of 'bad taste', or no taste, they are able to acknowledge informal creativity and dismiss it in the same breath. It becomes a product of deprivation, of 'not knowing any better', of making the best out of 'depressing environments'. It has value for the producers because it expresses identity and pride in home ownership, but its value in the realm of aesthetics and art is as quaint novelties. From the critics' position *House About Wollongong* affirms high culture and good taste.

The critical responses to *House About Wollongong* are a case study in how the cultural preferences and practices of different classes are valued. Drawing on Bourdieu's sociology of culture, Frow argues that distinctions between good and bad taste, between vulgar and sophisticated, between legitimate and illegitimate are evidence of the way in which class distinctions are transposed onto the apparently autonomous language of aesthetics (1987: 60). The fact of cultural difference is not the issue. Rather, it is the discourses of value which organise these differences hierarchically and establish certain cultural preferences as hegemonic. Value is always a relational category.

However, exposing definitions of taste as class-based does not automatically resolve the question of how to read working class cultural practice. The search for other standards of value has produced several related strategies. One is to reverse the scales, to read middle class taste as barren, restrained and aesthetically boring by placing it in a negative relation to the vitality, variety and self-confidence of the working class. This is Fiske, Hodge and Turner's approach (1987: 35). They extend this analysis by arguing that in bad taste's distinctively working class inflection there is resistance, specifically an opposition to middle class definitions of style. This is a well-worn path in much of cultural studies: the discovery and celebration of working class difference. It depends on a class-conscious populism that represents the working class in a constant state of warm, direct and resistant cultural practice.

Again Frow's (1987) critique of Bourdieu (1984) provides a way beyond this impasse. Although Bourdieu denounces populism, according to Frow his discussion of a 'working class aesthetic' implies that it is more authentic than both mass culture and high culture, and that it is formally and functionally autonomous. For Frow the implication of Bourdieu's argument is that the working class stand in a more 'natural', or less mediated, relation to experience. To Frow this claim can only be read as 'romantic obfuscation' (1987: 64). The most important point in this critique is Frow's insistence on the ideological and political *ambiguity* of popular cultural forms:

> It is the rigidity with which Bourdieu opposes two formally and functionally autonomous aesthetic universes that constitutes the problem. The immediate correlation of these aesthetic universes with social classes means that cultural forms are understood as non-contradictory expressive unities rather than as sites of political tension. (Frow, 1987: 66)

Frow's analysis is crucial for an evaluation of *House About Wollongong*. While the intentions behind this project were to affirm working class housing styles and practices, the documentation of different cultural expressions always takes place in relation to dominant discourses of value. The tensions this project generated about art are reflected not only in the reviews but also in the distribution strategies. The visual organisation and exhibition of this project inevitably aestheticise the house. But this aestheticisation is never complete. The presentation to the public in the form of an exhibition at Wollongong City Gallery challenged ideas about what is acceptable content for art galleries. It also attracted a new audience to the gallery, an audience formed by the content of the project: working class home owners in

Wollongong (Waller, 1985: 3). These are the progressive effects of this project. However, while *House About Wollongong* sought to extend meanings for culture and to recognise the creativity of everyday practices the counter attack from the critics in the form of descriptions about 'colourful kitsch' reveal the extent to which art will be defended.

Art and community

Each of these projects produces meanings for community arts within their specific field of production, distribution and reception. What is common in these meanings is a discourse of affirmation that is constituted through the recognition of different cultural practices, forms and producers. It is this process of recognition, of signalling and celebrating other sources of creativity that is significant because it shows how these projects emerge always in relation to other available discourses of art and community. The intention in this section is to investigate how these projects place these categories together and how, in the process, new meanings are produced for them.

Land of Promises, *Mothers' Memories* and *House About Wollongong* were all projects employing professional artists. They are symptomatic of the period in policy formation from 1980 on that saw community arts practice redefined as a particular way of artists working in and for communities. Yet the relationship of the artist to the community is different in each case. *Land of Promises* and *Mothers' Memories* were projects conceived by artists who wrote the original submissions, sought out a base to work from and had to attract participants through local networks and promotion of the project. These were artists committed to working 'in the community', committed to offering their skills as a resource for marginal groups:

> I am a visual artist who has opted to work for the most part in community situations rather than in isolation in a studio producing work for sale or inclusion in an art gallery . . . I am primarily interested in breaking down the distinction between the art of artists and art institutions on one hand and the art expression of people in general on the other. (Binns, no date: 1)

For Viv Binns and Andrew and Eugenia Hill community practice meant an opportunity to challenge those ideologies of the artist that valorise creative isolation and the production of commodities for the art market. It also meant the opportunity to work with specific constituencies, to use art as a means for cultural and political expression:

> Why not, instead of producing works about immigrant people, set up a situation in which they could create their own unmediated art pieces. (Hill, 1985: 1)

Here the artists' discourse constructs community as the site of authentic cultural practice. Working with people is placed in opposition to working for individual fame. 'The community' becomes something to be served but the community is not clamouring for committed artists, it has to be created by the artist. Notions of 'authenticity' are somewhat undermined by the realisation that the formation of constituencies for community arts practice is also the work of the artist.

Land of Promises and *Mothers' Memories* were participatory projects. The artists worked with groups in a collective creative process involving weekly meetings to discuss and exchange ideas. However, the end results were exhibitions of individual works, a distribution strategy little different from most bourgeois art. In this contradiction between an oppositional method of production and a traditional method of distribution, the authority of the artist is constantly shifting.

In the production process of *Land of Promises* the Hills' claims about facilitating 'unmediated art' are a little romantic. The artist's authority is never completely dislodged by the collective process. Their power as experts or professionals working with amateurs remains but it is constituted differently. Collaborative practice does not simply place the artist in the role of tutor. While the artist may teach skills, she or he also encourages recognition of the skills participants already have (Binns, no date: 3). Discussions about individual works often involve many members of the group. In this way there is a self-conscious attempt to break patterns of deference and dependency in relations between artists and non-artists, to deskill the artist and recognise the skills of participants.

Even so the artist remains the mediator, and the extent to which this role has been played is evident in the visual uniformity of *Land of Promises*. In this project the artists have exerted an obvious aesthetic control. This is not simply a product of using one form, issue-based silkscreen prints, it is also a result of repeated design techniques which signal the organising presence of the community artist, far more so than *Mothers' Memories'* eclectic forms and varying levels of skill. The difference between a project which allows great diversity in texts and one in which there is an implicit set of aesthetic standards signals the variety of methods deployed by artists in collective practice.

The use of the exhibition as the major device for public display also has different effects. *Land of Promises* opened in the Adelaide Festival Centre Gallery, a major and prestigious public gallery. The placement of a community arts project in a space traditionally devoted to the display of high art was regarded as a significant achievement. Each participant was granted the status of artist:

> I never thought when I started this project that the work I produced would hang in a public gallery. I feel like an artist (LOP participant quoted in Hill, 1985: 15).

For the Hills the pride participants experienced seeing their work displayed as art was one of the most important effects of the projec (A. and E. Hill, *Interview*, 18-11-87). This display strategy has to be considered as part of an aesthetics of affirmation. However, recognition from the world of high art was only momentary. After its opening, *Land of Promises* was exhibited mainly in educational organisations, at conferences and in community centres. The posters circulated, not so much as art, but as evidence of the 'migrant experience', and in these distribution strategies the producers' experiential authority spoke louder than their artistic authority.

The Blacktown stage of *Mothers' Memories* was exhibited at Westpoint Plaza shopping centre, Blacktown. Previous stages of the project had been exhibited at the University of NSW and Watters Gallery, Sydney. The use of the central foyer of a shopping centre to display a community arts exhibition about women, mothers and domestic creativity addressed women consumers as a captive audience. In this attempt at de-institutionalisation, the art was transported to the audience rather than the reverse. This exhibition strategy did not privilege the cultural authority of the producers, if anything it undermined it. With panels hung around the escalators, the effect was of a display of women's hobby or craft work rather than of individual artists.

The status of the artists who organised these projects also warrants scrutiny. It is not completely demolished by collaborative processes, rather it is reconstituted as 'community artist'. There is a tendency to refer to community arts projects by the name of the organising artist, for example: 'Viv Binns' *Mothers' Memories* Project'. The construction of a reputation for a project often depends on the invocation of the artist's name. That is what survives over time. The names of participants fade into oblivion. *House About Wollongong* was explicitly the work of Ruth Waller, the exhibition was promoted as the work of an artist. The houses photographed were identified by address and name of the occupants when this was available but it was Waller's role as photographer and designer that was privileged. The effect is a star system of community artists who are regarded as producing good work, in much the same way as appears in other Boards of the Australia Council. In some instances professional artists who opt to work in the community are regarded as jeopardising their reputations but the evidence here is of artists who move with ease from community contexts to individual production.

Just as art is interrogated by these projects so too is the idea of community. Each in different ways constructs representations of community and central to this process is the establishment of boundaries. The discourses of community constituted here imply both similarity and difference. In *Land of Promises* and *Mothers' Memories* it is the similar experiences of migrants and of women that signifies commonality, but this shared experience is also what distinguishes them as different, as 'other'. What is important about these projects is the way in which the expression of community provides a moment where 'others' become the centre, where margins are refused. Common interest and experience are the privileged voices.

In contrast, it is common locality rather than common experience that underpins the expression of community in *House About Wollongong*. However, while community is often given geographical meanings, in this project it is possible to see the problems inherent in equating community with place. In *House About Wollongong* a different 'regional identity' is established. Wollongong is represented through photos of houses, and in these images there is a challenge to the idea of the 'steel city', to the tendency to construct Wollongong as a site of steel mills, grime and male manual labour. The domestic architecture of Wollongong represents it as a place where people *live* as well as work.

Despite this domestic rather than occupational meaning for locality, 'community' remains a fairly unstable category in this project. The houses reflect both commonality and difference. There are the common class practices and preferences that are expressed in the working class suburb and which distinguish it from other suburbs. But there are also the differences between migrant and Anglo–Saxon housing styles, between owner-built and developer-built. This acknowledgement of internal differences undermines a discourse of community. While Wollongong may be unlike other suburbs it is also heterogeneous. Like most other regions 'community' is cut across with ethnic, gender and economic divisions. The meanings of Wollongong as place are multiple and contradictory. Grouping them together under the title of community depends on the invocation of an imaginary unity and denies the different relationships to place that are evident in *House About Wollongong*.

However, what remains so important about these varied invocations of community is how they place the idea of 'nation' at risk. In each of these projects cultural identity and expression emerge from specific contexts which ideologies of Australianness often depend on suppressing. The voice of women confronts the mateship ethos, migrants refuse the imposition of Anglo–Saxon cultural hegemony and a working class suburb exposes the illusion of the great outback, the frontier landscape. 'Australia' disintegrates.

Conclusion

These projects must be read as evidence of the shift in the discourses of community arts from cultural disadvantage to cultural difference. Their use of an aesthetics of affirmation is crucial to this shift. It refuses lack and legitimates other cultural producers and expressions. None of these projects is based on the assumption that Culture needs to be democratised, nor do they interpret access as improved methods for distributing high culture. Here access means the provision of resources and support to groups less able to express and maintain their cultural identity and preferences. Like policy, projects emerge in relation to dominant discourses of art but the meanings they produce for community arts are a product of their specific conditions of production and circulation. In seeking to acknowledge the identity and experience of marginalised groups these projects establish other standards of value. While these standards reiterate the themes of policy they also reveal complexity and contradiction. In the world of projects and local cultural practice the straightforward objectives of policy become far more complicated.

While policy establishes the centrality of valuing participation above products, each of these projects gives this objective a different meaning. In *Land of Promises* the aesthetic regulation and guidance of the Hills reflected the desire to exhibit the posters in a bastion of high culture. Here 'standards' were not to be sacrificed for participation. In *House About Wollongong* there was no 'community involvement'; instead an artist was employed to represent Wollongong back to itself. In all projects artists were a resource for marginalised constituencies but their skills were deployed differently. While Viv Binns describes herself as a community worker, using culture to organise women, Ruth Waller is the roving ethnographer and social historian exploring and representing an 'other' world. However, beyond these variations and contradictions an aesthetics of affirmation remains; an aesthetic committed to the use of creativity and expression to contest discourses of domination.

10

Community arts: legacies and limitations

The idea of art as a moral and spiritual storehouse for the nation ran deep in the earliest demands for access and participation. It informed the first strategies of the Community Arts Program. In investigating the 'problem' of uneven involvement in the arts the CAC diagnosed numerous social groups and regions as 'culturally disadvantaged'. While the concept of disadvantage was central to Whitlam's social democratic reforms its political effects within the field of arts policy were fundamentally conservative. The invocation of disadvantage in the earliest policies of the CAC worked to affirm the hegemony of 'high' culture. Those who were unaware of the value of art were deprived and lacking and it was the duty of the 'more cultural' to share 'excellence' with the 'less cultural' (Rowse, 1989: 14).

While policy explored the causes of cultural disadvantage, projects tried to ameliorate it. Various strategies were developed. Attempts to introduce communities to art were driven by the desire to universalise upper-middle class taste, taking art where it had never been before. Related to this were strategies to convert participation into appreciation. Popular tastes warranted improvement because watching sophisticated culture was uplifting and illuminating. In contrast, making your own culture was fun but insignificant. Art was also given various social objectives: it could be put to work to integrate the marginalised or to improve the quality of life for captive communities in prisons, old people's homes and factories. It could also rescue children from straying down the path of mass culture, never to be seen again. In these shifting policy and project formations various meanings for community arts were prescribed. Community arts were a form of cultural therapy for those outside the elite valuing community that recognised excellence. They were mechanisms for improving the distribution and awareness of 'high' culture and they were also a convenient administrative solution for difficult-to-categorise forms and constituencies.

In the gradual shift from disadvantage to difference that took place during the early 1980s access and participation were reinterpreted. With the institutional security of Board status and an influx of new personnel an alternative 'theory' of community arts emerged. The organising function of culture was asserted with a vengeance. In the spaces between elite culture and mass culture there was the potential to foster cultural practices that raised consciousness, affirmed identity and generated 'community'.

As the burden of cultural disadvantage was shed arguments about the spiritual qualities of art became impossible to sustain. Several years of grants disbursement revealed cultural diversity not cultural lack. It was obvious that those who were uninterested in 'high' culture were busy enjoying a myriad of other cultures unrecognised by the narrow confines of institutionalised and formal definitions of art. Difference and plurality took over from disadvantage. Approaches to access and participation shifted from the deficiencies of individuals to the systematic exclusions performed by funding institutions. The dilemma was how to organise subsidy in ways that acknowledged plural cultures. How to establish funding and policy guidelines that would support cultural traditions and constituencies that had been neglected or considered unworthy of public assistance.

The 1986 Programs of Assistance booklet of the CAB answered these questions. In this crucial text the transition from disadvantage to difference was established through an explicit rejection of earlier meanings for community arts. Community arts was not recreation, cultural welfare or a tool for increasing arts appreciation. It was 'communities making their own art' (CAB, 1986: 10). This definition exposed the fundamental contradiction in demands for access and participation. When the Community Arts Program took up the rhetoric of cultural diversity the illusion of democratising 'high' culture was exposed. Culture was a site where social differences were expressed not elided. In this reorientation community arts practice became a resource for expressing 'other' identities and experiences.

Central to this discursive shift was an anthropological meaning for culture that privileged process over and above products. Culture was not a discrete set of artefacts or canons warranting special protection and subsidy. It was 'the way we pass on, experience and explore our values and views . . . communicate with each other, interact with our environment and organise ourselves' (CAB, 1986: 9). The rejection of 'art' in favour of 'culture' created new problems. This category was so inclusive almost everything could have been eligible for subsidy. Anthropological meanings for culture produced a profound indeterminancy. Because public patronage is about systems of inclusion and exclusion this problem had to be resolved. Rationales had to be established that justified who and what was eligible for support from the Community Arts Program. The solution to this policy problem was to amplify the social justifications for subsidy that had always underpinned the Community Arts Program; to identify a set of non-aesthetic objectives for cultural practice.

In the 1986 Programs of Assistance booklet non-aesthetic measures of value were articulated with a force that directly opposed the hegemony of excellence. The discourses of the Community Arts Program expressed a militantly materialist perspective on art. Value was ascribed, it was a product of the conditions in which culture was produced and circulated. Local criteria of evaluation were established that eschewed any semblance of general or universal systems of value. In focusing on the processes of cultural production, on who was involved and how, the program established funding guidelines that recognised that different groups produced different cultures and cultural values. Access now meant the ability of various constituencies to represent themselves, to express and maintain their own cultural traditions and tastes.

The establishment of social or non-aesthetic discourses of value was the Community Arts Program's greatest achievement. These discourses remain as a significant alternative to the idea of art as a minority of 'excellent' forms at the top of a universal cultural hierarchy. By the mid-1980s the practices of the Community Arts Program began from the assumption of plural cultures, and subsidy was structured around the democratic recognition of diversity rather than the maintenance of the 'best'.

From its inception the Community Arts Program was persistently attacked for abandoning the aesthetic, for valuing participation over and above standards. But it continued to gnaw away at the organising assumptions of arts policy, resisting a variety of external and internal threats ranging from the McKinsey report to hostile Boards. Gradually aspects of its approach to arts support spread throughout the rest of the Australia Council. From the early 1980s the Incentive Funds and funding categories like 'community theatre', 'community music', 'community writing' and 'artist-in-community' surfaced in other Boards. These funding programs were evidence of the organisational capacities of community arts workers to lobby for funding and to demand change in the most hostile and recalcitrant Boards. They were also evidence of the success of the CAB and the CCDU in forcing the rest of the Australia Council to extend meanings for culture and to accept some responsibility, albeit minor, for other constituencies, other forms and other mechanisms of subsidy. The influence of the program in providing multiple examples of how to make arts funding more equitable was significant.

Since the late 1980s the rhetoric of arts funding has undergone substantial transformation. As 'support for excellence' has been exposed as self-serving elitism, arts funding has come under increasing pressure to serve all citizens rather than just the upper middle class. Terms like cultural rights, cultural democracy and cultural diversity have gained ascendancy, displacing 'access and participation' as the signs of a commitment to equity and social justice. The Community Arts Program has been one of the major forces responsible for this long-overdue shift. Yet this remains largely unrecognised.

Beyond the Australia Council the impacts of the Community Arts Program are evident in the thousands of cultural organisations, workers and artefacts enabled by community arts subsidies. In seeking to address cultural practices outside of the elite and the mass the Community Arts Program has nurtured an important cultural field. Naming this field is difficult, for it is dispersed across a multitude of practices and organisational structures ranging from the migrant women's embroidery group to the local government Cultural Planner. While grants have supported a vast assortment of forms their common link is the value they place on the expressive and organising potential of culture. As cultural workers, community artists have developed a significant body of skills in facilitating collaborative cultural production. These skills are manifest in the capacity of many community arts projects to express plural authorship, to establish democratic mechanisms for skilled and unskilled creativities to work together, and to collapse the social distance between producers and consumers.

While listing the achievements of the Community Arts Program is an essential part of any overview, so too is an assessment of constraints and limitations. Although this history has argued that the Community Arts Program was an innovation in arts funding this claim was always situated within the context of the Australia Council. Compared to the operations of the Music Board or the Theatre Board or the Visual Arts Board the Community Arts Program in the 1980s was 'radical'. However, beyond the fairly suffocating confines of the Australia Council broader issues emerge about the structures of a democratic cultural policy. What does this history of the Community Arts Program yield in terms of effective strategies for the reform of arts funding? Three categories central to the formation of the Community Arts Program require scrutiny in this wider analysis: 'community', non-aesthetic measures of value, and cultural democracy.

Community

Throughout the history of the Community Arts Program 'community' was a deeply ambiguous category. It was simultaneously the source of the program's opposition and its marginality. This was a product of the multiple meanings for community. This category functioned as an empty classificatory space that could be filled in too many different ways by too many different interests. Fixing progressive meanings for community depended on how this category was posed in relation to nation. Invocations of 'community' were only useful when they worked to disrupt and fragment the dominance of the national.

In the formation of the Community Arts Program oppositional meanings for community were not established until the middle of the 1980s. Prior to the acquisition of Board status 'community' was a sign of inferiority. It was a residual category in a negative relationship to nation and excellence; it was unequivocally lesser. The institutional insecurity of the program in its first five years reinforced this marginality. The pressure to devolve the program to state and local governments that escalated after the demise of the Labor government was a sign that 'community' could not claim a legitimate place in the nation. While the campaign for devolution appeared as a straightforward administrative reform, it was also an ideological attack on the validity of the objectives of access and participation in the Australia Council. As the McKinsey report so succinctly put it, these objectives represented 'goal conflict', they could not be reconciled with the pursuit of excellence (McKinsey and Co., 1976, Section 1: 2). In this contest the nation was not reducible to a series of regions or various publics, it was an imaginary unity over and above the parochialism of the community.

It was the development of Incentive Funds, particularly the Art and Working Life program, that finally established an oppositional meaning for community. This program asserted the right of different cultural traditions to equal recognition and public funds. AWL contested the unity of the nation with the argument that the privileging of some cultures over others was evidence not of the essential superiority of certain forms, not of some single national audience for art, not of some 'natural' hierarchy of taste, but of power relations. In AWL projects the 'trade union community' was identified as the primary audience. The value of cultural activity for this constituency was justified in terms of the role of cultural practice in maintaining a collective identity. The significance of AWL was that this collective identity was built around the unity of class, workplace or union in explicit opposition to the imaginary unity of the nation.

The problem in unravelling the shifting relations between nation and community, as the story of the Community Arts Program has revealed, was that community meant too much. Geographic meanings of community as suburb, locality or region jostled with qualitative meanings of community as a particular set of social relations or expressions of diversity. Problems of distance were too easily confused with problems of difference.

Each of these inflections requires specific policy strategies. If the persistent problem of metropolitan dominance in arts support is to be confronted then questions of regionalism need to be posed with far greater force than they have been in the past. 'Community' is not much use in this process. It simply adds another confusing layer onto an already overloaded geographic inventory: regional, local, community? The other dilemma with geographic meanings for community is that they too easily fuel distributional models of reform. Access becomes a matter of better touring policies or televised opera. While these strategies are not to be dismissed they do not get to the heart of equity in arts funding.

Non-aesthetic measures of value

The crucial issue at stake in relation to equity is how culture is defined. As this study has argued, aesthetic discourses of value occupy a hegemonic position within the Australia Council. The rhetoric of excellence attributes high status to certain objects and practices and to the audiences that recognise and appreciate these. In this context the ongoing problem for the Community Arts Program was how to legitimate 'other' forms and constituencies. Aesthetic meanings for art were exclusive and restrictive, denying the diversity of creative activities and valuing communities. As already outlined the solution to this dilemma was to establish non-aesthetic measures of value, to place the social benefits of cultural participation above aesthetic outcomes.

These social objectives for cultural funding had ambiguous effects. They were based on a series of measures of community involvement in and support of the funding application. To a certain extent this confronted the problem of indeterminacy, although measuring 'community involvement' was difficult. Despite these problems these criteria did insist on evidence of the *relevance* of the project to its intended constituency. The question of relevance was closely connected to 'community'. The relationship between these categories was used to signal the specificity of most arts whose origins and impacts are firmly rooted within particular times and within particular cultures. In this way the discourses of the Community Arts Program avoided some of the excesses of a crude class populism that often characterised left definitions of community arts. The CAB and CCDU did not champion community arts as a victory for majority culture over minority culture. It was recognised that the popular may well be a series of minorities (Rowse, 1985b). The importance of the Community Arts Program's social measures of value was that they showed how it was possible to define precise and modest constituencies around various structures of difference. This is the key to the democratic potential of non-aesthetic measures of value. Their aim should not be to replace aesthetic discourses with class discourses, to substitute the hegemony of excellence with the hegemony of 'working class' or 'majority' culture. Rather, they should facilitate flexible forms of arts support that are able to recognise and respond to various constituencies and creativities and acknowledge local criteria for cultural value.

Related to social measures of value were a series of political criteria for the disbursement of subsidy. These were organised around the recovery of community. One of the recurring motifs in the history of the Community Arts Program was the importance of generating or reviving community; it was represented as both the pretext for and outcome of collaborative cultural production. 'Community' was posed in opposition to the power and alienation of the state, the mass media or whatever. In this configuration the explicit purpose of subsidy was to establish communities, to organise and address various marginal groups not as audiences, not as consumers, but as self-determining 'communities'.

This insistence on the political importance of community drew on the discourses of radical welfare. In arts policy these discourses were remade. In this context the centrality of community was only maintained through a negative evaluation of both 'high' and mass culture. The policies of the Community Arts Program were littered with repeated representations of mass culture consumers as stupified dupes. Apart from the contempt these evaluations revealed for mass forms and their audiences, they also displayed an irritatingly reactionary understanding of the processes of mass cultural consumption which, as much audience research reveals, are both active and various. This positioning of mass cultural consumption as bad and community cultural participation as good had the effect of valorising the special space of 'community' as the source of authenticity. Unable to deal with the profound dominance of mass culture in most people's cultural experience, community arts rejected it completely. This made the invocation of community backward looking. The refusal to acknowledge the deep interconnections between elite, mass and community-based cultural fields led to a continual defence of the purity of 'community' as a space that needed to be protected from contamination by both television and opera. The nostalgic effects of this have already been noted: projects which often spoke only to themselves; which were unable to make connections between community and other social forces; and which often represented difference as isolated social enclaves that were both exotic and worthy.

This critique, however, does not mean that mobilisations around 'community' are inherently nostalgic. As the example of the Gay and Lesbian Mardi Gras revealed community can function as a shifting and strategic alliance. The production of a gay and lesbian public through a cultural event, through the pleasures of a ritualised performance, was thoroughly political. The power of this celebration was not only in its extensive parodies of mass, high and gay culture it was also, as Michaels (1988b) argues, in its capacity to collapse boundaries, to establish a utopian moment when distinctions between us and them, gay and straight, became meaningless.

The final issue surrounding non-aesthetic measures of value is the status of art. While community arts sidestepped this with an emphasis on culture, 'art' would still not go away. The progressive intent of the refusal to impose general aesthetic standards cannot be denied but it left the Community Arts Program open to interminable attacks. Formal diversity was read as an absence of 'standards', as aesthetic deregulation. The Community Arts Program's fear of art meant that it was unable to clearly articulate other standards and languages of critical evaluation in which the aesthetic was situated in its social conditions of production and reception. The representation of community arts as a distinctive cultural practice produced an over-valorisation of contexts that obliterated any consideration of texts.

This profound silence about texts is reflected in the absence of a critical language within the community arts complex. While this problem has recently been confronted there is still enormous resistance to the very idea of criticism. This was most evident in the hostile responses to Jude Adams' (1989) review of *Bitter Song*, a community arts project about the experiences of migrant women. In this review Adams queried the limitations of humanist realism as the dominant aesthetic strategy within community arts. She outlined the negative effects of this aesthetic, particularly the claims to 'truth' which it produced and the generation of a moralistic and guilt-ridden political discourse. For initiating a debate about the problems of the documentary form (a debate which has been around independent film-making for years) Adams was accused of being racist, condescending, theoreticist and paternalistic (Hill, 1989; Kalantzis, 1989; Lesses, 1989). So much for the possibilities of a critical language within community arts! Yet without this language projects will remain trapped in an aesthetics of affirmation that is unable to move beyond consensual or confessional modes of address.

The fundamental problem with non-aesthetic measures of value in the history of the Community Arts Program is their over-reliance on the rhetoric of radical welfare. This welfare rhetoric remains the framing discourse of community arts, structuring the way in which both policy and projects are known and understood. One of the aims of this history has been to explore the influences of this framing discourse on texts; to examine the aesthetic limitations of social objectives for cultural funding. While collective modes of social organisation and self-determination are extremely important political objectives, how these are expressed and inscribed in texts is a question that cannot be ignored. For too long the community arts movement has been obsessed with political processes and community development. When it has occasionally reflected on the nature of art and representation the answers posed have been predictably narrow. A 'good' community arts project is either harmlessly wholesome in its representation of unity, harmony and togetherness, or it is crudely rhetorical in its representations of us against them.

The reluctance to critically reflect on what constitutes 'radical' art has produced a certain aesthetic uniformity in community arts. Despite the great diversity of forms employed in projects and the multiple sites where they are produced there is often a profound lack of aesthetic vitality. It is as if documentary realism is the only aesthetic strategy acceptable for community-based cultural production. Few community artists seem interested in developing a more reflexive practice, in investigating the formal traditions and institutional supports which have shaped their practice. While there has been a great commitment to exploring progressive strategies for working with communities there has been little concern to explore related issues in the production of progressive art. The persistent refusal within community arts projects and policy to explore the avant-garde and other critical cultural practices is more evidence of a deep cultural conservatism. While the 1970s and 1980s have been characterised by a phenomenal expansion in cultural theory and debate, community arts has been generally blind to these developments, preferring instead to develop communities rather than a dynamic aesthetic able to explore and critique the nature of social order.

Culture and democracy

While community arts represents important possibilities for the reform of arts funding, its role in the wider struggle for cultural democracy is more ambiguous. This is because art is a long way from the real action in this campaign. As many commentators have pointed out the ownership and regulation of broadcasting and other mass media are the fundamental issues at stake (see Frow, 1986; Garnham, 1987; Mulgan and Worpole, 1986; and Dermody and Jacka, 1988b). Private broadcasting goods and services are the dominant cultural field. Fiddling around with the organisation of arts subsidy has little or no impact on this. As Mulgan and Worpole argue, the support of distinctive ethnic, women's or gay cultures does not address directly the most crucial cultural battlegrounds of the 1990s (1986: 119).

However, despite art's economic insignificance it remains ideologically privileged within the current structures of cultural policy. Contesting this privilege is crucial to effective reform. It is only by situating art within a wider cultural domain that it is possible to see it as one part of a continuum of creative forms, organisations and pleasures. The models proposed so far do not necessarily gaurantee this. Rowse's (1985a) promotion of decentralised patronage as a radical innovation in the structure of subsidy goes some way towards this. He argues that this model has a proven track record in fostering new patrons for culture and new constituencies. But what Rowse ignores is the incapacity of this model to confront the entrenched dualism between art and entertainment in cultural policy that he so carefully critiques. Rowse's vision implies an Australia Council dominated by the Community Arts Program's practices and discourses; an Australia Council where The Australian Opera is asked 'has there been significant community input into the development of the project and the determination of its structure?' (CAB, 1986: 34).

Another model gaining popularity is the cultural industries approach. While this approach is beginning to be tentatively explored in Australia (see DASET, 1992: 25–9) it has been most fully developed in proposals made by Nicholas Garnham (1987) and Mulgan and Worpole (1986). The fundamental difference with the cultural industries approach to intervention is its stand against the tradition of idealist cultural analysis (Garnham, 1987: 24). Garnham traces the influence of this tradition on the structures of cultural policies. He points out that the selection of certain activities for subsidy is officially justified on the grounds that these cultural forms possess inherent values which are damaged by the pressure of commercial forces. Policy also perpetuates the ideology of the unique talent of the creative artist and structures subsidy around the needs of cultural producers rather than cultural consumers. The end result is public intervention in the cultural sphere which not only perpetuates elitist views of culture but is also profoundly marginal to most people's cultural needs and aspirations (1987: 24–5).

In opposition to this tradition Garnham and Mulgan and Worpole propose cultural policies structured around industrial rather than aesthetic objectives. Their vision focuses on public intervention in the cultural economy or the dominant market sector. 'Culture' is not a treasure house of precious values and artefacts but 'the production and circulation of symbolic meaning, as a material process of production and exhange . . . determined by the wider economic processes of society' (Garnham, 1987: 25). The overriding emphasis is on markets, distribution techniques, public investment rather than subsidy, and regulation for diversity in ownership and forms. Subsidy dependence is replaced with different patterns of public support such as investment loans and assistance for common services such as marketing, management consultants and new technology. The fundamental aim of such strategies is to enhance the cultural choices of individuals and groups by putting cultural workers in touch with new audiences and markets. Rather than rejecting market-based culture this approach is geared at exploiting its contradictions. As Garnham argues:

> . . . even within the capitalist mode of production the market has, at crucial historical conjunctures, acted as a liberating cultural force. . . Indeed, the cultural market, as it has developed in the last 150 years in the UK as a substitute for patronage in all its forms, cannot be read either as a destruction of high culture by vulgar commercialism or as the suppression of authentic working-class culture, but should be read as a complex hegemonic dialectic of liberation and control . . . the only alternative to the market

which we have constructed, with the partial exception of broadcasting, has tended either simply to subsidize the existing tastes and habits of the better-off or to create a new form of public culture which has no popular audience. (Garnham, 1987: 34).

Related to this is Mulgan and Worpole's model for a Ministry of Arts and Communications, which outlines how the arts could be administered alongside other forms of culture and communications. This model completely undermines the aesthetic privileging of art and it shows how divisions between high and low and public and private could be contested. In this framework there would be no need for community arts because questions of difference and diversity would be foregrounded in all spheres of policy. Significantly, Mulgan and Worpole's vision does not eliminate aesthetic criteria for cultural funding. Rather, it places these alongside equally important social and industrial criteria. They propose four rationales for the public support of culture:

> *cultural* (aesthetic contribution, innovation, distinctiveness), *social* (contribution in terms of work or pleasure to social groups otherwise ignored by the market or mainstream institutions), *employment* (creation of flexible opportunities for paid work and training) *audience* (ability to meet unmet needs of hitherto neglected audiences). (Mulgan and Worpole, 1986: 125) [emphasis in the original]

These justifications for public intervention align the aesthetic, economic and pluralist possibilities for culture in an inspiring progressive vision.

In these arguments for the reform of cultural policy, community arts does not feature. In Garnham's proposal the emphasis on the market explicitly rejects grant-aid as a technique for disbursing public funds. Not only does grant-aid breed dependence but it also produces a special sphere of public culture removed from any demands for accountability beyond the requirements of the funding body. The alternative sector of community-based culture does not need subsidy but coordination in order to exploit economies of scale and to expand the reach of its innovative cultural repertoire. Questions of access and participation are focused on the broadcasting sector, 'the heartland of contemporary cultural practice'. The issue here is how to regulate for diversity of ownership and programming (Garnham, 1987: 36).

In contrast, Mulgan and Worpole recognise the enabling potential of subsidy—specifically, its role in supporting aesthetic innovation and addressing constituencies outside the market. However, what remains so important about their approach is the integration of these objectives into the wider economic development of the arts and culture.

For Mulgan, Worpole and Garnham community arts is most definitely a cultural program whose moment has passed. Radical reform of cultural administration has no place for art as a separate and privileged sphere. Nor does it have any place for notions of cultural disadvantage which implicitly affirm the hegemony of high culture. Apart from this, these models for reform recognise what community arts has always been unable to face: the centrality of the market and mass culture in most people's cultural experience.

It would be foolhardy, however, to dismiss community arts as the 1970s fad that never went away. For in its very persistence are some important lessons and models. The Community Arts Program has transformed the landscape of arts funding and in this process it has produced methods and rationales for disbursing grants that are far more democratic than the search for excellence. The program is also a significant example of the value of cultural participation as a resource for the expression and affirmation of social difference.

Ultimately, this history of the Community Arts Program is deeply ambiguous. While the creation of the program began a much needed challenge to the elitist structures of arts support, it also produced a space in cultural policy where those uninterested in art were constituted as lacking and deprived. Perhaps this is the fundamental problem with the term 'community'? It is a term that is both deeply nostalgic in its invocations of harmony and integration and profoundly political in its call to collective action and alliances.

Bibliography

Official Publications

Australia Council (1974–1992) *Annual Reports*

Australia Council (1975–1992) *Artforce* Arts Information Program of the Australia Council.

Australia Council (1978) *Ethnic Arts Directory* North Sydney: Australia Council.

Australia Council (1979) *Housing the Arts: Establishing Community Arts Centres or Performing Arts Facilities* North Sydney: Australia Council.

Australian Council for the Arts (1973) *First Annual Report*.

Australian Council for the Arts (1974) *Second Annual Report*.

Community Arts Committee (1973–1977) Minutes (unpublished).

Community Arts Board (1977–1987) Minutes (unpublished).

Community Arts Board (1978–1987) *Programs of Assistance Booklets* North Sydney: Australia Council.

Community Arts Board (1978) *Ethnic Arts Policy* North Sydney: Australia Council.

Community Arts Board (1980) *The Arts Council of Australia* Occasional Papers, Program Review Series, North Sydney: Australia Council.

Community Arts Board (1986) *Introducing Community Arts* North Sydney: Australia Council.

Community Arts Board (1979–1988) *Caper* A series of occasional papers about community arts.

Community Cultural Development Unit (1987-1992) *Programs of Assistance Booklets* Australia Council.

Community Cultural Development Unit (1990-1992) *Report Back* Redfern: Australia Council.

Department of the Arts, Sport, the Environment and Territories (1992) *The Role of the Commonwealth in Australia's Cultural Development: A Discussion Paper* Canberra: DASET.

Industries Assistance Commission (1977) *Assistance to the Performing Arts* Canberra: Parliamentary Paper No. 290.

Local Government and the Arts Taskforce (1991) *Local Governments Role in Arts and Cultural Development* Local Government and the Arts Taskforce.

Report of the Committee of Inquiry into Folklife in Australia (1987) *Folklife: Our Living Heritage* Canberra: Australian Government Publishing Service.

Report of the House of Representatives Standing Committee on Expenditure (1986) *Patronage, Power and the Muse: Inquiry into Commonwealth Assistance to the Arts* Canberra: Australian Government Publishing Service.

Review of Post-Arrival Programs and Services for Migrants (1978) *Migrant Services and Programs: Report of the Review of Post-Arrival Programs and Services for Migrants* Canberra: Australian Government Publishing Service.

UNESCO (1979) *Culture and Working Life: Experiences from Six European Countries* Paris: UNESCO.

Books and Articles

Adams, J. (1975) 'Art for Our Sake—Ann Newmarch Exhibition' *Refractory Girl* 8 (Autumn): 45–51.

——(1987) 'Community Arts—Time to Come Out of the Corner' *Community Arts National* 2, 2: 14–15.

——(1989) 'There is Always a Simple Solution and it's Always Wrong' *Artlink* 9, 1 (March/May): 39–43.

Alvarado, M. (1979/80) 'Photographs and Narrativity' *Screen Education* 32/33 (Autumn/Winter): 5–17.

Anderson, B. (1983) *Imagined Communities: Reflections on the Origin and Spread of Nationalism* London: Verso.

Andrews, B. (1982) 'The Federal Government as Literary Patron' *Meanjin* 41, 1, (April): 3–19.

Appleyard, B. (1984) *The Culture Club: Crisis in the Arts* London: Faber and Faber.

Bakhtin, M. (1984) *Rabelais and His World* (trans. H. Iswokky) USA: Midland Books.

Baldry, H. (1981) *The Case for the Arts* London: Secker & Warburg.

Barker, P. (ed.) (1977) *Arts in Society* Great Britain: Fontana.

Barrett, M., Corrigan, P., Kuhn, A. and Wolff, J. (eds) (1979) *Ideology and Cultural Production* London: Croom Helm.

Barry, J. and Flitterman, S. (1981/82) 'Textual Strategies: The Politics of Art Making' *LIP* 6: 29–34.

Barthes, R. (1977) *Image—Music—Text* (trans. S. Heath) Glasgow: Fontana/Collins.

——(1980) *Camera Lucida* (trans. R. Howard) New York: Hill and Wang.

Battersby, J. (1980) *Cultural Policy in Australia* Paris: UNESCO.

——(1983) 'Commonwealth Support for the Arts—Theory and Practice' (unpublished) Exhibit No. 39, Report of the House of Representatives Standing Committee on Expenditure, *Patronage, Power and the Muse: Inquiry into Commonwealth Assistance to the Arts* Canberra: Australian Government Publishing Service.

Baxandall, L. (ed.) (1972) *Radical Perspectives in the Arts* USA: Penguin.

Beilharz, P. (1987) 'Reading Politics: Social Theory and Social Policy' *Australian and New Zealand Journal of Sociology* 23, 3: 388–406.

Bell, D. and Hawkes, P. (1988) *Generations: Grandmothers, Mothers and Daughters* Australia: McPhee Gribble/Penguin.

Benjamin, W. (1973a) *Understanding Brecht* (trans. A. Bostock) London: New Left Books.

——(1973b) *Illuminations* London: Fontana.

Bennett, T. (1980) 'Popular Culture: A "Teaching Object" ' *Screen Education* 34 (Spring): 17–29.

——(1983) 'Marxist Cultural Politics: In Search of "the Popular" ' *Australian Journal of Cultural Studies* 1, 2 (December): 2–28.

——(1985) 'Really Useless "Knowledge": A Political Critique of Aesthetics' *Thesis Eleven* 12: 28–52.

——(1988a) 'Ozmosis: Looking at Pop Culture' *Australian Left Review* 104 (April/May): 33–5.

——(1988b) *Out of Which Past? Critical Reflections on Australian Museum and Heritage Policy* Griffith University: Institute for Cultural Policy Studies, Occasional Paper No. 3.

——(1988c) 'The Exhibitionary Complex' *New Formations* 4 (Spring): 73–102.

——(1989a) 'Museums and the Public Good: Economic Rationalism and Cultural Policy' *Culture and Policy* 1, 1 (August): 37–51.

——(1989b) 'Culture: Theory and Policy' *Media Information Australia* 53 (August): 9–11.

——(1989c) 'Museums and Public Culture: History, Theory, Policy' *Media Information Australia* 53 (August): 57–65.

——(1972) *Ways of Seeing* London: British Broadcasting Corporation and Penguin Books.

——(1979/80) 'The Authentic Image' *Screen Education* 32/33 (Autumn/Winter): 19–30.

Bertrand, I. and Collins, D. (1981) *Government and Film in Australia* Sydney: Currency Press.

Bezencenet, S. and Corrigan, P. (1986) *Photographic Practices: Towards a Different Image* London: Comedia.

Bhabha, H. (1983) 'The Other Question—The Stereotype and Colonial Discourse' *Screen* 24, 6 (November/December): 18–36.

Bianchini, F. (1987) 'GLC R.I.P. Cultural Policies in London 1981–1986' *New Formations* 1: 103–17.

Bianchini, F., Fisher, M., Montgomery, J. and Worpole, K. (1988) *City Centres, City Cultures* Manchester: Centre for Local Economic Strategies.

Binns, V. (1980) 'Mothers' Memories Others' Memories' *LIP* 5: 38–45.

——(no date) 'Mothers' Memories Others' Memories: A Project Combining Creative Expression, Memorabilia and Oral History' (unpublished) Notes Accompanying a Slide Tape Show on the Project.

Blainey, G. (1974) 'Government Patronage and Literature' *Overland* 57: 37–43.

Blonski, A., Creed, B. and Freiberg, F. (eds) (1987) *Don't Shoot Darling! Women's Independent Filmmaking in Australia* Australia: Greenhouse.

Bommes, M. and Wright, P. (1982) ' "Charms of Residence": The Public and the Past' in Johnson, R. et al. (eds) *Making Histories* London: Hutchinson and Centre for Contemporary Cultural Studies.

Bonney, B. and Wilson, H. (1983) *Australia's Commercial Media* Melbourne: Macmillan.

Bower, R. (1981a) 'The Community Arts Officer: What is it all About?' *Caper* 10 North Sydney: CAB

——(1981b) 'Community Arts: What Is It?' *Caper* 10 North Sydney: CAB.

Bourdieu, P. (1973) 'Cultural Reproduction and Social Reproduction' in Brown, R. (ed.) *Knowledge, Education and Cultural Change* London: Tavistock.

——(1980) 'The Aristocracy of Culture' *Media, Culture and Society* 2, 3 (July): 225–54.

——(1984) *Distinction: A Social Critique of the Judgement of Taste* (trans. R. Nice) London: Routledge & Kegan Paul.

Braden, S. (1978) *Artists and People* London: Routledge & Kegan Paul.

——(1983) *Committing Photography* London: Pluto Press.

Brecht, B. (1965) *The Messingkauf Dialogue* London: Eyre Methuen.

Brereton, K. (1981) *Photo-Discourse: Critical Thought and Practice in Photography* Sydney: Sydney College of the Arts.

Brett, J. (1982) 'ALP Arts Policy Workshop' *Meanjin* 41, 4 (December): 549–52.

Briggs, A. (1980) 'Problems and Possibilities in the Writing of Broadcasting History' *Media, Culture and Society* 2, 1 (January): 5–13.

Britain, I. (1982) *Fabianism and Culture: a Study in British Socialism and the Arts 1884–1918* Cambridge: Cambridge University Press.

Brophy, P. and Bishop, R. (1987) 'Creative Development' *Arena* 80: 64–7.

Browning, B. (1986) 'The Rise of the Paguts: Political Advocacy Groups Utilising Taxes' *Institute of Public Affairs Review* 40, 2 (Winter): 10–15.

Bryson, L. and Mowbray, M. (1981) ' "Community": The Spray On Solution' *Australian Journal of Social Issues* 16, 4: 255–67.

Burke, J. (1979) 'Six Women Artists' *Meanjin* 38, 3 (September): 305–20.

——(1981) 'Collaboration: Artists Working Collectively' *Art and Text* 1: 33–42.

Burn, I. (1982) 'ACTU National Conference: Art and Working Life' *Art Network* 5 (Summer/Autumn): 37–8.

——(1984) 'The Sixties: Crisis and Aftermath' in Taylor, P. (ed.) *Anything Goes: Art in Australia 1970–1980* Victoria: Art and Text.

——(1985) *Working Art: A Survey of Art in the Australian Labour Movement in the 1980s* Catalogue, Sydney: Art Gallery of NSW.

Burton, F. and Carlen, P. (1979) *Official Discourse* London: Routledge & Kegan Paul.

Burvill, T. (1984) 'Sidetrack: Theatre and Community' *The Bulletin of Australasian Drama Studies Association* 3, 1 (Autumn).

Cassidy, S. (1983) *Art and Working Life in Australia* North Sydney: Australia Council.

Castles, S., Kalantzis, M., Cape, B., Morrissey, M. (1988) *Mistaken Identity: Multiculturalism and the Demise of Nationalism in Australia* Australia: Pluto Press.

Chambers, I. (1980) 'Rethinking "Popular Culture" ' *Screen Education* 36 (Autumn): 113–17.

——(1986) *Popular Culture: The Metropolitan Experience* London: Methuen.

——(1987) 'Maps for the Metropolis: A Possible Guide to the Present' *Cultural Studies* 1, 1 (January): 1–21.

Chandler, A.M. (1985) 'Left on the Cutting Room Floor at the AFC' *Filmnews* (March): 3–4.

Chesterman, C. and Schwager, J. (1990) *Arts Development in Western Sydney* Redfern: Australia Council.

Church, J. (1986) 'Review of Truth Rules II' *Artlink* 6, 1 (March/April): 3–5.

Clarke, J. and Critcher, C. (1985) *The Devil Makes Work: Leisure in Capitalist Britain* London: Macmillan.

Clifford, J. (1983) 'On Ethnographic Authority' *Representations* 1, 2 (Spring): 118–46.

——(1986) 'On Ethnographic Allegory' in Clifford, J. and Marcus, G. (eds) *Writing Culture* California: University of California Press.

Clifford, J. and Marcus, G. (eds) (1986) *Writing Culture* California: University of California Press.

Cochrane, P. and Goodman, D. (1988) 'The Great Australian Journey: Cultural Logic and Nationalism in the Postmodern Era' in Janson, S. and Macintyre, S. (eds) *Making the Bicentenary* Melbourne: University of Melbourne.

Cockburn, C. (1977) *The Local State* London: Pluto Press.

Cohen, A.P. (1985) *The Symbolic Construction of Community* England: Ellis Horwood Ltd and Tavistock.

Connell, R.W. (1983) 'Democratising Culture' *Meanjin* 42, 3 (September): 295–307.

Coombs, H.C. (1969) 'The Australian Council for the Arts—Progress and Plan' UNESCO and ANU Seminar on Public Support for the Arts 25–31 May.

——(1970–1971) 'The Economics of the Performing Arts' *Economic Papers* 35 (September–June).

——(1981) *Trial Balance* Australia: Macmillan.

Couzens Hoy, D. (ed.) (1986) *Foucault: A Critical Reader* London: Basil Blackwell.

Coward, R. (1984) *Female Desire: Women's Sexuality Today* UK: Paladin.

Cunningham, S. (1992) *Framing Culture* North Sydney: Allen & Unwin.

——(1987) 'Australian Cinema Studies: Writing the Revival' *Media Information Australia* 45 (August): 38–43.

——(1989) 'Cultural Critique and Cultural Policy: Handmaiden or No Relation?' *Media Information Australia* 54 (November): 7–12.

Dauth, L. (1982) 'Posters: A Partial Picture' *Art Network* 5 (Summer/Autumn): 21–7.

Davidson, J. (1981) 'The Great Arts-Funding Debate' *Meanjin* 40, 4 (December): 456–60.

Dermody, S., Docker, J., and Modjeska, D. (eds) (1982) *Nellie Melba, Ginger Meggs and Friends: Essays in Australian Cultural History* Australia: Kibble Books.

Dermody, S. and Jacka, E. (1987) *The Screening of Australia: Anatomy of a Film Industry* Vol.1, Australia: Currency Press.

——(1988a) *The Screening of Australia: Anatomy of a National Cinema,* Vol.2 Australia: Currency Press.

——(1988b) *The Imaginary Industry: Australian Film in the Late '80s* Australia: AFTRS Publications.

Dimaggio, P. (1981) *The Impact of Public Funding of Organizations in the*

Arts Yale University: Institution for Social and Policy Studies, Program on Non-Profit Organizations, Working Paper 31.

——(1982) 'Cultural Entrepreneurshp in Nineteenth-Century Boston: the Creation of an Organizational Base for High Culture in America' *Media, Culture and Society* 4, 1 (January): 33–50.

——(1982) 'Cultural Entrepreneurship in Nineteenth-Century Boston, Part II: the Classification and Framing of American Art' *Media, Culture and Society* 4, 4 (October): 303–22.

Dimaggio, P. and Useem, M. (1978) 'Social Class and Arts Consumption: The Origins and Consequences of Class Differences in Exposure to the Arts in America' *Theory and Society* 5, 2 (March): 141–61.

Dimech, M. (no date) 'Policies and Procedures of the Australia Council with Respect to "Arts for a Multicultural Australia" ' Redfern: Australia Council.

Docker, J. (1988) 'Popular Culture and Bourgeois Values' in Burgmann, V. and Lee, J. (eds) *Constructing a Culture—A Peoples' History of Australia since 1788* Australia: McPhee Gribble/Penguin.

Dolk, M. (1982) 'Aspects of Socially Engaged and Community Art' *Art Network* 5 (Summer/Autumn): 17.

Dreyfus, H. and Rabinow, P. (1982) *Michel Foucault: Beyond Structuralism and Hermeneutics* Chicago: University of Chicago Press.

Duncan, G. (1986) 'Whitlam and the Problems of Social Democracy' *Meanjin* 45, 4 (December): 469–77.

Dunstan, G. (1979) 'In Search of the Sacred' *Caper* 3 North Sydney: CAB.

Dutton, G. (1968) 'The Work and Prospects of the Australian Council for the Arts' in Whitelock, D. (ed.) *Government Aid to the Arts* Adelaide: Department of Adult Education, University of Adelaide.

Edmonds, M. (1981) *Local Government and the Arts* North Sydney: Australia Council.

Enzenberger, H.M. (1977) *Raids and Reconstructions* London: Pluto.

Ewington, J. (1984) 'Political Postering' in Taylor, P. (ed.) *Anything Goes: Art in Australia 1970–1980* Victoria: Art and Text.

——(1982) 'Fragmentation and Feminism: the Critical Discourses of Postmodernism' *Art and Text* 7 (Spring): 61–73.

——(1987) *Domestic Contradictions* Catalogue, Sydney: Power Foundation Gallery.

Fabian Papers (1986) *The Whitlam Phenomenon* Fitzroy: McPhee Gribble/Penguin.

Field, M. (1980) 'The Geography of Arts Funding' *Meanjin* 40, 1 (April): 57–65.

Fensham, R. (1987) 'The Need for a Language Continues' *Community Arts National* 2, 1 (June): 12.

——(1989) 'Framing the Impossible Questions' *Artlink* 9, 3 (Spring): 59–60.

——(1990) 'Why Do Angels Fly Anti-Clockwise?' *Artlink* 10, 3 (Spring): 10–13.

Fiske, J., Hodge, B. and Turner, G. (1987) *Myths of Oz* Australia: Allen & Unwin.

Footscray Community Arts Centre (1980) *The Next Ten Years: Report on the National Community Arts Conference Melbourne, 1980* Footscray: Community Arts Centre.

Fotheringham, R. (ed) (1987) *Community Theatre in Australia* Australia: Methuen.

Foucault, M. (1977) *Discipline and Punish: the Birth of the Prison* Harmondsworth: Penguin.

——(1978) 'Politics and the Study of Discourse' *Ideology and Consciousness* 3 (Spring): 7–26.

——(1979a) 'On Governmentality' *Ideology and Consciousness* 6 (Autumn): 5–21.

——(1979b) *Power, Truth and Strategy* (trans. and edited by M. Morris and P. Patton) Sydney: Feral Publications.

——(1980a) *Power/Knowledge* (trans. C. Gordon) New York: Pantheon.

——(1980b) 'What is an Author?' in Haran, J. (ed.) *Textual Strategies* London: Methuen.

——(1981) 'Questions of Method: An Interview with Michel Foucault' *Ideology and Consciousness* 8 (Spring): 3–14.

——(1982) 'The Subject and Power' in Dreyfus, H. and Rabinow, P. *Michel Foucault: Beyond Structuralism and Hermeneutics* Chicago: University of Chicago Press.

Freudenberg, G. (1978) *A Certain Grandeur: Gough Whitlam in Politics* Australia: Macmillan.

——(1986) 'The Program' in Fabian Papers *The Whitlam Phenomenon* Fitzroy: McPhee Gribble/Penguin.

Frow, J. (1986) 'Class and Culture: Funding the Arts' *Meanjin* 45, 1 (March): 118–28.

——(1987) 'Accounting for Tastes: Some Problems in Bourdieu's Sociology of Culture' *Cultural Studies* 1, 1 (January): 59–73.

——(1988) 'Some Versions of Foucault' *Meanjin* 47, 1 (Autumn): 144–56.

Galbraith, L. (1990) 'It Didn't Happen Overnight' *Gay and Lesbian Mardi Gras Program* Sydney: Sydney Gay and Lesbian Mardi Gras Association.

Garnham, N. (1977) 'Towards a Political Economy of Culture' *New Universities Quarterly* 31, 3 (Summer): 341–57.

——(1987) 'Concepts of Culture: Public Policy and the Culture Industries' *Cultural Studies* 1, 1: 23–37.

Gillen, P. (1984) 'Reading, Writing and Cultural Democracy' *Meanjin* 43, 4 (December): 525–30.

Gold, S. (1987) 'Policy and Administrative Change in the Arts in Australia' *Prometheus* 5, 1: 146–54.

Goodman, D. (1990) 'Fear of Circuses: Founding the National Museum of Victoria' *Continuum* 3, 1: 18–34.

Grace, H. (1981/82) 'From the Margins: A Feminist Essay on Women's Art' *LIP* 6: 13–18.

Grace, H. and Stephen, A. (1981) 'Where Do Positive Images Come From? (and what does a woman want?)' *Scarlet Woman* 12 (March): 15–22.

Grant, B. (1986) 'Introduction' in Fabian papers *The Whitlam Phenomenon* Fitzroy: McPhee Gribble/Penguin.

Green, M. and Wilding, M. (1970) *Cultural Policy in Great Britain* Paris: UNESCO.

Greenberg, C. (1969) 'The Avant Garde and Kitsch' in Dorfles, G. (ed.) *Kitsch: The World of Bad Taste* USA: Universe Books.

Greenwood, T. (1983) 'Is Community Action an Essential Ingredient in Community Arts?' *Meanjin* 42, 3 (September): 309–13.

Gunew, S. (1982) 'Re-Viewing the Migrant Story: Place (St. Albans, 3021)' in Creed, B. et al. (eds) *Papers and Forums on Independent Film and Asian Cinema* Australian Screen Studies Association and Australian Film and TV School.

——(1983) 'Migrant Women Writers: Who's on Whose Margins?' *Meanjin* 42, 1 (March): 16–26.

——(1985a) 'Framing Marginality—Distinguishing the Textual Politics of the Marginal Voice' *Southern Review* 18, 2 (July): 142–56.

——(1985b) 'Multicultural Writers: Where Are We Writing From and Who Are We Writing For?' in Literature Board *Writing in Multicultural Australia* North Sydney: Australia Council.

Hakim, C. (1983) 'Research Based on Administrative Records' *Sociological Review* 31, 3 (August): 489–519.

Hall, L. (1989) 'Who is Bill Posters?' *Caper* 27 North Sydney: CAB.

Hall, S. (1980b) 'Cultural Studies: Two Paradigms' *Media, Culture and Society* 2, 1 (January): 57–72.

Ham, C. and Hill, M. (1984) *The Policy Process in the Modern Capitalist State* Great Britain: Wheatsheaf Books.

Harper, K. (1984) 'The Wonthaggi Celebration: a Community Theatre Event' *Meanjin* 43, 1 (March): 95–104.

——(1984) 'The Useful Theatre: The New Theatre Movement in Sydney and Melbourne 1935–1983' *Meanjin* 43, 1 (March): 57–71.

Hawkes, J. (1984) 'Definitions' *Artlink* 4, 4 (Summer): 8–9.

——(1986) 'State Support for Community Arts, What Next?' (unpublished) CAB.

——(1988) 'Self Sufficiency: Reality or Myth?' *Community Arts National* 4, 2 (August): 3–4.

Hawkins, G. (1987) 'Why Write a History of Community Art?' (unpublished) Paper presented to the NSW Community Arts Association, Annual Conference: University of NSW.

——(1989) 'Reading Community Arts Policy: From Nimbin to the Gay Mardi Gras' *Media Information Australia* 53 (August): 31–5.

——(1990) 'Community Arts: the Seventies Fad that Never Went Away' *Artlink* 10, 3 (Spring): 14–17.

Hebdige, D. (1979) *Subculture: the Meaning of Style* London: Methuen.

Heks, R. (1982) 'Mural Painting in Australia' *Art Network* 5 (Summer/Autumn): 29–33.

——(1985a) *Community Arts Officer Review* North Sydney: CAB.

——(1985b) 'Rethinking Community Arts' *Meanjin* 44, 4 (December): 553–5.

——(1987) 'Community Arts and Standards of Excellence: the Need for a Language' *Community Arts National* 2, 1 (June): 8–9.

Henderson, S. (1979) 'The Community Arts Officer' *Caper* 1 North Sydney: CAB.

Herd, N. (1983) *Independent Film-making in Australia 1960–1980* Sydney: AFTRS.

Hicks, P. (1982) 'Community Arts, False Freedom and a Fight For Our Lives' *Art Network* 5 (Summer/Autumn): 42–3.

Hill, A. (1985) 'Land of Promises' (unpublished) Draft Text for a *Caper* Paper.

——(1987) 'Towards a Multicultural Arts Practice' *Community Arts National* 2, 2: 9–11.

——(1989) 'Response to Jude Adams' Review of a Bitter Song' *Artlink*, 9, 3 (Spring): 61–3.

Hill, A., Hill, E., Hopkinson, J. (1983) *Land of Promises* Exhibition Catalogue, Adelaide: Community Media Association.

Hobsbawm, E. (1978) 'Man and Woman in Socialist Iconography' *History Workshop* 6 (Autumn): 121–38.

——(1983a) 'Introduction: Inventing Traditions' in Hobsbawm, E. and Ranger, T. (eds) *The Invention of Tradition* Cambridge: Cambridge University Press.

——(1983b) 'Mass Producing Traditions: Europe 1870–1914' in Hobsbawm E. and Ranger, T. (eds) *The Invention of Tradition* Cambridge: Cambridge University Press.

Hobsbawm, E. and Ranger, T. (eds) (1983) *The Invention of Tradition* Cambridge: Cambridge University Press.

Hodge, B. (1984) 'Historical Semantics and the Meanings of "Discourse" ' *Australian Journal of Cultural Studies* 2, 2 (November): 124–30.

Hoggart, R. (1978) 'Gamekeepers or Poachers?' *New Universities Quarterly* 32, 1 (Winter): 207–12.

——(1979) 'Excellence and Access and the Arts Council' *New Universities Quarterly* 33, 4 (Autumn): 389–401.

Holst, G. (1976) *A Survey of Support for the Ethnic Arts in Australia* North Sydney: Australia Council.

Horne, D. (1964) *The Lucky Country* Sydney: Angus & Robertson.

——(1980) *Time of Hope: Australia 1966–1972* Australia: Angus & Robertson.

——(1984) *The Great Museum* London: Pluto Press.

——(1985) 'The Arts and the Australian Economy' *Artforce* 49: 10–12.

——(1986) *The Public Culture* London: Pluto Press.

——(1991) 'Coming Out of the Culture Bunker' in Australia Council *Extending Parameters*.

——(1988) *Arts Funding and Public Culture* Griffith University: Institute for Cultural Policy Studies, Occasional Paper No. 1.

Hull, A. (1974) *Report on the Compost Conference, Macquarie University* North Sydney: CAC.

——(1981a) *A Report on Pilot Projects: 1977–1981* (unpublished) CAB.

——(1981b) 'Principles, Priorities and Practices—The Community Arts Board Four Years On' (unpublished) Address to the Council of the Australia Council.

——(1982) 'The Arts in Context: Director of the Community Arts Board, Andrea Hull, Interviewed by Peter Thorn' *Art Newwork* 5 (Summer/Autumn): 34–6.

——(1983) 'Community Arts: A Perspective' *Meanjin* 42, 3 (September): 315–24.

Hull, A. and Kefala, A. (1987) 'The Australia Council's Multicultural Program' (unpublished) CAB.

Hunter, I. (1989) 'Accounting for Humanities' *Meanjin* 48, 3 (Spring): 438–48.

Hutchinson, N. (1982) *The Politics of the Arts Council* London: Sinclair Browne.

Inglis, K.S. (1983) *This is the ABC* Melbourne: Melbourne University Press.

Johnson, L. (1979) *The Cultural Critics: From Mathew Arnold to Raymond Williams* London: Routledge & Kegan Paul.

Johnson, L. (1982/83) 'Images of Radio: The Construction of the Radio Audience by Popular Radio Magazines' in *Melbourne Working Papers* No. 4: Melbourne University.

——(1982) ' "Sing 'em muck Clara" Highbrow Versus Lowbrow on Early Australian Radio' *Meanjin* 41, 2 (June): 210–22.

——(1986) 'The Study of Popular Culture: The Need for a Clear Agenda' *Australian Journal of Cultural Studies* 4, 1 (June): 1–13.

——(1988) *The Unseen Voice: A Cultural Study of Early Australian Radio* London: Routledge.

Johnson, R., McLennan, J., Schwarz, B., Sutton, D. (eds) (1982) *Making Histories* London: Hutchinson and the Centre for Contemporary Cultural Studies.

Johnson, T. (1985) 'An Impossible Vision: Conceptual Art in the '70s' *On the Beach* 9: 7–13.

Kalantzis, M. (1989) 'Reception Theory: The Simple Solution' *Artlink* 9, 3 (Spring): 64.

Kalantzis, M., Cope, B. and Hughes, C. (1984/85) 'Pluralism and Social Reform: A Review of Multiculturalism in Australian Education' *Thesis Eleven* 10–11: 195–215.

Kefala, A. (1977) 'A Survey of Funding, Preservation and Research of Ethnic Arts in Australia' (unpublished) Report prepared for the Australia Council.

——(ed.) (1986) *Multiculturism and the Arts* North Sydney: Australia Council.

Kelly, O. (1984) *Community, Art and the State: Storming the Citadels* London: Comedia.

King, N. and Rowse, T. (1983) ' "Typical Aussies": Television and Populism in Australia' *Framework* 22–3 (Autumn): 37–42.

Kirby, S. (1982) 'Directions in Australian Radical Art: Affirmation and Opposition' *Art Network* 5 (Summer/Autumn): 39–41.

Kuhn, A. (1982) *Women's Pictures* London: Routledge & Kegan Paul.

——(1988) *Cinema, Censorship and Sexuality 1909–1925* London: Routledge.

Lachlau, E. (1980) 'Populist Rupture and Discourse' *Screen Education* 34 (Spring): 97–3.

Langer, B. (1988) *The Culture Industry: High Culture as Mass Culture* Department of Sociology, La Trobe University, Working Paper No. 79.

Laurie, R. (1984) 'A Thousand Bloomin' Flowers No Stopping Now' *Meanjin* 34, 1 (March): 81–5.

Lees, R. and Mayo, M. (1984) *Community Action for Change* London: Routledge & Kegan Paul.

Lewis, J., Morley, D., Southwood, R. (1986) *Art—Who Needs It? The Audience for Community Arts* London: Comedia.

MacCabe, C. (ed.) (1986) *High Theory/Low Culture: Analysing Popular Television and Film* Manchester: Manchester University Press.

McDonald, J. (1985) 'Two-Headed Monster on the Prowl Again', Review of R. Waller's Exhibition 'House About Wollongong' in *The Sydney Morning Herald*, 20/12/1985.

Macdonell, D. (1986) *Theories of Discourse: An Introduction* Oxford: Basil Blackwell.

Macdonnell, J. (1992) *Arts Minister? Government Policy and the Arts* Sydney: Currency Press.

Macintyre, S. (1986) 'The Short History of Social Democracy in Australia' *Thesis Eleven* 15: 3–4.

McKinnon, E. (1983) 'Review of Land of Promises' *Artlink* 3, 11 (Spring): 40–1.

McKinsey and Company (1976) *Strengthening Operations: Report of a Study Commissioned by the Australia Council* Sydney: McKinsey and Co. Inc.

Marsh, A. (1984) 'Art and Society: An Analysis of Community Art' *Artlink* 4, 5 (October/November): 5–7.

Mennell, S. (1976a) 'Cultural Needs and Municipal Initiative' *Social and Economic Administration* 10, 2 (Summer): 123–34.

——(1976b) *Cultural Policy in Towns* Strasbourg: Council of Europe.

——(1979) 'Theoretical Considerations on the Study of Cultural Needs' *Sociology* 13, 2: 235–57.

Mercer, C. (1986) 'The Popular is Plural' *Australian Left Review* 97 (Spring): 11–18.

Merewether, C. (1977) 'Social Realism: The Formative Years' *Arena* 46: 65–80.

——(1984) *Art and Social Commitment—An End to the City of Dreams 1931–1948* Catalogue, Sydney: Art Gallery of NSW.

——(1987a) 'Contemporary Visual Arts in the Art and Working Life Program' (unpublished) Report prepared for the Visual Arts/Craft Board of the Australia Council.

——(1987b) 'The Avanzada: Nelly Richard's Account of Art in Chile' *Age Monthly Review* 7, 8 (December): 23–5.

Merewether, C. and Stephen, A. (eds) (1977) *The Great Divide* Melbourne: The Great Divide.

Merkel, K. (1987) 'A Brief Look at Community Arts and Aesthetics' *Community Arts National* 2, 1 (June): 5–6.

Michaels, E. (1987a) *For a Cultural Future* Melbourne: Artspace.

——(1987b) 'Aboriginal Content—Who's Got It—Who Needs It?' *Art and Text* 23–4 (March/May): 58–79.

——(1988a) 'Bad Aboriginal Art' *Art and Text* 18 (March/May): 57–73.

——(1988b) 'Carnivale in Oxford Street' *New Theatre: Australia* 5 (May/June): 4–8.

Mills, D. (1980) 'A Review of the Extensions Program and a Proposal for Future Directions' (unpublished) Report prepared for the CAB.

——(1985) 'Preface' in Burn, I. *Working Art: A Survey of Art in the Australian Labour Movement in the 1980s* Catalogue, Sydney: Art Gallery of NSW.

——(1986) 'An Evaluation of the Australia Council's Art and Working Life Program' (unpublished) Report prepared for the Australia Council.

——(1992) 'Overview Paper for CCDC/CCDB Handover Meeting' (unpublished) Australia Council.

Milner, A., Thomson, P., and Worth, C. (eds) (1988) *Postmodern Conditions* Melbourne: Centre for General and Comparative Literature, Monash University.

Minihan, J. (1977) *The Nationalization of Culture: the Development of State Subsidies to the Arts in Great Britain* London: Hamish Hamilton.

Moore, C. (1988) *Aspects of Feminist Photography in Australia 1972–1987* (unpublished) PhD Thesis: University of Sydney.

Moore, F. (1986) *Putting Art to Work* Melbourne: Publicity Works/Australia Council.

Moores, S. (1990) 'Texts, Readers and Contexts of Reading: Developments in the Study of Media Audiences' *Media, Culture and Society* 12, 1 (January): 9–29.

Moran, A. (1982) 'Localism and Australian Television' in Dermody, S., Docker J. and Modjeska, D. (eds) *Nellie Melba, Ginger Meggs and Friends: Essays in Australian Cultural History* Australia: Kibble Books.

——(1983) 'A State Capitalist Venture: The South Australian Film Corporation' *Framework* 22/23 (Autumn): 43–6.

Moran, A. and O'Regan, T. (1983) 'Two Discourses of Australian Film' *The Australian Journal of Screen Theory* 15/16: 163–73.

Moran, A. and O'Regan, T. (eds) (1985) *An Australian Film Reader* Sydney: Currency Press.

Morgan, K. (1977) 'A Community Arts Program or Not?' (unpublished) Report prepared for the CAC.

Morley, D. (1986) *Family Television: Cultural Power and Domestic Leisure* London: Comedia.

Morley, D. and Worpole, K. (eds) (1982) *The Republic of Letters: Working Class Writing and Local Publishing* London: Comedia.

Morris, M. (1988) *The Pirate's Fiancee* London: Verso.

Morrow, D. (1987) 'Symbols, Images and Poster Design' *Community Arts National* 2, 1 (June): 7–8.

Mowbray, M. (1984) 'Localism and Austerity—"The Community Can Do It" ' *Journal of Australian Political Economy* 16 (March): 3–14.

Mulgan, G. and Worpole, K. (1986) *Saturday Night or Sunday Morning: From Arts to Industry—New Forms of Cultural Policy* London: Comedia.

Mulhern, F. (1980) 'Notes on Culture and Cultural Struggle' *Screen Education* 34 (Spring): 31–5.

Muecke, S. (1982) 'Available Discourses on Aborigines' in Botsman, P. (ed.) *Theoretical Strategies* Sydney: Local Consumption Publications.

——(1987) 'All About Yves' in Brophy, P., Dermody, S., Hebdige, D. and Muecke, S. *Streetwise Flash Art: Is There a Future for Cultural Studies?* Occasional Paper No. 6 Sydney: Power Institute of Fine Arts, University of Sydney.

Muir, K. (no date) 'Ann Newmarch—Artist in Community' *Caper* 20 North Sydney: CAB.

Netzer, D. (1978) *The Subsidized Muse: Public Support for the Arts in the United States* London: Cambridge University Press.

Noble, R. (1988) 'The History of the Workers' Cultural Action Committee' (unpublished) Paper presented at the '14 Years On . . . Looking Backward to Look Forward' Conference, Newcastle 26,27-3-1988.

O'Neill, E. (1984) 'The Popular Theatre Troupe: Freedom of Expression and Community Theatre' *Meanjin* 43, 1 (March): 86–93.

O'Regan, T. (1983) 'Australian Filmmaking: Its Public Circulation' *Framework* 22/23 (Autumn): 31–6.

——(1984) *Writing on Australian Film History: Some Methodological Notes* Sydney: Local Consumption Publications, Occasional Paper No. 5.

Owusu, K. (1986) *The Struggle for Black Arts in Britain* London: Comedia.

Parker, R. and Pollock, G. (1987) *Old Mistresses: Women, Art and Ideology* London: Routledge & Kegan Paul.

Parry, J. and Parry, N. (eds) (1986) *Leisure, the Arts and the Community* Papers from the Leisure Studies Association Conference, London: City University.

Paroissien, L. (no date) 'Provincialism, Pluralism and Professionalism' in Paroissien, L. (ed.) *Australian Art Review* Australia: Warner Associates.

Parsons, P. (ed.) (1987) *Shooting the Pianist: The Role of Government in the Arts* Sydney: Currency Press.

Pascoe, T. (1983) 'Setting Priorities for the Second Decade', *Artforce* 44 (Spring): 8–10.

Patton, P. (1984–85) 'Michel Foucault: The Ethics of an Intellectual' *Thesis Eleven* 10/11 (March): 71–80.

Pearse, W. (1983) *Retrenchment—Denying Skills* Catalogue, Newcastle: Workers' Cultural Action Committee.

——(1984) 'Art and Working Life' *Photofile* 2, 3 (Spring): 7.

Pearson, N. (1982) *The State and the Visual Arts* Milton Keynes: Open University Press.

Perrier, R. (1982) 'Finding an Audience: The Murray River Performing Group' *Meanjin* 41, 1 (April): 29–39.

Phillips, A.A. (1972) 'Neo Patronage of the Arts' *Meanjin* 31, 2 (June): 237–9.

——(1973a) 'Stimulants or Tranquillizers? A Choice for Literary Patronage' *Meanjin* 32, 2 (June): 239–40.

——(1973b) 'A Chance for the Artist' *Meanjin* 32, 1 (March): 127–8

Phillips, C. (1990) 'From the President' *Gay and Lesbian Mardi Gras Program* Sydney: Sydney Gay and Lesbian Mardi Gras Association.

Pick, J. (ed) (1980) *The State and the Arts* East Sussex: John Otford Publications and City University Centre for the Arts.

Pick, J. (1986) *Managing the Arts* Great Britain: Rhinegold.

Pike, A. (1975) *Development of Arts Activities in the Sydney Western Region* Community Arts Committee, Australian Council for the Arts.

Plant, R. (1974) *Community and Ideology* London, Routledge & Kegan Paul.

Pollock, G. (1977) 'What's Wrong with Images of Women' *Screen Education* 24 (Autumn): 25–34.

Popular Memory Group (1982) 'Popular Memory: Theory, Politics, Method' in Johnson, R., McLennan, G., Schwarz, B. and Sutton, D. (eds) *Making Histories* London: Hutchinson and The Centre for Contemporary Cultural Studies.

Poster, M. (1984) *Foucault, Marxism and History: Modes of Production Versus Modes of Information* Cambridge: Polity Press.

Powell, D. (1989) 'Bunging It On: Public Manners and Private Taste' in Wilson, H. (ed.) *Australian Communications and the Public Sphere* Australia: Macmillan.

Price, D. (1983) 'Photographing the Poor and the Working Classes' *Framework* 22/23 (Autumn): 20–5.

Rew, W. (1987) 'The Chance Element: Aesthetics and Photography' *Community Arts National* 2, 1 (June): 10–11.

Richard, N. (1986) *Margins and Institutions: Art in Chile Since 1973* Melbourne: Art and Text.

Roberts, B. (1983) 'Community Writing' *Meanjin* 42, 3 (September): 283–93.

——(1985) 'Defining Community Arts' *Meanjin* 44, 4 (December): 548–52.
Robertson, T. (1982) 'Community Arts: A History' *Art Network* 5 (Summer/ Autumn): 18–20.
Roberts-Floyd, C. (1984) 'Access is Not a Dirty Word' *Filmnews* November/December.
Robinson, J. (1985) 'The Rise and Fall of Access Video' *Filmnews* May.
Rhodie, S. (1983) 'The Australian State: A National Cinema' *Framework* 22/23 (Autumn): 28–30.
——(1987) 'The Film Industry' in Wheelwright, T. and Buckley, K. (eds) *Communications and the Media in Australia* Sydney: Allen & Unwin.
Rolston, B. (1987) 'Politics, Painting and Popular Culture: The Political Wall Murals of Northern Ireland' *Media, Culture and Society* 9, 1: 5–28.
Rowe, D. (1985) 'Rock Against the Clock: Independent Cultural Production' *Social Alternatives* 4, 4: 58–61.
Rowley, S. (1989) 'Mind over Matter: Reading the Art/Craft Debate' *West* 1, 1: 3–7.
Rowse, T. (1978a) *Australian Liberalism and National Character* Melbourne: Kibble Books.
——(1978b) 'Heaven and a Hills Hoist: Australian Critics on Suburbia' *Meanjin* 37, 1 (April): 3–13.
——(1981a) 'Culture and Democracy: The Economists and the Performing Arts' *Media Interventions* Sydney: Interventions Publications.
——(1981b) 'The Great Arts Funding Debate' *Meanjin* 40, 4 (December): 450–53.
——(1985a) *Arguing the Arts* Australia: Penguin.
——(1985b) 'Doing Away with Ordinary People' *Meanjin* 44, 2 (June): 161–9.
——(1986) 'The Future of the Australia Council' *Island Magazine* 29 (Summer): 3–7.
——(1988) 'Culture as Myth, Criticism as Irony: The Middle Class Patriotism of Donald Horne' *Island Magazine* 36 (Spring): 12–22.
——(1989) 'Cultural Policy and Social Theory' *Media Information Australia* 53 (August): 13–22.
Rowse, T. and Moran, A. (1984) ' "Peculiarly Australian"—The Political Construction of Cultural Identity' in Encel, S. and Bryson, L. (eds) *Australian Society* Melbourne: Longman Cheshire (4th edition).
Ryan, S. (1981) 'The Great Arts Funding Debate' *Meanjin* 40, 4 (December): 453–5.
Rydon, J. and Mackay, D. (1984) 'Federalism and the Arts' *Australian Cultural History* 3: 87–103.
Said, E. (1978) *Orientalism* England: Penguin.
——(1983) 'Opponents, Audiences, Constituencies and Community' in Foster, H. (ed.) *The Anti-Aesthetic: Essays on Postmodern Culture* Washington: Bay Press.
——(1986) 'Foucault & the Imagination of Power' in Couzens Hoy, D. (ed.) *Foucault: A Critical Reader* London: Basil Blackwell.
Samuel, R. (ed) (1981) *People's History and Socialist Theory* London: Routledge & Kegan Paul.
Sanders, N. (1981) 'Notes on Photoportraiture' in Brereton, K. *Photo-Discourse* Sydney: Sydney College of the Arts.
Sekula, A. (1983) 'Photography Between Labour and Capital' in Buchloh, B.

and Wilkie, R. (eds) *Mining Photographs and Other Pictures* Halifax: Nova Scotia College of Art and Design and the University College of Cape Breton Press.

Selle, P. and Svassand, L. (1987) 'Cultural Policy, Leisure and Voluntary Organizations in Norway' *Leisure Studies* 6, 3: 347–64.

Shaw, R. (1987) *The Arts and the People* London: Jonathan Cape.

Sheridan, S. (ed.) (1988) *Grafts: Feminist Cultural Criticism* London: Verso.

Smith, B. (1975) 'Notes on Elitism and the Arts' *Meanjin* 34, 2 (June): 117–20.

——(1988) *The Death of the Artist as Hero* Australia: Oxford University Press.

Smith, T. (1975) 'Official Culture and the Visual Arts Board' *Meanjin* 34, 2 (June): 121–8.

——(1976) ' "It's Still Privileged Art!"': New York Notes' *Meanjin* 35, 1 (April): 23–33.

——(1980) 'Photography and Politics: The English Situation' *Art Network* 2 (Spring): 65–6.

——(1984) 'Photographic Practice in the Trade Union Movement—A Report' *Photofile* 2, 2 (Winter): 7.

Sontag, S. (1977) *On Photography* London: Allen Lane.

Stanwell, J. and Jones, A. (1987) 'The Logan City Story' in Fotheringham, R. (ed.) *Community Theatre in Australia* Australia: Methuen.

Stephen, A. (1984) 'A Process of De-Neutralising' in Taylor, P. (ed.) *Anything Goes—Art in Australia 1970–1980* Victoria: Art and Text.

——(1987) 'Representing Women' *Scarlet Woman* 23: 24–8.

Stephen, A. and Reeves, A. (1984) *Badges of Labour Banners of Pride* Sydney: Museum of Applied Arts and Sciences and Allen & Unwin.

Tagg, J. (1980) 'Power and Photography: Part One: The Photograph as Evidence in Law' *Screen Education* 36 (Autumn): 17–55.

——(1980/81) 'Power and Photography: Part Two: A Legal Reality: The Photograph as Property in Law' *Screen Education* 36 (Autumn): 17–27.

Taylor, P. (1981) 'Lip Reading' *Meanjin* 40, 4 (December): 529–33.

——(1981) 'On Criticism' *Art and Text* 1: 5–11.

——(ed) (1984) *Anything Goes—Art in Australia 1970–1980* Victoria: Art and Text.

Thornley, J. (1987) 'Past, Present and Future: The Women's Film Fund' in Blonski, A., Creed, B. and Freiberg, F. (eds) *Don't Shoot Darling! Women's Independent Filmmaking in Australia* Australia: Greenhouse.

Thorpe, R. and Petruchina, J. (eds) (1985) *Community Work or Social Change?* London: Routledge & Kegan Paul.

Throsby, D. and Withers, G. (1979) *The Economics of the Performing Arts* Melbourne: Edward Arnold.

——(1984) *What Price Culture?* North Sydney: Australia Council.

Tribe, K. (1988) 'Government Support for the Arts—Practices, Principles and Proposals' *Australian Cultural History* 7: 18–36.

Underhill, N. (1987) 'Art on the Agenda: A Survey of Peter Kennedy's Art-Making' *Praxis* 16: 29–34.

UNESCO (1979) *Culture and Working Life Experiences from Six European Countries* Paris: UNESCO.

Valentine, A. (1990) 'The Gay Glasnost' *Gay and Lesbian Mardi Gras Program* Sydney: Sydney Gay and Lesbian Mardi Gras Association.

Vernon, K. (1990) 'Redback Graphix Retrospective' *Art Monthly* (March): 17–18.

Waites, B., Bennett, T. and Martin, G. (eds) (1982) *Popular Culture: Past and Present* London: Croom Helm in association with the Open University Press.

Walker, J.A. (1983) *Art in the Age of the Mass Media* London: Pluto.

Waller, R. (1985) 'How About a Residency?' *Against the Grain* Canberra: Photo-Access Centre.

Watson, B. (1963) 'On the Nature of Art Publics' *International Social Science Journal* 20, 4: 667–81.

Watson, S. (ed) (1990) *Playing the State* Sydney: Allen & Unwin.

Westmore, T. (1990) 'The Association: Fitting the People and Pieces Together' *Gay and Lesbian Mardi Gras Program* Sydney: Sydney Gay and Lesbian Mardi Gras Association.

Whitlam, E.G. (1985) *The Whitlam Government 1972–1975* Australia: Penguin.

Wickham, G. (1987) 'Foucault, Power, Left Politics' *Arena* 78: 146–61.

Wilenski, P. (1980) 'Reform and its Implementation: the Whitlam Years in Retrospect' in Evans, G. and Reeves, J. (eds) *Labour Essays 1980* Melbourne: Allen & Unwin.

Williams, M. (1984) 'The Alternative Theatre (1966–1980)' in Love, H. (ed.) *The Australian Stage: A Documentary History* Sydney: NSW University Press.

Williams, R. (1958) *Culture and Society 1780–1950* England: Penguin Books in association with Chatto and Windus.

——(1962) *Britain in the Sixties: Communication* England: Penguin.

——(1975) *The Country and the City* Great Britain: Paladin.

——(1976) *Keywords* Great Britain: Fontana/Croom Helm.

——(1977) *Marxism and Literature* Oxford: Oxford University Press.

——(1979) 'The Arts Council' *The Political Quarterly* 50 (Spring): 157–71.

——(1980) *Problems in Materialism and Culture* London: Verso.

——(1981) *Culture* Great Britain: Fontana.

——(1983) *Towards 2000* London: Chatto and Windus and The Hogarth Press.

Willis, A. (1981) 'The Visual Arts Board and Contemporary Australian Photography' in Brereton, K. *Photo-Discourse* Sydney: Sydney College of the Arts.

——(1984) 'The Local and the Ordinary: Community Photography in Caulfield' *Photofile* 2, 3 (Spring): 6–7.

Willis, P. (1977) *Learning to Labour* England: Saxon House.

——(1978) *Profane Culture* London: Routledge & Kegan Paul.

——(1979/80) 'The Authentic Image: An Interview with John Berger and Jean Mohr' *Screen Education* 32/33 (Autumn/Winter): 19–30.

Willmott, P. and Thomas, D. (1984) *Community in Social Policy* London: Policy Studies Institute, Discussion Paper No. 9.

Wilson, H. (ed.) (1989) *Australian Communications and the Public Sphere* Australia: Macmillan.

Withers, G. (1977) 'Let Art and Genius Weep: The Matter of Subsidising the Performing Arts' *Australian Quarterly* 49, 4 (December): 66–79.

——(1981a) 'The Great Arts Funding Debate' *Meanjin* 40, 4 (December): 442–9.

——(1981b) 'Principles of Government Support of the Arts' *Australian Cultural History* 1: 53–8.

Wolff, J. (1981) *The Social Production of Art* London: Macmillan.

——(1982) 'The Problem of Ideology in the Sociology of Art: A Case Study of Manchester in the Nineteenth Century' *Media, Culture and Society* 4, 1 (January): 63–75.

——(1989) *Women's Knowledge and Women's Art* Griffith University: Institute for Cultural Policy Studies.

Worpole, K. (1984) *Reading By Numbers: Contemporary Publishing and Popular Fiction* London: Comedia.

Wright, P. (1985) *On Living in an Old Country* London: Verso.

Zuzanek, J. (ed) (1979) *Social Research and Cultural Policy* Waterloo: Otivan Publications.

Index